C
Programmer's Guide to
NetBIOS

C
Programmer's Guide to
NetBIOS

W. David Schwaderer

HOWARD W. SAMS & COMPANY

A Division of Macmillan, Inc.

11711 North College, Suite 141, Carmel, IN 46032 USA

Send code corrections that may be incorporated into the sample programs, helpful insights, suggestions, and requests for technical assistance to:

W. David Schwaderer
c/o Howard W. Sams & Company
A Division of Macmillan, Inc.
11711 North College, Suite 141
Carmel, IN 46032 USA

Please note the author may use and distribute the material you submit in any way he believes is appropriate without incurring any obligation.

©1988 by W. David Schwaderer

FIRST EDITION
FIFTH PRINTING—1990

International Standard Book Number: 0-672-22638-3
Library of Congress Catalog Card Number: 88-62228

Acquisition Editor: *James S. Hill*
Development Editor: *James Rounds*
Production Coordinator: *Marjorie Colvin*
Editor: *Albright Communications, Incorporated*
Illustrator: *Donald B. Clemons*
Cover Artist: *Ned Shaw*
Keyboarder: *Lee Hubbard, Type Connection, Indianapolis*
Indexer: *Brown Editorial Service*
Compositor: *Shepard Poorman Communications Corporation*

Printed in the United States of America

Trademark Acknowledgments

To my family: Barbara, Greg, and Melissa
and
To the incandescent intellects
of James T. Brady and Larry K. Raper

Contents

Appendixes

Foreword

NetBIOS is an extremely important network programming interface. In the PC-DOS arena NetBIOS provides a consistent interface for communication systems using IBM, XNS, TCP, IEEE and OSI protocols, among others. As we networkers migrate our systems to new protocols such as OSI, to new LAN operating systems such as the OS/2 LAN Manager, and to new hardware platforms such as the PS/2 and Macintosh II, NetBIOS's importance expands.

Schwaderer's *C Programmer's Guide to NetBIOS* gives clarity and stability to a heretofore illusory de facto standard. It provides historical perspective as well as a working NetBIOS reference. It illustrates principles and techniques for developing the growing variety of NetBIOS applications that operate on the many evolving LAN systems.

Dr. Robert M. Metcalfe
Ethernet Inventor
Founder, 3Com Corporation

Preface

Network Basic Input/Output System (NetBIOS) is nearly a communication programmer's dream come true. Is NetBIOS perfect? I doubt it, but it takes so little effort to master and provides such a remarkably powerful LAN communications programming platform that I feel compelled to share it with the uninitiated—its innate simplicity as well as some of its more obscure areas.

With the information in this book, you will learn

- a history of NetBIOS and how it interrelates with other IBM hardware and software
- NetBIOS commands
- the Ncb fields
- name, datagram, and session support programming
- LAN data security and integrity
- CRC fundamentals

Example listings throughout the book demonstrate application principles and the Appendixes provide ready reference tables and programs.

Acknowledgments

Two friends are mentioned in the dedication. The first, Jim Brady, is currently my second-level manager. I am especially indebted to him for assigning me to LAN-related projects for most of the two and one-half years I have worked in IBM's disk-drive division. My assignments allow me to keep abreast of developments in LAN technology in a way that is presumably useful to our division. Thankfully, Jim has not wandered too far into communication subjects, or my life at work would be doubly difficult.

The second fellow is Larry Raper. He occasionally calls me at midnight to suggest an approach for a program I am working on. This is remarkable because midnight in San Jose means Larry is calling at 3:00 A.M. from the east coast. The sample C Post Routine in Appendix B is a direct consequence of one of these calls. Larry is one of the most brilliant programming craftsmen and system designers in the industry. Simply put, there are some as good, but none better anywhere. The internal clarity, design elegance, and concussion of Larry's programs can reduce even the most gifted programmers to despondency.

I am most grateful that the paths of these two fellows have crossed mine to change it immeasurably for the better. In the event that you know or come to know them, you might not want to mention this tribute to them as they would likely immolate in crimson distress. It can be a secret we share.

Finally, my deepest thanks to Nancy Albright for her remarkable editing skills, to Jim Rounds and Marj Colvin for their coordinating efforts, to Ned Shaw for his spectacular cover, and to my acquisition editor, Jim Hill. His personal integrity is the principal reason I initially signed with Howard W. Sams, and my regard for him has yet to change.

This book was written on an IBM PC-AT using Wordproof and the Personal Editor II. The programs were compiled using the Microsoft C 5.0 compiler and were debugged using the compiler's CodeView debugger assisted by an Atron Miniprobe.

Good luck with NetBIOS and drop a line if you will. I'd love to hear your thoughts on what might have been done better in this book or how you are using NetBIOS to improve your work. If you find any errors or have any suggestions, please write me in care of the publisher. I will do everything I can to personally reply and fix the problem in the next printing. Thanks in advance.

W. David Schwaderer
San Jose, California
August 1988

Introduction to NetBIOS

Chapter 1

Overview

The Network Basic Input/Output System (NetBIOS) is an application programming interface for data exchange between data sources and data sinks. Loosely speaking, NetBIOS is a programming gateway to sets of services that allow computer applications and devices to communicate. Application programs must generally invoke these various NetBIOS services using specific command sequences. Hence, NetBIOS has explicit, though minimal, protocols associated with some of its services.

Typically, data exchange occurs between NetBIOS applications residing within separate machines connected by a Local Area Network (LAN). However, two applications within the same machine can also use NetBIOS for data communication without a LAN. Thus, though all IBM NetBIOS implementations require a LAN adapter, NetBIOS use is not restricted to LAN environments.

Where Does NetBIOS Fit in the Scheme of Things?

If you are familiar with data communication theory, you might recall the International Standards Organization (ISO) Open Systems Interconnection (OSI) Reference Model depicted in Figure 1-1. This conceptual model divides the various activities, typically required to effect orderly data communication between two applications residing in distinct machines, into seven discrete processes or "layers." NetBIOS's location within this conceptual model is also illustrated in Figure 1-1.

During application-to-application communication, each layer within a given machine directly coordinates message-passing activities with the

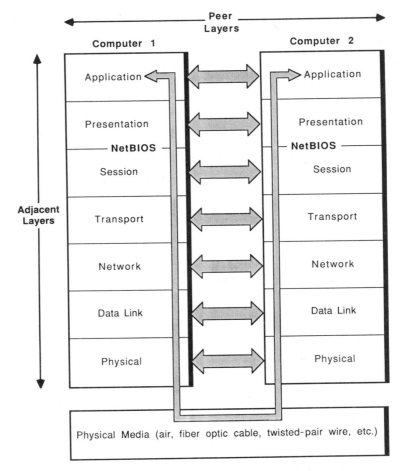

Fig. 1-1. ISO/OSI Reference Model.

adjacent layers immediately above and below it. This type of communication is called adjacent-layer communication. In addition, each layer within a machine also indirectly coordinates its message-passing activities with its peer-level counterpart within the other machine. This type of communication is called peer-layer communication.

NetBIOS is situated high within the reference model hierarchy, so applications that program to the NetBIOS interface are largely isolated and essentially insulated from the precise way the lower layers interact with their peer and adjacent layers. For example, two NetBIOS applications may communicate using IBM PC Network adapters. The underlying communication may be accomplished using the native Session Management Protocol (SMP) located on the adapter card. The applications may also use the IBM PC LAN Support Program which uses IEEE 802.2 Logical Link Control (LLC) protocols. In any event, the application programs are insulated from the precise protocols used.

This immunity allows general NetBIOS application portability across a spectrum of communication environments, though the portability is usually not total. For example, each type of IBM LAN has a specific NetBIOS implementation, or will have according to one of IBM's statements of direction issued at the introduction of the IBM PC Network. Because of the variety of IBM's LAN offerings, the precise effect of some NetBIOS commands does vary by LAN offering and the same is generally true for other NetBIOS implementations within other communication environments. However, because of the significant portability of NetBIOS applications and NetBIOS's intuitive simplicity, NetBIOS has rapidly become an uncontested de facto industry standard. Moreover, while not a perfect fit, NetBIOS interfaces are also appearing for other communication environments such as the popular TCP/IP and emerging MAP/TOP environments.

NetBIOS is rapidly becoming a pervasive data communication programming platform within a variety of operating environments such as PC-DOS, OS/2, and UNIX. Thus, if you are facile with NetBIOS programming, you possess a very marketable skill within an exploding market.

Where Did NetBIOS Come From?

NetBIOS first appeared in August 1984 with the IBM PC Network adapter card designed for IBM by Sytek Inc. The IBM PC Network was IBM's first LAN. It provides a 2-megabit per second data transmission burst rate across a broadband coaxial cable, using the popular industry standard Carrier Sense Multiple Access Collision Detect (CSMA/CD) access method that first appeared with IEEE 802.3 Ethernet.

Located on the IBM PC Network LAN Adapter (LANA) is an extended BIOS ROM referred to as the LANA's Network Adapter BIOS. This ROM module occupies 8K bytes of memory, starting at memory segment CC00h, and contains the LANA initialization routines, diagnostics, coprocessor and PC memory interface routines, and part of the first NetBIOS implementation. The remainder of this implementation is located on a second adapter ROM referred to as the adapter's protocol ROM. The adapter ROM also contains routines that allow a medialess (no bootable hard disk or available diskette) IBM PC to boot from a boot-server connected to the same network. The surrogate diskette boot process is referred to as Remote Program Load (RPL) and invokes the coresident ROM NetBIOS services to achieve its purpose.

What Is "True NetBIOS"?

The industry standard TCP/IP NetBIOS implementations, first demonstrated in December 1987, required NetBIOS extensions for resolution of internetwork routing between, and name resolution within, interconnected network environments. Because the MAP/TOP implementations are in their embryonic stages as of this writing, differences are likely to appear there as well.

Within the IBM product line, the current version of the IBM LAN Support Program provides the "true NetBIOS" implementation because it provides NetBIOS support for all of IBM's LAN adapters through a variety of PC-DOS device drivers.

One significant advantage of this program is that it allows IBM's various adapters to communicate with each other via an intermediary PC or PS/2* running the IBM Token-Ring/PC Network Interconnect Program. This enables IBM PC Network LAN workstations to communicate with Token-Ring based workstations, among other things. Thus, strategic reasons alone dictate that the IBM LAN Support Program's NetBIOS implementation supersede the original implementation as the true NetBIOS industry standard.

How Do I Get NetBIOS?

If you are using an IBM LAN, the answer to this question requires a historical product survey, which follows. Otherwise, consult your system vendor.

Original PC Network LANA Card

NetBIOS is automatically included on each IBM PC Network Adapter LANA card. However, because the LANA ROM is a PC BIOS extension, it, like the PC-XT Fixed Disk Adapter, Extended Graphics Adapter (EGA), etc., requires the presence of the PC BIOS Extended BIOS Option. This feature is automatically included with every IBM PC model except the original IBM PC (i.e., is available with the IBM PC-XT, IBM PC-AT, etc.).

In the case of the original IBM PC, this requires a BIOS-ROM upgrade

---

*PC includes the IBM PC family (excluding the PC Junior) and the PS/2 family, unless explicitly stated otherwise.

before the NetBIOS is usable. The effect of the upgrade is that after executing its Power-On-Self-Tests (POST) and initialization routines—but before loading PC-DOS—the PC scans PC memory for BIOS extensions. The BIOS starts at memory location C800:0000 and looks for the extended ROM signature value of AA55h every 2K bytes. Because IBM no longer provides BIOS ROM upgrade kits, check with your systems supplier for alternate ways to install this capability.

If the AA55h value is found, a BIOS extension is detected and executed by calling the instruction three bytes beyond the AA55h value. This permits the ROM extension to perform various activities, such as adapter and interrupt vector initialization. When complete, each ROM extension returns to the PC BIOS, allowing the PC BIOS to continue its memory scan for more ROM extensions. Hence, individual or multiple BIOS extensions initialize in an orderly manner.

Subsequent to the availability of the first LANA NetBIOS, IBM upgraded the Network Adapter BIOS with another version of the ROM. If you have a LANA adapter, you can determine whether you have the initial NetBIOS ROM or the upgraded one. Using PC-DOS's DEBUG.COM program, you can display the value at memory location CC00:0000. Near that location you see the Network Adapter BIOS part number, which is either 6360715 for the original version or 6480417 for the upgraded version.

You can also visually inspect the actual LANA NetBIOS chip, which is positioned in an upside-down orientation on the lower edge of the card immediately above the lefthand side of the adapter's PC bus connector. Figure 1-2 illustrates the position of the ROM chip.

The original ROM's copyright date has the year 1984 and the updated version, 1985. These dates are also displayed in memory near the Network Adapter BIOS part number.

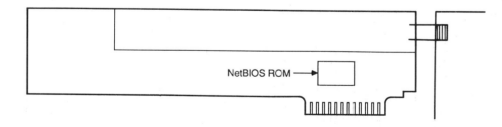

NetBIOS ROM →

Fig. 1-2. Location of the PC Network LANA NetBIOS ROM chip.

NETBIOS.COM

NETBIOS.COM is a complete NetBIOS replacement for the PC Network LANA NetBIOS. It is included with versions of the IBM PC LAN Program. Unlike the NetBIOS ROM version, NETBIOS.COM occupies memory within the 640K PC memory address space. When the IBM PC LAN Program executes, and when the adapter's NetBIOS ROM has an earlier date than the NETBIOS.COM module, the IBM PC LAN Program automatically loads and executes NETBIOS.COM as part of its initialization process. This completely replaces the ROM's NetBIOS services, upgrading the NetBIOS ROM.

Note that NETBIOS.COM can be executed as part of an AUTOEXEC. BAT initialization procedure (or AUTOUSER.BAT in instances where the IBM PC LAN Program has usurped AUTOEXEC.BAT) if you wish to use NetBIOS prior to running your licensed copy of the IBM PC LAN Program.

In the event you have the original NetBIOS and do not have an authorized copy of NETBIOS.COM, contact your authorized IBM sales representative for replacement policy information.

The IBM Token-Ring's NETBEUI

When IBM introduced the IBM Token-Ring in October 1985, it provided it with a NetBIOS programming interface. The NetBIOS support appeared as a separately purchased module named NETBEUI.COM, which is an acronym for NetBIOS Extended User Interface.

NETBEUI.COM requires another module named TOKREUI.COM (Token-Ring Extended User Interface). TOKREUI.COM is included on the Token Ring Guide To Operations Diskette and provides another communication programming interface known as Data Link Control (DLC), which uses a different set of communication protocols than LLC. NETBEUI.COM translates NetBIOS commands into DLC commands and presents them to the DLC interface. The *Token-Ring's Technical Reference Manual* documents NETBEUI.COM's services, which have minor deviations from the IBM LANA NetBIOS services.

The IBM LAN Support Program

IBM's latest implementation of NetBIOS is an IBM LAN Support Program component named DXMT0MOD.SYS which works in conjunction with other Program *modules*. All DLC and NetBIOS support is provided by combinations of members within the Program's PC-DOS device drivers families. The specific device drivers you select depend on your particular PC and optional software. DXMT0MOD.SYS can have 26 parameters which customize the installation of the Program.

What IBM NetBIOS Reference Material Is Available?

The *PC Network Technical Reference Manual*, the *Token-Ring Network PC Adapter Technical Reference Manual*, and the *IBM NetBIOS Application Development Guide* provide documentation and assistance in application and implementation of NetBIOS

PC Network Technical Reference Manual

The *PC Network Technical Reference Manual* (IBM Part Number 6322505) documents the original PC Network LANA NetBIOS programming interface and includes a Network Adapter BIOS listing in Appendix D. However, the LANA protocol ROM largely implements the actual NetBIOS and no LANA protocol ROM listing is provided. Using PC-DOS DEBUG.COM to examine the code shipped on the first version of the Network Adapter BIOS, and comparing it to the code in the listing, quickly reveals that the two are not identical. On page D-17, the listing mentions two PC-DOS include files that are not listed in the manual. One of them, NETBIOS.LIB, is present on the IBM PC Network Sample Program Diskette accompanying the *Manual*. The other, LANAS.INC, is undocumented.

For these and other reasons, the *Manual* has limited utility in providing an example NetBIOS implementation, although it has important RPL information as well as RPL sample program listings on the Diskette. Curiously enough though, the 1984 LANA NetBIOS code listing compares the BIOS model signature byte to an FCh constant (for a PC-AT) and asks the question "On a PC-3?" as a comment.

Token-Ring Network PC Adapter Technical Reference Manual

Chapter 5 of the *Token-Ring Network PC Adapter Technical Reference Manual* (IBM Part Number 69X7830) documents the NETBEUI.COM programming interface, which varies slightly from the original PC Network LANA NetBIOS programming interface. Specifically, two additional commands are provided, as well as additional return codes, use of a previously reserved area, and different status information reflecting the differences between a CSMA/CD and Token-Ring environment. The Sample Diskette contains some of the same program listings as the *PC Network Technical Reference Manual* Sample Diskette.

IBM NetBIOS Application Development Guide

The *IBM NetBIOS Application Development Guide* (IBM Part Number S68X-2270) describes the NetBIOS programming interface and provides pseudocode for the NetBIOS commands as well as the NetBIOS commands used with the PC Network Protocol Driver Program. The PC Network Protocol Driver Program allows PC Network II and PC Network II/A adapters to communicate with the original PC Network LANA adapter cards using the original LANA protocols.

DXMINFO.DOC

The IBM LAN Support Program device drivers are provided on a PC diskette along with a printable file named DXMINFO.DOC. This file contains several pages of critical late-breaking NetBIOS and adapter configuration information. It also documents the 26 DXMT0MOD.SYS NetBIOS input parameters (discussed in Chapter 5). Be warned the information has a definite LLC terminology orientation.

NetBIOS is a pervasive communications programming interface available within a variety of operational environments. Its several implementations vary in minor ways, reflecting differences within specific communication environments. Because of its innate simplicity and intuitive approach, NetBIOS has become an uncontested industry de facto standard. For the sake of simplicity, this book only discusses IBM's PC LANs, though the discussion is generally extendable to numerous other environments.

Chapter 2

NetBIOS and IBM's LAN Adapters

IBM offers a variety of PC LAN adapters spanning five LAN environments:

- Token-Ring
- PC Network Broadband
- PC Network Baseband
- Ethernet
- the IBM Industrial Network

IBM currently provides a NetBIOS implementation for each of these offerings except the Industrial Network and issued an August 1984 statement of direction that it would provide a NetBIOS interface for an "IBM Industrial local area network using the token-bus protocol."

The following hardware discussion is brief and illustrates the wide spectrum of IBM LAN adapter offerings. For a more detailed discussion of the individual adapters and the LAN technologies involved, consult *IBM's Local Area Networks: Power Networking and Systems Connectivity* (Schwaderer 1988).

Token-Ring Environment

IBM's strategic LAN, the Token-Ring, provides a 4-megabit burst transmission rate on shielded and unshielded twisted-pair wiring using a token access method within a *ring topology*. All IBM Token-Ring adapters transmit data signals on shielded twisted-pair copper wire using electrical voltage-level variations.

IBM has also announced work on a 16-megabit shielded twisted-pair version, as well as a 100-megabit fiber optic Token-Ring based on the ANSI X3T9.5 Fiber Distributed Data Interface (FDDI) draft standard.

Currently, IBM provides five Token-Ring Adapters:

- IBM Token-Ring Network PC Adapter I
- IBM Token-Ring Network PC Adapter II
- IBM Token-Ring Network Adapter/A
- IBM Token-Ring Network Trace and Performance Adapter II
- IBM Token-Ring Network Trace and Performance Adapter/A

The IBM Token-Ring Network PC Adapter operates in IBM PCs, PC-XTs, PC-ATs, and PS/2 models 25 and 30, and contains 8K bytes of on-board shared-RAM for network functions and an empty socket which allows installation of an 8K-byte RPL feature EPROM.

The 8K bytes are referred to as shared-RAM because both the PC's microprocessor and the LAN adapter's microprocessor directly access this memory. The RPL EPROM feature's protocols are LLC-based. Hence, they are incompatible with the PC Network LANA RPL protocols that are NetBIOS/SMP-based. However, they are compatible with the onboard RPL capability of the IBM PC Network Broadband Adapter II(/A) adapters and the IBM PC Network Baseband Adapter(/A) adapters.

The IBM Token-Ring Network PC Adapter II also operates in IBM PCs, PC-XTs, PC-ATs, and PS/2 models 25 and 30, and contains 16K bytes of onboard shared-RAM for network functions as well as an empty socket for an 8K-byte RPL feature EPROM.

The additional 8K bytes of shared-RAM on the Adapter II allows it to use larger size transmission packets (essentially 2K bytes versus 1K bytes) than the Adapter I. Therefore, in high-transmission rate applications typical for file servers, bridges, and gateways, the Adapter II has a significant performance advantage over the Adapter I.

The IBM Token-Ring Network Adapter/A operates in all IBM PS/2s except PS/2 models 25 and 30, and contains 16K bytes of shared-RAM for improved network performance as well as an empty socket for an 8K-byte LLC-protocol RPL feature EPROM.

The IBM Token-Ring Network Trace and Performance Adapter II operates in members of the original PC, PC-XT, PC-AT, and PS/2 models 25 and 30, and with the IBM Token-Ring Network Trace and Performance Program. It also functions as a normal network adapter.

The IBM Token-Ring Network Trace and Performance Adapter/A operates in members of the PS/2 except models 25 and 30, and with the

IBM Token-Ring Network Trace and Performance Program. It also functions as a normal network adapter.

IBM PC Network Broadband Environment

The IBM PC Network provides a 2-megabit burst rate on broadband cabling using the popular industry-standard IEEE 802.3 CSMA/CD access method within a branching-tree topology. IBM PC Network broadband adapters transmit data signals on coaxial cable using radio frequency (RF) techniques. Currently, IBM provides three PC Network broadband adapters, though two of them can operate at different frequencies by changing their adapter transceiver (RF modem):

- IBM PC Network Adapter
- IBM PC Network Adapter II
- IBM PC Network Adapter II/A

The IBM PC Network Adapter was discussed in Chapter 1. The IBM PC Network Adapter II operates in IBM PCs, PC-XTs, PC-ATs, and PS/2 models 25 and 30, and contains 8K bytes of shared-RAM for network functions.

The IBM PC Network Adapter II/A operates in all IBM PS/2s except models 25 and 30, and contains 8K bytes of shared-RAM for network functions.

Both the Adapter II and the Adapter II/A are available with transceivers that operate at one of three different frequencies. Table 2-1 illustrates the relationships.

Table 2-1. IBM PC Network Adapter II and Adapter II/A
Frequency Options

Broadband Channels	IBM PC Adapter	IBM PS/2 Adapter
Chan. T14 & J	IBM PC Network Adapter II	IBM PC Network Adapter II/A
Chan. 2' & 0	IBM PC Network Adapter II Frequency 2	IBM PC Network Adapter II/A Frequency 2
Chan. 3' & P	IBM PC Network Adapter II Frequency 3	IBM PC Network Adapter II/A Frequency 3

IBM PC Network Baseband Environment

The IBM PC Network Baseband provides 2-megabit burst transmission rates on twisted-pair wiring using the popular industry-standard IEEE 802.3 CSMA/CD access method within star and single-bus topologies. Currently, IBM provides two PC Network baseband adapters:

- IBM PC Network Baseband Adapter
- IBM PC Network Baseband Adapter/A

The IBM PC Network Baseband Adapter operates in IBM PCs, PC-XTs, PC-ATs, and PS/2 models 25 and 30, and contains 8K bytes of shared-RAM for network functions.

The IBM PC Network Baseband Adapter/A operates in all IBM PS/2s except PS/2 models 25 and 30, and contains 8K bytes of shared-RAM for network functions.

The individual members of the IBM PC Network baseband family of adapters are low-cost and have nearly identical counterparts within the IBM PC Network broadband family of adapters. The only essential difference is that the baseband adapter transceivers drive twisted-pair media and the broadband adapter transceivers drive broadband media. In this sense, Adapter II(/A) and the Baseband Adapter(/A) are excellent examples of "layered hardware" design. In fact, applications that use Broadband II and II/A adapters must go to some length to determine whether they are actually running on Baseband Adapter and Baseband Adapter/A, respectively.

An application must read the LAN adapter Transceiver Interface Register at the primary (alternate) port address 0626h (062Eh). If the two high-order bits have a value of 00, then the adapter's transceiver is a broadband transceiver. Otherwise, the two high-order bits have a value of 01 and the transceiver is a baseband transceiver. This inconsequential difference clearly illustrates that base adapters are absolutely identical, differing only in their transceivers, which are attached in the final assembly phases.

Indeed, you could switch transceivers between an Adapter II(/A) and a Baseband Adapter(/A) and reinstall the adapters in the appropriate network without application impact other than changing the network adapter's serial number. Thus, assumptions that given applications can run on IBM PC Network Broadband Adapter IIs (/As) but not on IBM PC Network Baseband Adapters (/As) are largely statements of support, not capability. In the final analysis, nothing prevents applications from going the extra mile to detect that they are executing on a PC Network baseband adapter and to terminate execution on that basis. Caveat emptor.

Ethernet Environment

IBM markets Ethernet adapters manufactured by Ungermann-Bass of Santa Clara, California. The adapters are available from a business unit known as IBM Academic Computing Information Systems (ACIS), which works closely with academic institutions under joint development agreements involving a variety of technologies and communication environments.

IBM LAN Programming Interfaces

NetBIOS is one of five communication programming interfaces provided by IBM for its LANs. The various interfaces are

- adapter card
- Advanced Program-to-Program Communications (APPC)
- Data Link Control (DLC)
- direct
- NetBIOS

The relationships of these interfaces to NetBIOS are illustrated in Figure 2-1. Detailed discussion of the other four major interfaces is beyond the scope of this book, but the following discussion summarizes their purposes.

Adapter Card Interface

The adapter card interface is the most difficult programming interface, requiring timing-sensitive logic, tricky interrupt processing, and nimble management of shared-RAM. For example, the IBM Token-Ring PC Adapter has a variety of independent interrupts that must be correctly handled in isolation or in mass. The adapter's interrupt fecundity, combined with an error in the PC BIOS's timer tick handler, eventually led IBM to introduce the CONFIG.SYS STACKS parameter (with DOS 3.2) and the TIMERINT.SYS device driver (with the IBM LAN Support Program), respectively. In other words, this is an interface of last resort, though it is the interface used by LAN monitors to observe network traffic.

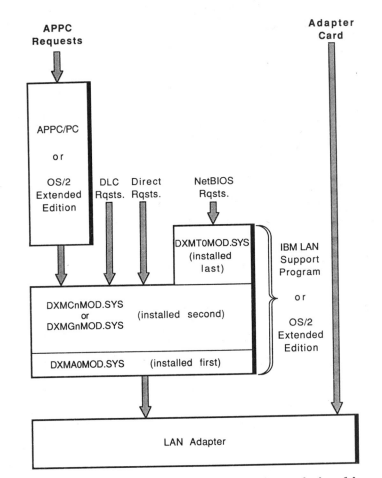

Fig. 2-1. IBM PC LAN programming interface relationships.

APPC Interface

APPC is the interface provided for Systems Network Architecture (SNA) communication. It has numerous command sequences and control blocks associated with it, and is useful for peer-to-peer communications with IBM mainframes and other IBM processor applications that require SNA LU 6.2 communication capability.

DLC Interface

DLC provides the IEEE 802.2 LLC communication interface for IBM's LAN adapters, which supports the IEEE type 2 LLC protocol guaranteeing notification of unsuccessful transmissions. DLC also provides the IEEE type 1 "connectionless" communications, sometimes referred to as "send and pray" communication, in which no guarantee of message delivery is provided and no notification is given in the event of transmission problems.

DLC offers the potential of higher performance communication than NetBIOS because it is "closer to the adapter." As earlier indicated, NetBIOS commands are converted into one or more DLC commands and then presented to the DLC interface. This is why NetBIOS data transmission throughput rates often cannot exceed DLC data transmission throughput rates.

Direct Interface

The direct interface provides the ability to open, initialize, and close adapters, and permits programs to read and reset adapter logs, trace adapter activities, obtain status information, and operate adapter timers.

IBM provides a wide spectrum of LAN adapters and programming interfaces, including NetBIOS. Clearly, a mechanism is needed to support these diverse adapters while simultaneously presenting a stable, uniform set of programming interfaces to applications. This is provided by the IBM LAN Support Program, which insulates applications from implementation details of the specific LAN they operate on, allowing users to select the appropriate LAN for their requirements.

Chapter 3

Application Services

NetBIOS provides four categories of application services:

- name support
- datagram support
- session support
- general command

NetBIOS Name Support

An individual NetBIOS LAN adapter is distinguished from other adapters on its respective network by one or more network names, which allow LAN applications to direct their messages to specific adapters and indicate that their adapter originated the message.

Each network name consists of 16 characters. Within a network name, each of the 16 characters is significant and uppercase is different than lowercase. The names you can create cannot have a value of binary zero or an asterisk (*) as the first character. IBM reserves the values of 00h to 1Fh for the 16th character and uses some of the reserved character values with the IBM PC LAN Program. This is why you can only have a 15-character IBM PC LAN Program machine name. Finally, IBM reserves the use of "IBM" as the first three characters of any name. For a more complete discussion of NetBIOS naming considerations, refer to the NetBIOS Adapter Status Program discussion in Part II, of this book.

The number of names an adapter can use (or is using) will vary, as can the number of adapters using a given name, but before an adapter can use any name, it must acquire the rights to register and use the name on the LAN.

NetBIOS initiates name registration activities in response to either of the two types of NetBIOS add-name commands: Add Name and Add Group Name. An adapter registers a network name by first broadcasting a network petition (a name-claim packet) to use the name. The type of packet, Name_Claim or Add_Group_Name_Claim, indicates whether the adapter wants to register the name as a *unique name* or as a *group name* respectively.

Finally, once a name is successfully registered, any registered name except the first can be deregistered by issuing a NetBIOS Delete Name command. NetBIOS Adapter Reset commands erase the NetBIOS name table (except the first name), as does a system reset (Ctrl-Alt-Del) and powering off the workstation.

Unique Names

If an adapter tries to register a name as a unique name, then no other adapter operating on the LAN can have the same registered name or the registration attempt fails. If the name is currently registered, either as a unique name or as a group name, the offended adapter(s) issues a network complaint and the pending name registration command is refused. Otherwise, the adapter has the exclusive right to use the name on its LAN.

Group Names

If an adapter tries to register a name as a group name, then no other adapter can be using that name as a unique name or the registration attempt fails. If the name is in use as a unique name, the offended adapter issues a network complaint and the command to use the name is refused. Otherwise, the adapter has the nonexclusive right to use the name on the LAN. This allows other adapters to register the name as a group name, though not as a unique name. Group names are useful for sending messages to collections of workstations such as departments or teams.

The Name Table and Name Number

If an attempted name registration fails, the failure is reported to the workstation application for subsequent analysis along with an appropriate error return code. In the absence of network complaints, the adapter's NetBIOS support places the name in a locally maintained, internal table known as the NetBIOS *name table*. It then reports the name registration success to the LAN application along with a one-byte value.

The one-byte value is an unsigned number referred to as the name's NetBIOS *name number*. The name number is subsequently used in various NetBIOS commands associated with the name. NetBIOS assigns the value of the name number in an incremental, modulo 255, roundrobin manner. The values zero and 255 are never assigned, and the first entry is permanently assigned by the adapter based on its internal serial number. Thus, the numbers are assigned in the order 1, 2, 3, . . . 254, 2, 3, 4, . . . 254, etc.

Placing the name in the name table authorizes the adapter to subsequently scrutinize registration petitions of other adapters wishing to register names. And, once added, a name can be deleted from the table, potentially allowing some other name to use it as a unique name.

Note that the NetBIOS name table is a temporary table contained within RAM and is reconstructed after each system boot or adapter reset. Because each adapter has its own private name table, NetBIOS name resolution is highly autonomous across the LAN, requiring no central name administration. If a NetBIOS module is supporting more than one LAN adapter within a workstation, each adapter also has its own independent NetBIOS name table.

The Permanent Node Name

All IBM LAN adapters have a unique six-byte number associated with them, guaranteed to be unique for every IBM LAN adapter and contained in an adapter ROM. The number is referred to by a variety of names:

- permanent node name
- permanent node address
- burned-in address (BIA)
- universally administered address
- unit identification number
- physical address
- local node name

For all IBM LAN adapters other than the PC Network LANA card, this address is in the range that is universally administered by the standards committees for LANs and has the two high-order bits set to zero. Under the native ROM NetBIOS, PC Network LANA adapter cards always have two bytes of binary zeros as the last two bytes of their permanent node name. The values of the two high-order bits in the remaining four bytes vary by adapter.

The permanent node name can be overridden at boot time with a six-byte locally administered address whose high-order bytes must have a value of X'4000'. This provides a new LAN hardware address for the adapter that replaces the permanent node name and is accomplished by specifying an appropriate value on the LAN adapter's IBM PC LAN Support Program device driver. DXMINFO.DOC has the appropriate details.

If overridden, the locally administered address temporarily replaces the permanent node name as the adapter's LAN hardware address until the system is rebooted. This provides the opportunity to omit or respecify the overriding locally administered address value or to replace the adapter with another that uses the same locally administered address.

Note: NetBIOS applications cannot detect when a permanent node name has been overridden either on a local or remote adapter. NetBIOS always uses and returns the original permanent node name when an application obtains an adapter's name. The only way to obtain both the permanent node name and the current LAN hardware address is to issue a local DIR.STATUS request. This is not a NetBIOS request and is beyond the scope of this book.

When any LAN adapter is initialized and active on a LAN, it has a unique six-byte number associated with it, the burned-in permanent node name. The number is also guaranteed to be unique on the LAN because it is registered in the NetBIOS name table as a unique name during adapter initialization (the six bytes are appended to 12 bytes of binary zeros to construct a unique 16-byte name). Because the registration happens during system initialization, the permanent node name is always the first entry in an adapter's NetBIOS name table. Zero is an invalid NetBIOS name number value, so permanent node name always has a name number value of one.

The permanent node name serves as a LAN address that fingerprints all messages transmitted *by* an adapter, and serves as an identification anchorpoint for all messages transmitted *to* an adapter. Specifically, it is used to tell the adapter's communication circuitry which messages should be ignored and which messages should be admitted into the workstation. This unique 48-bit value constitutes an adapter's electronic message sieve.

Symbolic Names

Suppose you wrote a program to send a message to an associate named Melissa and you wished to send it to her workstation's permanent node name, which you believe is X'4001020003404'.

This type of approach would be error prone because X'4001020003404' is an invalid address (it has one too many digits), and the program may need rewriting if Melissa's workstation adapter is changed, perhaps for maintenance reasons. Thus, it would be convenient to personalize the LAN adapter address by using your associate's natural name, Melissa. Such pseudonyms are called symbolic names and are registered in the NetBIOS name table as either unique names or group names.

Adapters can receive messages that are addressed to it using only

- their 48-bit unique address derived from their unique serial number
- an indiscriminate general broadcast address of X'FFFFFFFFFFFF'
- bit-mapped functional addresses
- one value-mapped group address

The last two of these methods are beyond the scope of this book.

The name registration process is actually a LAN protocol for early name-usage conflict detection, and is an indiscriminate broadcast protocol in preparation for subsequent communication requiring translation of symbolic names to 48-bit LAN addresses.

Once a symbolic name has been resolved into an appropriate 48-bit address, NetBIOS needs only that address to conduct the communication. The name used to make the association is nonessential until it is needed to resolve another, perhaps a different 48-bit address, to the symbolic name. Remember, symbolic names can be registered and deregistered.

Datagram and Session Support

Once an adapter becomes active in a network, application programs within the workstation can use NetBIOS to communicate with other applications residing in the same or different workstations. The applications can communicate using either *datagrams* or *sessions*.

Datagram Support

Datagrams are short messages whose size varies by NetBIOS implementation and have no guarantee of delivery beyond a "best effort" by the adapter. Regardless of whether the messages arrive safely, no receipt indication is provided by NetBIOS. The intended recipient machine may

- not exist
- be powered off
- not be expecting a datagram

In these instances, and in the case of network problems, the datagram may never be received by any workstation. Datagram communication is "send and pray" communication unless the receiving application takes explicit action to transmit a receipt acknowledgment. The primary advantage of datagram communication is that it can consume less workstation resource than session communication.

There are two types of datagram communication: *broadcast datagrams* and *plain datagrams*. In both cases, the NetBIOS datagram transmission command references an existing local NetBIOS name number, perhaps the permanent node name's, that serves as the *datagram's origin name*. This name number may be associated with a local unique or group name. Finally, plain datagrams transmitted to group names and broadcast datagrams have a very low level of data security because they can be intercepted with very little effort.

Broadcast Datagrams

Broadcast datagrams are totally indiscriminate datagrams transmitted with a NetBIOS Send Broadcast Datagram command. Any adapter, including the transmitting adapter, can receive a broadcast datagram if it has previously issued a NetBIOS Receive Broadcast Datagram command.

In general, broadcast datagram communication should be avoided because two applications within the same workstation could easily receive broadcast datagrams intended for the other application. In addition, applications that execute in workstations running the IBM PC LAN Program are specifically warned against using broadcast datagram communication.

Plain Datagrams

Plain datagrams are discriminate datagrams transmitted with a NetBIOS Send Datagram command. Unlike NetBIOS Send Broadcast Datagram commands, applications specify a recipient NetBIOS name with the Send Datagram command. Any adapter, including the transmitting adapter, can receive a datagram if it has previously added the appropriate recipient name and issued a Receive Datagram command to NetBIOS referencing the number of the name specified in the command.

If an application specifies a name number of FFh in a receive datagram, the application can receive a datagram for any name in the NetBIOS name table. This is referred to as a *receive-any* datagram. However, Receive Datagram commands for a specific name number have priority over Receive-Any Datagram commands. Figure 3-1 summarizes the relationship between the two forms of Receive Datagram commands.

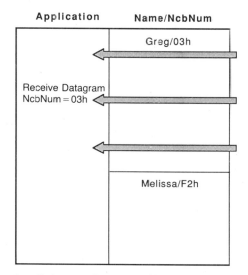

Receive Datagram for a specified name number

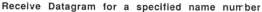

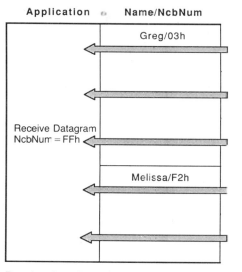

Receive-Any Datagram (lowest priority)

Fig. 3-1. Receive Datagram command flavors.

Finally, plain datagrams can be transmitted to adapters using the name as a unique name, or to groups of adapters that share a group name.

Session Support

The second form of NetBIOS application communication is session communication. NetBIOS session support creates a reliable two-way data communication connection between two applications that can exist for extended periods. Such connections are sometimes referred to as *virtual circuits*.

The communicating applications may reside within the same workstation (local sessions) or within different workstations (remote sessions). Each application constitutes one *half* or *side* of the session.

The primary advantage of session communication over datagram communication is that message-receipt status is presented to the transmitting application for every message it transmits. Datagram communication provides message transmission status. However, session communication reliability comes with the slight overhead of creating and maintaining sessions and the packet acknowledgment protocol between adapters.

Creating Sessions

Sessions are created when one application issues a NetBIOS Listen command referencing a name in its NetBIOS name table. The application may use an existing name in the table such as the permanent node name or add one of its own.

The Listen command also specifies the remote name that a petitioning application must use to qualify as a session partner, and may use an asterisk (*) as the first character of the remote name. In this case, the remaining 15 characters are ignored and the local NetBIOS allows the second application to use any name to qualify as a session partner. (Since session security depends on matching both names, one might correctly suspect such promiscuous behavior has its hazards.)

A second application then issues a NetBIOS Call command, which references the name in its NetBIOS name table that the first application is expecting as a partner's name. The Call command also references the name the first application referenced in its own NetBIOS name table. The double name match fulfills the criteria of both applications to create a session and the pending Listen and Call commands then complete. Note the sequence: first the Listen, then the Call. This sequence cannot be successfully reversed.

Each application then receives notification of session establishment and a one-byte unsigned value referred to as the NetBIOS Local Session Number (LSN) that the adapter associates with the session. The LSN is analogous to a PC-DOS file handle.

NetBIOS assigns the LSN value in an incremental, modulo 255, round-robin manner. The values zero and 255 are never assigned. Thus, the numbers are assigned in the order 1, 2, 3, . . . 254, 1, 2, 3, 4, . . . 254, etc.

Even if both sides of the session are local sessions, note that two numbers are assigned—one for each side. In this case, either application can use either LSN. In general, there is no restriction that the two LSNs have the same value, even if they are both local sessions. The session creation procedure is summarized in Figure 3-2.

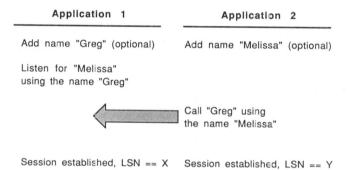

Fig. 3-2. Session establishment.

Receive Command Flavors

After establishing a session, both sides can issue NetBIOS Send and Receive commands to transfer data. If a given name is used to create several sessions, an application can also issue a NetBIOS Receive-Any-for-a-Specified-Name (Receive-Any) command, which provides received data from any session associated with a specified name. More generally, the application can issue a NetBIOS Receive-Any-for-Any-Name (Receive-Any-Any) command, which provides received data from any existing session the adapter has actively established.

In the event a message arrives that could satisfy more than one of these types of NetBIOS Receives, the following hierarchy is observed:

1. Receive (highest priority)
2. Receive-Any-for-a-Specified-Name
3. Receive-Any-for-Any-Name (lowest priority)

The behavior of the various Receive flavors is summarized in Figure 3-3.

Send Command Flavors

Applications issue NetBIOS Send commands to transfer data to the other application. The Send command allows the application to send messages ranging in size from zero bytes to 64K minus 1 bytes of data; the data must be in contiguous memory. The application can also issue a NetBIOS Chain Send command that allows data to reside in buffers located in two different storage areas.

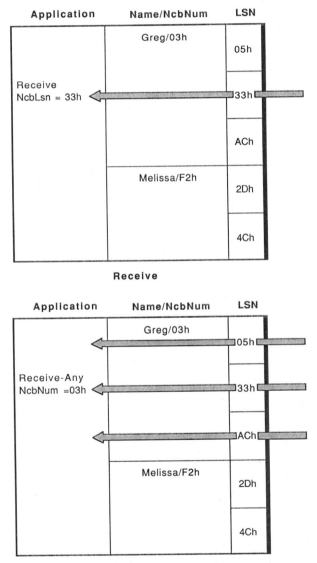

Fig. 3-3. Receive command flavors.

With a Chain Send command, data within each of the buffers must be in contiguous memory, though the two buffers themselves do not have to be contiguous. Moreover, each data block can range from zero bytes to 64K minus one bytes, allowing up to 128K minus two bytes to transfer with one Chain Send command.

Send and Receive Considerations

First note that a NetBIOS Chain Send command exists, but a NetBIOS "Chain Receive" command does not. NetBIOS allows applications to receive part of a transmission and issue subsequent NetBIOS Receives to receive the remainder of the message. This is true for messages that originate from both Send and Chain Send commands. Conversely, a single NetBIOS Receive command can usually receive messages transmitted with a Chain Send command provided the message is not too large. In any event, the receiving application cannot detect whether a message was transmitted with a Send versus a Chain Send unless the size of the total message exceeds 64K minus one bytes. This is because Chain Send command data originating in two separate buffers always arrives seamlessly with no indication of the original buffer boundaries.

The only stipulation for an application that partially receives a message is that it not delay "too long" to receive the entire message. Specifically, when the session is established, each side specifies Receive and Send time-out threshold periods. If the Send threshold period is exceeded be-

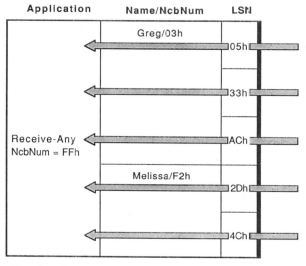

Receive-Any-for-Any-Name (lowest priority)

Fig. 3-3. (Cont.)

fore the message is completely received, the Send times-out and the entire session is terminated by the sending adapter. In this instance, both sides of the session are notified of the consequences of the receiver's lethargy.

Send No-Ack and Chain Send No-Ack Considerations

The Send No-Ack and Chain Send No-Ack commands first appeared with version 1.02 of the IBM LAN Support Program. They differ from the Send and Chain Send commands, respectively, by eliminating unnecessary NetBIOS-to-NetBIOS data-receipt acknowledgments occurring with prior IBM NetBIOS implementations.

Caution: The Send No-Ack and Chain Send No-Ack commands are not in the original NetBIOS definition and may not be universally recognized by other NetBIOS implementations, including prior IBM NetBIOS implementations and the IBM PC Network Protocol Driver Program. Using them may produce nonportable results because they require new command codes and generate new return code values for themselves and the Send, Chain Send, Receive, and Receive-Any commands.

Ending Sessions Gracefully

Sessions are ended by one or both sides issuing a NetBIOS Hang Up command that specifies the LSN of the session to be terminated. The other application is notified of the session termination when it issues a subsequent session command. An application can issue a NetBIOS Session Status command that will indicate the status of a session—existing or cancelled.

General Commands

The NetBIOS general commands provide such NetBIOS services as

- Reset
- Adapter Status
- Cancel and Unlink
- Find Name
- Trace

Reset Command

The Reset command forces the adapter to an initialized state. This terminates all sessions and removes all names from the NetBIOS name table except for the permanent node name. The Reset command optionally specifies the maximum allowable number of NetBIOS commands that can be pending at one time as well as the maximum number of sessions that concurrently exist within the adapter. Minimizing these values can increase performance by freeing up valuable work space for more network buffers. OS/2 use of the Reset command is discussed in Appendix F.

Adapter Status Command

The Adapter Status command allows you to query a NetBIOS adapter and retrieve operational information such as detected LAN error counts and the adapter's NetBIOS name table. The queried adapter could be a local adapter or a remote adapter on the LAN. In some environments, using the Adapter Status command to query a remote adapter is an excellent way to determine whether the adapter *and* a workstation is hung or just the workstation is hung. (Adapters can sometimes operate from LAN interrupts though the workstation is hung.)

Cancel and Unlink Commands

The NetBIOS Cancel command allows applications to cancel commands that have not completed. The NetBIOS Unlink command allows a PC Network LANA adapter that has booted using RPL to disconnect from the RPL server machine. The Unlink command is intercepted by the PC Network LANA NetBIOS and converted to a Hang Up command that uses information stored in high RAM.

The Unlink request is only valid for the primary adapter and always returns a zero (successful) return code. For all other IBM LAN adapter NetBIOS implementations, the Unlink command is provided as a compatibility feature for the PC Network LANA card and performs no function. See Part III for a complete discussion of the RPL process.

Find Name Command

The NetBIOS Find Name command locates adapters that are using a symbolic name specified in the Find Name command. This is similar to an Adapter Status command except NetBIOS returns one adapter response at most to an Adapter Status command. (Several adapters sharing a group name may respond, but only one response is returned to a requesting application.)

In the case of the Find Name command, several adapters can also reply if they share a group name, but theoretically speaking, all the responses are eligible to be returned to the requesting application. An Adapter Status command returns all names within the target adapter's NetBIOS name table and the NetBIOS Find Command returns the adapter routing information for the adapters that are using the name.

The adapter routing information is only relevant in interconnected LANs such as the IBM Token-Ring because the information indicates the route(s) a message can take to arrive at a specific workstation. This routing information identifies the bridges connecting separate physical rings. Messages must traverse these bridges to reach the LAN the recipient workstation is on.

Trace Command

The Trace Command activates a trace of all commands issued to the Net-BIOS interface. Its primary objective is to provide support for diagnostic programs. In the event your implementation does not have a Trace command, you can write one yourself by intercepting all INT 5C requests. You should only analyze interrupt requests where the ES:BX register pair point to a byte in memory that has a value greater than 02h. When ES:BX point to values of 00h, 01h, and 02h, the request is a DLC IEEE 802.2 LLC request. This topic and the general Trace command is beyond the scope of this book.

Issuing NetBIOS Commands

Applications issue NetBIOS commands by first zeroing out a 64-byte area of memory. This prevents residual data from causing NetBIOS to wildly branch into random memory when the command completes. The application then uses the area to construct a NetBIOS Control Block or Ncb. Completing the control block consists of filling various fields that are required by the particular command that will be issued. Failure to complete the Ncb fields correctly can hang the user's machine because uncompleted fields are initialized to all zeros. For example, in the case of PC-DOS, if the Ncb specifies a Receive command and the receive data buffer address is inadvertently not specified, the arriving data will obligingly be placed at address 0000:0000 overlaying and corrupting your machine's interrupt vectors. That can be a difficult error to isolate though its effect is more than somewhat obvious.

After filling in the Ncb, the application then points the ES:BX register pair at the Ncb and issues an INT 5C interrupt request. When NetBIOS can report status on the request, it does. However, the particular way it does this varies with the way the particular request was issued.

C Example

Listing 3-1 shows how to issue a NetBIOS interrupt request using the C language. This particular figure issues a NetBIOS interrupt directly to the native NetBIOS interrupt. For IBM PCs, an alternate method uses a PC-DOS INT 2Ah request specifying a value of 0400h or 0401h in the AX register. In both cases, the ES:BX register pair point to a valid Ncb.

**Listing 3-1. C Fragment Illustrating a Direct NetBIOS
Interrupt Request**

```
#define USGC   unsigned char
#define USGI   unsigned
#define USGL   unsigned long

#define NetbiosInt21FunctionCode   ((USGC) 0x2A)
#define NetbiosInt5C               ((USGC) 0x5C)

void NetbiosRequest(NcbPointer)
struct Ncb *NcbPointer;
{
 struct SREGS SegRegs;
 union  REGS  InRegs, OutRegs;  /* defined in dos.h */
 struct Ncb far *NcbPtr = (struct Ncb far *) NcbPointer;

    segread(&SegRegs);

    SegRegs.es  = FP_SEG(NcbPtr);
    InRegs.x.bx = FP_OFF(NcbPtr);

    int86x(NetbiosInt5C, &InRegs, &OutRegs, &SegRegs);
}
```

An AX value of 0401h indicates PC-DOS should not automatically retry the command if the command failed. An AX value of 0400h indicates PC-DOS should retry the command if the command failed because

- the adapter does not have the resources necessary to complete the command successfully
- the adapter is busy and cannot handle the request

- the other workstation rejected our application's attempt to start a communication session with it

The INT 2A approach is sometimes necessary for total coexistence with the IBM PC LAN Program. However, before first using this interface, an application must test the version of PC-DOS to verify it is version 3.1 or later, and then determine whether the IBM PC LAN Program is installed (see Chapter 6).

MASM Example

Listing 3-2 illustrates how to issue a NetBIOS interrupt request using MASM. Again, this particular figure issues a NetBIOS interrupt directly to the native NetBIOS interrupt in lieu of a PC-DOS INT 2Ah request with AH set to 0400h or 0401h.

Listing 3-2. MASM Fragment Illustrating a Direct NetBIOS Interrupt Request

```
NetbiosInt     equ 5Ch                       ; NETBIOS interrupt vector


               mov     BX,offset Ncb


               mov     AX,CS
               mov     ES,AX          ; ES:BX ==> Ncb


               int     NetbiosInt
```

Testing for the Presence of NetBIOS

Before an application can safely issue a NetBIOS request, it must determine if NetBIOS is present. For IBM PCs, this process varies with the model.

The Original IBM PC and PC-XT Test

The original IBM PC and PC-XT BIOS POST procedures initialize interrupt vectors that BIOS does not need to OFFSET:SEGMENT values of 0000:0000. Issuing a NetBIOS request in one of these machines to an uninitialized interrupt is virtually guaranteed to hang the machine.

The Test for Other IBM PCs

The IBM PC-AT and follow-on machine BIOS POST procedures point the interrupt vectors that BIOS does not need at an immediate IRET instruction. The SEGMENT value of the IRET instruction is always F000h. Thus, issuing a NetBIOS request to an uninitialized interrupt in one of these machines is harmless though unproductive. Chapter 4 contains a program that tests correctly for NetBIOS presence.

To summarize, there are four categories of NetBIOS commands, each with several members:

Name Support	Add Name
	Add Group Name
	Delete Name
Datagram Support	Receive Datagram
	Receive Broadcast Datagram
	Send Datagram
	Send Broadcast Datagram
Session Support	Call
	Listen
	Send
	Send No-Ack
	Chain Send
	Chain Send No-Ack
	Receive
	Receive-Any
	Hang Up
	Session Status
General Commands	Reset
	Cancel
	Adapter Status
	Unlink

Chapter 4

Ncb/Mcb Fields

IBM Token-Ring literature refers to the Ncb as the Message Control block or Mcb, but we will use the term Ncb exclusively.

The Ncb is 64 bytes, with 13 fields and one 14-byte reserved area. Table 4-1 diagrams the Ncb and its fields. The C language Ncb structure is illustrated in Listing 4-1 and the MASM structure is illustrated in Listing 4-2. The chart on the inside front cover illustrates when a field is an input field and when it is an output field. The fields are discussed in greater detail in Part IV.

Table 4-1. The Ncb Fields

Offset	Field Name	Length in Bytes	Field Structure
+00	Command	1	☐
+01	Return Code	1	☐
+02	Local Session Number	1	☐
+03	Name Number	1	☐
+04	Buffer Address	4	☐☐☐☐
+08	Buffer Length	2	☐☐
+10	Call Name	16	☐☐☐☐☐☐☐☐☐☐☐☐☐☐☐☐
+26	Name (Local)	16	☐☐☐☐☐☐☐☐☐☐☐☐☐☐☐☐
+42	Receive Time Out	1	☐
+43	Send Time Out	1	☐

Table 4-1. (cont.)

Offset	Field Name	Length in Bytes	Field Structure
+44	Post Routine Address	4	□□□□
+48	LANA Number	1	□
+49	Command Complete Flag	1	□
+50	Reserved Field	14	□□□□□□□□□□□□□□

Listing 4-1. A C Ncb Structure

```
#define USGC   unsigned char
#define USGI   unsigned
#define USGL   unsigned long

struct Ncb
    {
        USGC    NcbCommand;          /* command code                    */
        USGC    NcbRetCode;          /* return code                     */
        USGC    NcbLsn;              /* local session number            */
        USGC    NcbNum;              /* Datagram ADD NAME table entry    */

        char *  NcbBufferOffset;     /* I/O buffer offset               */
        USGI    NcbBufferSegment;    /* I/O buffer segment              */

        USGI    NcbLength;           /* length of data in I/O buffer    */

        char    NcbCallName[16];     /* remote system name for CALL     */
        char    NcbName[16];         /* local adapter network name      */

        USGC    NcbRto;              /* receive timeouts in 1/2 second units */
        USGC    NcbSto;              /* send    timeouts in 1/2 second units */

        char *  NcbPostRtnOffset;    /* offset  of post routine         */
        USGI    NcbPostRtnSegment;   /* segment of post routine         */

        USGC    NcbLanaNum;      /* network adapter number to execute cmd  */
        USGC    NcbCmdCplt;      /* 0xFF ==> command pending, else cmplted */

        char    NcbReservedArea[14]; /* work area for network card      */
    } ZeroNcb;                       /* prototype NCB for sizeof calcs */
```

Listing 4-2. A MASM Ncb Structure

```
;                    Ncb Structure

Ncb              struc
    Ncb_Command    db   00h           ;Ncb command field
    Ncb_RetCode    db   00h           ;Ncb return code
    Ncb_Lsn        db   00h           ;Ncb local session number
    Ncb_Num        db   00h           ;Ncb name number from AddName
    Ncb_BufferOff  dw   0000h         ;Ncb message buffer offset
    Ncb_BufferSeg  dw   0000h         ;Ncb message buffer segment
    Ncb_Length     dw   0000h         ;Ncb message buffer length (in bytes)
    Ncb_CallName   db   16 dup(0)     ;Ncb remote name
    Ncb_Name       db   16 dup(0)     ;Ncb AddName
    Ncb_Rto        db   00h           ;Ncb receive timeout
    Ncb_Sto        db   00h           ;Ncb send timeout
    Ncb_PostOff    dw   0000h         ;Ncb post routine offset
    Ncb_PostSeg    dw   0000h         ;Ncb post routine segment
    Ncb_Lana_Num   db   00h           ;Ncb adapter number
    Ncb_Cmd_Cplt   db   00h           ;Ncb 0FFh ==> command pending indicator
    Ncb_Reserve    db   14 dup(0)     ;Ncb reserved area
Ncb              ends
```

Command

The Ncb command field is a one-byte field containing the NetBIOS *command code* for the desired operation. If the high-order bit of the command code is zero, NetBIOS accepts the request and returns to the application when the command is completed. This is referred to as the wait option. Clearly, only one wait-option command can be pending at a time.

Although some commands such as Reset, Cancel, and Unlink are guaranteed to complete, other commands only complete under certain conditions. If such a command never completes, NetBIOS never returns and the machine hangs in an infinite NetBIOS command completion spin-loop. To avoid this, applications can set the high-order bit of the command field to a binary one value for all commands except the Reset, Cancel, and Unlink commands. This is referred to as the no-wait option. In this situation, NetBIOS returns immediately with an initial return code (in AL for the IBM PC) and expects that the Ncb and all associated data areas will remain undisturbed until the command can complete.

If NetBIOS accepts the command, it queues it for subsequent action which allows several requests to be pending at one time. It also places an FFh in the Ncb command complete field, indicating the command has been queued but has not completed. When the command completes, NetBIOS posts the final return code in both the Ncb return code field and the Ncb command complete field. It also inspects the Ncb post routine address field to see if it is all zeros. If it is not, NetBIOS immediately enters the code in a disabled state as if the code were an interrupt routine.

The code must subsequently return to NetBIOS with an IRET instruction and should enable interrupts if its activities require any significant time to accomplish. Moreover, a post routine should not issue PC-DOS requests because they may have been interrupted to invoke the post routine and PC-DOS is not reentrant. However, a post routine can issue other NetBIOS requests.

Finally, some programs occasionally terminate execution and return to the operating system with NetBIOS commands still pending. This is equivalent to leaving without disabling enabled hardware interrupts. NetBIOS will destroy memory in the 64-byte Ncb area if the Ncb eventually completes. At the very worst, NetBIOS will see that the NetBIOS post routine address is not zero when the command completes, perhaps because your word processor has overlaid the area where the Ncb resided. Thus, NetBIOS might wildly branch into memory based on the unpredictable post routine address value, causing your machine to periodically hang for inexplicable reasons, such as divide-by-zero interrupts during periods of apparent workstation inactivity.

Be warned. Pending NetBIOS requests must be canceled before an application completes and returns to the operating system. This is done by explicitly canceling all pending Ncbs or possibly by issuing an adapter Reset command. Failing to do this can result in debugging sessions that are memorably excruciating.

Return Code

The Ncb return code field is a one-byte field that eventually contains the value of the command's final return code. If it is zero after command completion, the command completed successfully. Otherwise, a problem was detected, though it may not be of any consequence. Appendix C lists the NetBIOS Ncb return codes.

Local Session Number

The Ncb local session number field is a one-byte field containing the local session number associated with a command. NetBIOS assigns the
value of the local session number in an incremental, modulo 255, roundrobin manner. The values zero and 255 are never assigned.

Name Number

The Ncb name number field is a one-byte field containing the NetBIOS
name table name number associated with a command. NetBIOS assigns
the value of the name number in an incremental, modulo 255, roundrobin manner. The values zero and 255 are never assigned. The first entry's number, name number one, is always the permanent node name's
number.

Buffer Address

The Ncb buffer address field is a four-byte field containing a memory
pointer to a data buffer. In the case of the IBM PC, the data is in the OFF-
SET:SEGMENT format.

Buffer Length

The Ncb buffer length field is a two-byte field indicating the size of the
buffer pointed at by the Ncb buffer address field.

Call (Remote) Name

The Ncb call name field is a 16-byte field typically, but not always, containing a remote name associated with the request. All 16 bytes are significant and are used. In some instances, such as local session creation, the
name may be a local name instead of a remote name.

In the case of a Chain Send Command, the Ncb call name field does not contain a name. The first two bytes are used to indicate the length of the Chain Send's second buffer. The next two bytes contain the second buffer's offset, and the last two bytes contain the buffer's segment address. While using the Ncb call name field in this manner may seem a bit odd, it has the advantage of minimizing the Ncb size while satisfying field alignment requirements for many C compilers.

(Local) Name

The Ncb (local) name field is a 16-byte field containing a local name associated with the request. All 16 bytes are significant and are used. The first character cannot have a value of binary zero or be an asterisk (*). In addition, IBM reserves the values of 00h to 1Fh for the 16th character and the values "IBM" as the first three characters of any name.

Receive Time Out

The Ncb receive time out field is a one-byte field used with Call and Listen commands. It specifies the number of half-second periods that a Receive (Receive, Receive-Any) command can wait for completion before timing-out and returning an error. The time-out threshold is established at session creation and cannot be subsequently altered. Specifying a value of 00h indicates that there is no time-out threshold for Receive commands associated with the session.

Send Time Out

The Ncb send time out field is a one-byte field used with Call and Listen commands. It specifies the number of half-second periods that a Send command (Send, Send No-Ack, Chain Send, Chain Send No-Ack) can wait for completion before timing-out and returning an error. The time-out threshold is established at session creation and cannot be subsequently altered. If a Send command times-out, the session is terminated. Specifying a value of 00h indicates that there is no time-out threshold for Send commands associated with the session.

Post Routine Address

The Ncb post routine address field is a four-byte field containing a memory pointer to a routine that is executed when the command completes. NetBIOS only inspects this field when the command has specified the no-wait option; otherwise, it is ignored. In the case of the IBM PC, the data is in the OFFSET:SEGMENT format. See the related Ncb command field for more information.

LANA Number

The Ncb LANA number field is a one-byte field indicating which adapter should handle the command. In the case of the IBM PC LAN adapters, there are at most two adapters. The primary adapter is LANA adapter zero; the alternate adapter is LANA adapter number one.

Command Complete Flag

The Ncb LANA number field is a one-byte field that indicates whether a command that specified the no-wait option has completed. If the value in this field is FFh, the command has not completed. Otherwise, the field contains the final command return code. See the Ncb command field for more information.

Reserved

The Ncb reserved field is a 14-byte reserved area that NetBIOS may use to return extended error information. In addition, NetBIOS uses it as an intermittent scratchpad during request processing. Application programs should never use the Ncb reserved field because if it is tampered with, NetBIOS's behavior may be unpredictable.

Sample C Program to Test for NetBIOS Presence

We now look at our first C NetBIOS program. Listing 4-3, PRESENCE.C, is a sample C program that should correctly test for the presence of Net-BIOS on all IBM PC models. In the event that this program does not work correctly with your machine or future IBM machines, you should use a debugger to inspect the INT 5C interrupt vector at segment 0000h, offset 0170h, and correct to program accordingly.

Listing 4-3. PRESENCE.C

```c
#define LINT_ARGS

#include <dos.h>
#include <stdio.h>
#include "netbios2.h"

struct SREGS SegRegs;

#if defined(LINT_ARGS)
extern   int main(int argc,char * *argv);
extern   int CheckDosIVs(void);
extern   void IssueInvalidNetbiosRequest(void);
extern   void ClearNcb(struct Ncb *NcbPtr);
extern   void NetbiosRequest(struct Ncb *NcbPointer);
extern   void Logo(void);
#endif

int main(argc, argv)
int    argc;
char *argv[];
{
    unsigned char temp;

    Logo();

    if (CheckDosIVs())
        IssueInvalidNetbiosRequest();

    printf("\n\nProgram ending...\n");

    return 0;
}

#define DOS_INT_21    0x21
#define DOS_FETCH_IV 0x35
```

Listing 4-3. (cont.)

```
int CheckDosIVs()
{
    union  REGS  InRegs, OutRegs;
    struct SREGS SegRegs;

    InRegs.h.ah = DOS_FETCH_IV;
    InRegs.h.al = NetbiosInt5C;

    int86x(DOS_INT_21, &InRegs, &OutRegs, &SegRegs);

     printf("\n\nNetBIOS Int 5Ch IV SEGMENT:OFFSET == %04X:%04X...",
                                    SegRegs.es, OutRegs.x.bx);

    switch (SegRegs.es) {

      case 0x0000 : printf("\n\nNetBIOS IV segment == 0x0000\x07");
                    return FAILURE;
                    break;
      case 0xF000 : printf("\n\nNetBIOS IV segment == 0xF000\x07");
                    return FAILURE;
                    break;
      default :     printf("\n\nNetBIOS IV segment appears valid...");
                    return SUCCESS;
                    break;
    }
}


#define ERROR_INVALID_COMMAND 0x03

void IssueInvalidNetbiosRequest()
{
    struct Ncb  PresenceNcb;

    ClearNcb(&PresenceNcb);

    PresenceNcb.NcbCommand = NETBIOS_INVALID_COMMAND;

    NetbiosRequest(&PresenceNcb);

    if (PresenceNcb.NcbRetCode == ERROR_INVALID_COMMAND)
       printf("and NetBIOS is present...");
    else
       printf("but NetBIOS is not present...\x07");
```

Listing 4-3. (cont.)

```
}

void ClearNcb(NcbPtr)
struct Ncb *NcbPtr;
{
    int   i;
    char *CharPtr;

    CharPtr = (char *) NcbPtr;

    for ( i = 0; i < sizeof(ZeroNcb); i++ )
       *CharPtr++ = 0x00;
}

void NetbiosRequest(NcbPointer)
struct Ncb *NcbPointer;
{
 union  REGS  InRegs, OutRegs;  /* defined in dos.h */
 struct Ncb far *NcbPtr = (struct Ncb far *) NcbPointer;

    segread(&SegRegs);

    SegRegs.es  = FP_SEG(NcbPtr);
    InRegs.x.bx = FP_OFF(NcbPtr);

    int86x(NetbiosInt5C, &InRegs, &OutRegs, &SegRegs);
}

void Logo()
{
    printf("\n*- NetBIOS Presence Test Program");
    printf(" © Copyright 1988 W. David Schwaderer -*");
}
```

Note that the program also issues an invalid NetBIOS request to ensure that the NetBIOS interrupt vector is actually being used by NetBIOS and has not been captured by some other program. However, if the interrupt vector has been captured by another program that reflects the request to an uninitialized NetBIOS interrupt, the results may be catastrophic. The NetBIOS presence testing process is significantly complicated by the existence of the NETBIOS.COM module. NETBIOS.COM can be loaded anywhere and is generally indistinguishable from a debugging program that may pass the interrupt (reflect) to an uninitialized interrupt vector.

Chapter 5

The IBM PC-DOS LAN
Support Program

As indicated in Figure 2-1, the IBM LAN Support Program provides support for the NetBIOS, DLC, and direct interfaces in PC-DOS environments. It replaces the predecessor NETBEUI.COM and TOKREUI.COM programs and provides communication interface support for all of IBM's LAN adapters.

The IBM LAN Support Program can simultaneously support up to two adapters within the same machine and they do not have to be of the same type. One adapter is referred to as the *primary* and has a programming address of zero, and the other, if present, is referred to as the *alternate* adapter and has a programming address of one.

Since a given adapter requires specific support programming, the IBM LAN Support Program provides families of device drivers that enable users to configure the specific support they require. As an example, this allows the original IBM PC Network LANA card to use standard LLC protocols.

Conversely, using another program named the IBM PC Network Protocol Driver allows IBM PC Network Adapter II and II/A cards to communicate with IBM PC Network LANA cards using the original SMP protocols. In any event, the protocol used is invisible to NetBIOS applications unless an application that uses one protocol tries to communicate with an application using another. That would never work in any circumstance. Hence, the operative concept throughout IBM LAN system offerings is communication flexibility within protocols.

What Is Its Role?

The IBM LAN Support Program provides users of IBM LAN adapters a significant degree of independence from the specific programming and operating characteristics of the particular LAN they are using. This enables users to select the appropriate type of media and LAN topology for their environments, independent of their particular application requirements. However, this independence is not universally granted without restrictions.

It is rather remarkable to folks familiar with the original PC Network LANA card's design that it can communicate using the 802.2 LLC protocols. Among other things, this capability enables PCs using the original PC Network LANA card to communicate with Token-Ring devices via an intermediary PC running the IBM Token-Ring/PC Network Interconnect Program. However, the PC Network adapter card used in the gateway cannot be an original PC Network LANA card. It has to be a PC Network Broadband Adapter II or II/A because there must be no other communication adapter in a PC if an original PC Network LANA card using LLC protocols is present.

The IBM LAN Support Program provides the "glue" for the various IBM LAN adapters, and that is a very significant role though it sometimes involves a few restrictions.

NetBIOS Parameter Summary

The IBM LAN Support Program NetBIOS device driver, DXMT0MOD. SYS, is one of eight device drivers included on the Program diskette. DXMT0MOD.SYS has 26 parameters that can optionally appear on the CONFIG.SYS device driver specification line. One of the parameters, STATIONS, helps determine the number of transmit buffers as well as the size of both the transmit and receive buffers. This parameter can significantly affect NetBIOS performance. Other parameters such as DLC. MAXIN, DLC.MAXOUT, DLC.T1, and DLC.T2 parameters affect NetBIOS performance as well.

The rest of the parameters either affect memory consumption or performance during error recovery (see Table 5-1). Consult DXMINFO.DOC for details concerning the other device drivers and how to specify the parameter values for primary and alternate adapters.

DLC, LLC, SAPs, and Link Stations Preliminaries

A Service Access Point (SAP) is a constructed code point that identifies applications to the DLC and LLC software (see Table 5-1). All 802.2

Table 5-1. Effect of the DXMT0MOD.SYS STATIONS Parameter

Link Station Count	Transmit Buffer Count	Transmit Buffer Size	Receive Buffer Size
Token-Ring I Adapter (8K-byte shared-RAM)			
01–06	2	1048	280
07–12	1	1048	192
13–18	1	600	144
19–24	1	600	112
〉24	1	600	96
Token-Ring II Adapter and Token-Ring/A Adapter (16K-byte shared-RAM)			
01–32	2	2040	280
33–48	2	1048	280
49–64	1	1048	280
〉64	1	600	144
PC Network Adapter			
01–32	2	2040	280
33–48	2	1048	280
49–64	1	1048	280
〉64	1	600	144

Source: DXMINFO.DOC version 1.02

frames (transmitted packets) contain a one-byte SAP value. DLC and LLC logic use this value to determine the destination application and where to obtain resources (e.g., storage) to handle a frame. The NetBIOS SAP value is 0Fh and the SNA value is 04h; there are others. DLC and LLC software both permit multiple simultaneous active SAPs.

SAPs own link stations and can own more than one link station simultaneously. Link stations are components which DLC and LLC use to identify communicating adapters. When NetBIOS establishes a session, a local link station connects with a remote link station, establishing a path. The session uses this path for all frames associated with the session. LLC insures the integrity of the data and handles the acknowledgment and sequencing of the frames. When a session abnormally ends, there is a connection problem between two link stations.

For each of the parameters we are going to discuss, the expression in parentheses indicates the parameter's abbreviation as well as its allowable range or values. Where appropriate, the value following the "default =" is the default value. Parameters that begin with DLC are given to LLC software to specify characteristics of NetBIOS link stations. Note that this information is extracted from the DXMINFO.DOC version 1.02 and is subject to change. For more current information, consult the DXMINFO.DOC file on your current IBM PC LAN Program Diskette.

ADAP.ADDR.NOT.REVERSED

The ADAP.ADDR.NOT.REVERSED (ANR=Y/N, default = N) parameter specifies the order in which an Adapter Status command should present the bytes composing an adapter's permanent node name.

PC Network LANA Adapter Cards

Using native ROM NetBIOS, PC Network LANA adapter cards always have two bytes of binary zeros as the last two bytes of their permanent node name. If a PC Network LANA adapter has a permanent node name of X'112233440000', specifying ANR=Y causes an Adapter Status to present the value as X'000011223344'. Otherwise, the value is presented as X'443322110000'. This means, with either selection of the ANR value, the PC LAN Program version 1.02 does not provide the value a native LANA NetBIOS provides. (Refer to Figure 5-1.)

Non-LANA Permanent Node Name ⟶ X'112233445566'

ANR = Y ⟶ X'112233445566'
ANR = N ⟶ X'665544332211'

LANA Permanent Node Name ⟶ X'112233440000'

ANR = Y ⟶ X'000011223344'
ANR = N ⟶ X'443322110000'

Fig. 5-1. Effect of ANR parameter, LAN Support Program version 1.02.

Other Network Adapter Cards

If the ADAP.ADDR.NOT.REVERSED parameter is specified as Y, an Adapter Status command presents the adapter's permanent node name the way it exists on the adapter. If omitted or specified as N, an Adapter Status command presents the adapter's permanent node name in a byte-reversed format. (Refer to Figure 5-1.)

CLOSE.ON.RESET

The CLOSE.ON.RESET (CR=Y/N, default = N) parameter specifies whether NetBIOS should close and reopen the adapter whenever a NetBIOS Reset command is issued. An adapter close and reopen can take a few seconds to complete.

If omitted or specified as N, the close and reopen is not performed when the adapter is Reset. In this case, the Reset command takes significantly less time to complete because it only clears the NetBIOS name table and changes the resettable maximum command and session values. This also does not disrupt DLC communication that may exist at the time of the Reset command.

COMMANDS

The COMMANDS (0 <= C <= 254, default = 12) parameter specifies the maximum number of Ncbs that may be waiting for completion at one time. If omitted or specified as 0, the default value of 12 is used.

DATAGRAM.MAX

This DATAGRAM.MAX (DG=Y/N, default = N) parameter specifies that the maximum length datagram transmitted by NetBIOS is computed from the adapter's transmit buffer size (data hold buffer or DHB) rather than arbitrarily using the normal 512 bytes. If specified as Y, a datagram's maximum length is the transmit buffer's size less 96 bytes (DHB Size − 96).

DHB.NUMBER

The DHB.NUMBER (DN, default = NetBIOS selected) parameter specifies the number of adapter transmit buffer(s). If omitted or specified as 0, the value is determined by the NetBIOS device driver.

DHB.SIZE

The DHB.SIZE (0 or 200 <= DS <= 9999, default = NetBIOS selected) parameter specifies the size of the adapter's transmit buffer(s) data hold buffer(s) or DHB(s). If omitted or specified as 0, the value is determined by the NetBIOS device driver.

DLC.MAXIN

The DLC.MAXIN (1 $\langle=$ MI $\langle=$ 9, default $=$ 1) parameter specifies the MAXIN value for all NetBIOS device driver link stations. If omitted or specified as 0, the default value of 1 is used.

DLC.MAXOUT

The DLC.MAXOUT (1 $\langle=$ MO $\langle=$ 9, default $=$ 2) parameter specifies the MAXOUT value for all NetBIOS device driver link stations. If omitted or specified as 0, the default value of 2 is used.

DLC.RETRY.COUNT

The DLC.RETRY.COUNT (1 $\langle=$ RC $\langle=$ 255, default $=$ 8) parameter determines the number of retry attempts to be made by the adapter's LLC code. If omitted or specified as 0, the default value of 8 is used.

DLC.T1

The DLC.T1 (DLC.tee-one) (0 $\langle=$ T1 $\langle=$ 10, default $=$ 5) parameter determines the value of the T1 (response) timer in the adapter's LLC code. If omitted or specified as 0, the default value of 5 is used. For more information on the response timer, consult the *Token-Ring Technical Reference Manual*.

DLC.T2

The DLC.T2 (0 $\langle=$ T2 $\langle=$ 11, default $=$ 2) parameter determines the value of the T2 (receiver acknowledgment) timer in the adapter's LLC code. If the value is 11, the T2 timer function is not used. If omitted or specified as 0, the default value of 2 is used. For more information on the receiver acknowledgment timer, consult the *Token-Ring Technical Reference Manual*.

DLC.TI

The DLC.TI (DLC.tee-eye) (0 ⟨= TI ⟨= 10, default = 3) parameter determines the value of the Ti (inactivity) timer in the adapter's LLC code. If omitted or specified as 0, the default value of 3 is used. For more information on the inactivity timer, consult the *Token-Ring Technical Reference Manual*.

ENABLE

The ENABLE (E, positional parameter) parameter is the only DXMT0MOD.SYS positional parameter, and must be the first parameter if it is present and can be abbreviated E. The ENABLE parameter should be present when the host PC has an asynchronous communication adapter that is operating at "high-speed" (a speed equal to or greater than 1,200 bits per second according to IBM's field support representatives). The effect of this parameter, when present, is a potential "loss in performance" according to the DXMINFO.DOC documentation.

EXTRA.SAPS

The EXTRA.SAPS (0 ⟨= ES ⟨= 99, default = 0) parameter requests that the NetBIOS device driver obtain additional SAPs when it implicitly opens the adapter by first attempting to execute a command before the adapter is open. These SAPs are not used by the NetBIOS device driver. If omitted or specified as 0, no additional SAPs are requested.

EXTRA.STATIONS

The EXTRA.STATIONS (0 ⟨= EST ⟨= 99, default = 0) parameter requests the NetBIOS device driver to obtain additional link stations when it implicitly opens the adapter. These link stations are not used by the NetBIOS device driver. If omitted or specified as 0, no additional stations are requested.

NAMES

The NAMES (0 ⟨= N ⟨= 254, default = 17) parameter specifies the maximum number of NetBIOS names that may exist in the NetBIOS name table, including the universally administered address in the case of the Token-Ring. If omitted or specified as 0, the default value of 17 is used.

OPEN.ON.LOAD

If the OPEN.ON.LOAD (O=Y/N, default = Y) parameter is specified as Y, the NetBIOS device driver opens the adapter at load time during CON-FIG.SYS processing. This eliminates the delay caused by an adapter open when the first Ncb is subsequently issued. If omitted, the default value of Y is used.

RECEIVE.BUFFER.SIZE

The RECEIVE.BUFFER.SIZE (R, default = NetBIOS selected) parameter specifies the size of the adapter's receive buffers. If omitted or specified as 0, the value is determined by the NetBIOS device driver.

REMOTE.DATAGRAM.CONTROL

The REMOTE.DATAGRAM.CONTROL (RDC=Y/N, default = N) parameter is meaningless if the REMOTE.NAME.DIRECTORY (RND) (0 ⟨= RND ⟨= 255) parameter is omitted or specified as 0.

If specified as Y, Send Datagram also uses the remote name directory for transmitting to remote nodes. If omitted or specified as N, Send Datagram does not use the RND.

REMOTE.NAME.DIRECTORY

If omitted or specified as 0, all Calls, Status Queries, and Send Datagrams are broadcast to all NetBIOS nodes, as in previous levels of NetBIOS.

If a nonzero value is coded, the RND value specifies the number of remote names that may be saved by the local node. Note, the minimum number of name entries is 4 and the value of 4 is used if it is specified as 1, 2, or 3. After the local station has located a remote name, the remote node address is saved in the remote name directory.

Subsequent Calls, Status Queries, and Send Datagrams to that name are to the specific node rather than broadcast to all nodes. Issuing a Find Name command with a receive buffer-length of zero forces a remote name directory update when there is a failing bridge in the transmission path.

RESET.VALUES

If specified as Y, the RESET.VALUES (RV=Y/N, default = N) parameter has two options.

When the number of sessions is specified as 0 in a subsequent Reset, the default is the SESSIONS value rather than the normal default value of 6. When the number of commands is specified as 0 in a subsequent Reset, the default is the COMMANDS value rather than the normal default value of 12.

If omitted or specified as N, RESET works as it does in earlier releases of NetBIOS.

RING.ACCESS

The RING.ACCESS ($0 \langle= RA \langle= 3$, default = 0) parameter specifies a Token-Ring adapter's ring access priority for NetBIOS device driver messages. Higher numbers indicate a higher priority. If omitted or specified as 0, the default value of 0 is used.

SESSIONS

The SESSIONS ($0 \langle= S \langle= 254$, default = 6) parameter specifies the maximum number of NetBIOS sessions that may be defined. If omitted or specified as 0, the default value of 6 is used.

STATIONS

The STATIONS ($0 \langle= ST \langle= 254$, default = 6) parameter specifies the maximum number of NetBIOS link stations that may be defined. If omitted or specified as 0, the default value of 6 is used.

TRANSMIT.COUNT

The TRANSMIT.COUNT ($1 \langle= TC \langle= 10$, default = 6) parameter specifies the number of times queries (Call, Remote Adapter Status Query, Add Name, Add Group Name, and Find Name) are transmitted. If omitted or specified as 0, the default value of 6 is used.

TRANSMIT.TIMEOUT

The TRANSMIT.TIMEOUT (0 <= TT <= 20, default = 1) parameter specifies the number of half-second intervals between transmission of queries (Call, Remote Adapter Status Query, Add Name, Add Group Name, and Find Name). If omitted or specified as 0, the default value of 1 is used for a half-second interval.

DLC.MAXIN, DLC.MAXOUT, DLC.T1, and DLC.T2 Relationship

DLC.MAXIN is the number of frames a local link station receives before issuing an acknowledgment. The DLC.T2 timer specifies how long the receiving LLC component waits before sending the acknowledgment. If DLC.MAXIN is five and the local link station has received two frames, LLC acknowledges the two received frames when DLC.T2 expires.

The DLC.MAXOUT specifies the number of frames a local link station sends before expecting an acknowledgment. The DLC.T1 timer specifies how long the transmitting LLC component waits for this acknowledgment. If DLC.T1 expires before an acknowledgment, the link station enters checkpointing which causes a sequence-information exchange and network integrity validation by the link stations.

The DLC.MAXOUT and DLC.MAXIN default values of 2 and 1, respectively, allow NetBIOS and LLC to operate in maximum parallel mode. A transmitting link station sends two back-to-back frames to a receiving link station. The receiving station receives the first frame and immediately acknowledges it. Typically, by the time the second frame is transmitted, the acknowledgment for the first has arrived. This allows maximum utilization of the network.

IBM provides a wide spectrum of LAN adapters. Combined with the IBM LAN Support Program's versatility, IBM's LAN system offerings provide a significant degree of isolation from the underlying hardware support, including LAN media. This allows users to select the hardware and topology best suited to their requirements, confident that their programs will function correctly independent of their specific hardware choices.

Chapter 6

NetBIOS Relationships to Other IBM Products

There is a common misconception that NetBIOS requires some version of PC-DOS. Since NetBIOS operates on UNIX-based operating systems, this is clearly false. Moreover, if you use an IBM PC Network LANA adapter, you can write NetBIOS programs that execute on PC-DOS 1.0.

IBM PC-DOS Version Requirements

PC-DOS 3.1, and later PC-DOS versions, contain LAN considerations for the PC-DOS *redirector*. The redirector provides PC-DOS services necessary for the operation of the IBM PC LAN Program. REDIR.EXE module actually provides the redirector services and is an IBM PC LAN Program component.

IBM PC LAN Program Considerations

The IBM PC LAN Program expects to be the first NetBIOS user of a LAN adapter. If there are any existing sessions or names registered in the NetBIOS name table, the Program will not provide network services and terminates operation. This happens because the Program may reset a LAN adapter in an attempt to increase the maximum number of sessions and pending commands.

Appendix B of the *IBM PC Local Area Network Program User's Guide* contains a list of additional restrictions that must be observed by coexisting NetBIOS applications if the IBM PC LAN Program is to operate correctly in a server configuration.

Coexistence Restrictions

NetBIOS applications may need to determine if the IBM PC LAN Program is operating. If it is, the applications should observe the following considerations as mentioned in the *Guide*.

- They should not use all the available sessions and pending commands, because the IBM PC LAN Program needs some.
- They should not issue a NetBIOS Reset command because this removes the names the IBM PC LAN Program has added to the NetBIOS name table.
- They should not use any of the names added to the NetBIOS name table by the IBM PC LAN Program.
- They should not use the Receive-Any-for-Any Name command because the IBM PC LAN Program needs to receive its messages.
- They should not use the values 00h to 1Fh for the 16th byte value in NetBIOS names because these are reserved for the IBM PC LAN Program. Application programmers are encouraged to use a blank (20h) as the 16th character in NetBIOS Names.
- They should carefully reflect appropriate captured hardware and software interrupts and do so in a disabled state to simulate correct entry into the IBM PC LAN Program.
- To avoid overlaid data problems, destroyed FATs, and destroyed directories, they must not do direct disk or diskette accesses to write data.
- They should not directly program the display controller (e.g., 6845) to avoid the possibility of the IBM PC LAN Program's improperly restoring the display settings. The controller settings should be changed only with application BIOS calls.
- They should not use the NetBIOS Receive Broadcast Datagram command. Application designers are warned that using Receive Broadcast Datagram "will probably result in PC LAN or application failures that will require the user to reset (Ctrl-Alt-Del) the machine." Application designers are advised to use plain datagrams sent to group names if necessary.
- Where appropriate, they should use DOS file-handle functions with sharing modes and avoid using FCBs because FCBs do not support file sharing or locking functions. If this is not possible,

applications should not construct their own FCBs, change FCB reserved areas, or close the FCB and continue to use it as though it were still open. The last restriction includes saving an FCB in a file for use at another time. Moreover, to insure data integrity, applications should periodically close and reopen files that are accessed via FCBs.

- They should use the PC-DOS Create Unique File function (INT 21h AH=5Ah) to create temporary files. To avoid file contention and collisions in multiuser environments, they should not use fixed names for temporary files.
- They should use the PC-DOS Create New File function (INT 21h AH=5Bh) to create a file instead of simply creating one to see if it already exists.
- To avoid "unpredictable problems" they should not change the timer tick rate from its natural 18.2 times per second rate.

For more information, consult Appendix B of the *Guide*.

Detecting the Program

The IBMLANPG.C sample program in Listing 6-1 illustrates the proper way a program should determine whether the IBM PC LAN Program is installed. The application should first check that the PC-DOS version is 3.10 or later, then check to see if the Program is installed. If so, the application can request the machine name that the Program is using.

The machine name is returned as a 15-character name, padded at the end with blanks. A 16th byte holds an ASCII zero. In reality, the 16th byte of the machine name in the NetBIOS name table is a blank. For more details, check the *Guide* and the *PC-DOS Technical Reference Manual*, which documents the Get Machine Name function.

Listing 6-1. IBMLANPG.C

```
#define LINT_ARGS

#include <dos.h>
#include <stdio.h>
#include "netbios2.h"

#if defined(LINT_ARGS)
extern  int main(int argc,char * *argv);
extern  int CheckDosVersion(void);
extern  void CheckForIbmLanProgram(void);
```

Listing 6-1. (cont.)

```c
extern  void GetMachineName(void);
extern  void Logo(void);
#endif

#define DOS_INT_21        0x21
#define DOS_INT_2A        0x2A
#define DOS_INT_2F        0x2F

#define PC_LAN_PGM_CHECK  0xB800
#define DOS_FETCH_VERSION 0x30
#define GET_MACHINE_NAME  0x5E00

#define REDIRECTOR_FLAG   0x0008
#define RECEIVER_FLAG     0x0080
#define MESSENGER_FLAG    0x0004
#define SERVER_FLAG       0x0040

int main(argc, argv)
int   argc;
char *argv[];
{

    Logo();

    if (CheckDosVersion())
        CheckForIbmLanProgram();

    printf("\n\nProgram ending...\n");

    return 0;
}

int CheckDosVersion()
{
    union  REGS  InRegs, OutRegs;

    InRegs.h.ah = DOS_FETCH_VERSION;

    int86(DOS_INT_21, &InRegs, &OutRegs);

    printf("\n\nThe PC-DOS Version is %u.%u... ",
                        OutRegs.h.al, OutRegs.h.ah);

    if (OutRegs.h.al < 3)    /* check the major version number */
```

Listing 6-1. (cont.)

```
      return FAILURE;

   if (OutRegs.h.ah < 10)   /* check the minor version number */
      return FAILURE;

   InRegs.h.ah = 0;

   int86(DOS_INT_2A, &InRegs, &OutRegs);

   if (OutRegs.h.ah != 0)
      printf("\n\nThe INT 2A NetBIOS interface is available...");
   else
      printf("\n\nThe INT 2A NetBIOS interface is not available...\x07");

   return SUCCESS;
}


void CheckForIbmLanProgram()
{
   USGC temp;
   union  REGS  InRegs, OutRegs;

   InRegs.x.ax = PC_LAN_PGM_CHECK;

   int86(DOS_INT_2F, &InRegs, &OutRegs);

   if (OutRegs.h.al == 0) {
      printf("\n\nThe IBM PC LAN Program is not installed...\x07");
      return;
   }

   printf("\n\nThe IBM PC LAN Program is installed ");
   printf("and operating as a ");

   temp = OutRegs.h.bl & (REDIRECTOR_FLAG | RECEIVER_FLAG |
                          MESSENGER_FLAG | SERVER_FLAG);

   /*   The order of testing is important because
        the bit settings are cumulative as are the
        configurations.
   */

   if (SERVER_FLAG & temp)
```

Listing 6-1. (cont.)

```c
            printf("Server.");
    else if (MESSENGER_FLAG  & temp)
            printf("Messenger.");
    else if (RECEIVER_FLAG   & temp)
            printf("Receiver.");
    else if (REDIRECTOR_FLAG & temp)
            printf("Redirector.");
    else {
        printf("and operating in an unknown configuration.\x07");
        return;
    }
    GetMachineName();
}


void GetMachineName()
{
    struct SREGS SegRegs;
    union  REGS  InRegs, OutRegs;
    char   Buffer[16], far *BufferPtr = Buffer;


    InRegs.x.ax = GET_MACHINE_NAME;

    SegRegs.ds  = FP_SEG(BufferPtr);
    InRegs.x.dx = FP_OFF(BufferPtr);

    int86x(DOS_INT_21, &InRegs, &OutRegs, &SegRegs);

    if (OutRegs.h.ch != 0) {
        printf("\n\nThe machine name is ==>%s<== ", Buffer);
        printf("\n\nThe machine name's NetBIOS Name Number is %u."
                                                ,OutRegs.h.cl);
    } else
        printf("\n\nThe machine name is not defined...");

}


void Logo()
{
    printf("\nIBM Local Area Network Program Presence Test Program");
    printf("\n© Copyright 1988 W. David Schwaderer ");
}
```

Chapter 7

LAN Data Integrity and Security

This material merits its own discussion because the issues of LAN data integrity and security are becoming critical as LANs become more pervasive within business environments.

LAN Data Integrity

The good news is that LAN communication is typically very reliable. However, some LAN adapters do not have Cyclic Redundancy Checking (CRC) for message transmission and reception verification, and some do not have parity checking for onboard adapter memory.

The chilling fact is that if sections of a network's transmission path do not have these or comparable facilities, end-to-end data integrity cannot be guaranteed without some extra application programming effort. It may be worthwhile to check with your potential vendor to see if your LAN has sufficient data integrity features to satisfy your requirements.

LAN Data Security—A Word to the Wise

LANs provide all the data security that cordless telephones provide their users. Just as a cordless phone broadcasts conversations for passers-by and neighbors to monitor, all LAN communication is broadcast to all LAN adapters.

The adapter determines whether the data enters the workstation's memory or is simply discarded. Given enough guidance from a determined programmer, many LAN adapters can be coaxed into what is referred to as promiscuous mode, receiving all LAN-transmitted data for subsequent distribution to and leisurely review by affluent or otherwise interested third parties. Consider the following IBM statements.

IBM Statement 1

Above the copyright notice, the *Token-Ring Network PC Adapter Technical Reference Manual* states:

> Note: This product is intended for use within a single establishment and within a single, homogeneous user population. For sensitive applications requiring isolation from each other, management may wish to provide isolated cabling or to encrypt the sensitive data before putting it on the network.

Remember that achieving, not to mention maintaining, user population homogeneity could present a challenge.

IBM Statement 2

The *IBM NetBIOS Application Development Guide* Introduction states:

> It is the responsibility of the operating system or application program to make sure that data or devices are secure on the network as network security is not built into the NetBIOS.

Permanent Node Name Capers

You might suppose you can use an adapter's permanent node name to identify workstations involved in communication activities. However, unfriendly LAN users may alter their locally administered name or even covertly exchange LAN adapters among workstations.

This potentially allows a user to obtain a coveted permanent node name and subsequently "impersonate" other LAN users authorized with special LAN privileges by virtue of their permanent node names. Such privileges might include using the LAN to silently eavesdrop on other LAN workstation activities and inspection or manipulation of sensitive files—all unobtrusively from behind closed doors.

Thus, while IBM LAN adapter initialization procedures and supporting software guarantee that a node's permanent node name or locally administered ID is unique on a given LAN, be vigilant when you use adapter numbers as the only mechanism for user identification or LAN-user privilege administration.

You may not know who is really using a privileged permanent node name. While you might want to keep these numbers confidential from users, this is generally a futile effort against determined or sophisticated LAN penetrations.

The Uneasy Conclusion

As of this writing, portable LAN monitors are commercially available that can selectively or indiscriminately record and display everything transmitted on an Ethernet and IBM Token-Ring LAN. Though they are somewhat expensive, you should not discount their eventual use within your establishment.

If you would not project your spreadsheets, personal mail, financial data, etc., on a neighborhood drive-in theater's screen, you would be well advised to consider encrypting your data before transmitting it on a LAN.

Part II

NetBIOS Support Programming

Chapter 8

General Support Programming

Our first NetBIOS program resets an adapter that is assumed to be controlled by the IBM LAN Support Program. Examine this program in detail because it presents many NetBIOS programming principles used, but not discussed, in later programs. If you only study one program completely, this should be it. Note that all programs assume compatibility with Microsoft Corporation's C 5.0 compiler.

First note the #define LINT_ARGS statement. All programs contain this statement to include subsequent function prototype statements in the compilation. The compiler produces these statements when invoked with the /Zg parameter. (Redirecting the compiler output to a file allows the generated prototypes to be included in the source listing or separate header file.) All program function declarations observe pre-ANSI X3J11 conventions but can easily be replaced by modified function prototype statements if supported by your compiler.

Second, note the test for the adapter in the main( ) routine. To eliminate repetition, all subsequent program listings do not include this test.

Finally, note that the netbios2.h include file listed in Appendix A defines all symbolic values (e.g., SUCCESS, MAX_ADAPTER_NUMBER, etc.).

The NetBIOS RESET Sample Program

The RESET.C program in Listing 8-1 resets a NetBIOS adapter, and accepts three integer parameters. In order, they are:

1. the number of the adapter to reset (0 or 1)

2. the maximum session count (0 to 254)

3. the maximum pending command count (0 to 255)

If no parameter or an incorrect parameter is entered, the program displays a usage message. Note, the actual maximum allowable values for the session and command counts varies and may be controlled by IBM LAN Support Program /S and /C parameter values, respectively. Exceeding the ceiling values specified as IBM LAN Support Program parameter values forces NetBIOS to compute its own values. To dynamically determine these ceiling values, a program must issue an Adapter Status request.

Listing 8-1. RESET.C

```
#define LINT_ARGS

#include <dos.h>
#include <stdio.h>
#include "netbios2.h"

#if defined(LINT_ARGS)
extern   int main(int argc,char * *argv);
extern   void Logo(void);
extern   int CheckDosIVs(void);
extern   int IssueInvalidNetbiosRequest(void);
extern   int EditParms(int argc,char * *argv);
extern   void ResetAdapter(unsigned int AdapterNumber,
                           unsigned int SessionCount,
                           unsigned int CommandCount);
extern   void ClearNcb(struct Ncb *NcbPtr);
extern   void NetbiosRequest(struct Ncb *NcbPointer);
extern   void AnalyzeResetError(int ResetErrorCode);
extern   void Explain(void);
extern   void ExitNow(void);
#endif

struct Ncb ResetNcb;

struct SREGS SegRegs;

int main(argc, argv)
int    argc;
char *argv[];
{
```

Listing 8-1. (cont.)

```c
  Logo();

  if ((!CheckDosIVs()) || (!IssueInvalidNetbiosRequest())) {
    printf("\n\nNetBIOS not present...program ending...\n\n\x07");
    ExitNow();
  }

  if (!EditParms(argc, argv)) {
    Explain();
    ExitNow();
  } else ResetAdapter(atoi(argv[1]),
                      atoi(argv[2]),
                      atoi(argv[3]));

  return 0;
}

void Logo()
{
  printf("\n            NETBIOS Adapter Reset Sample Program");
  printf("\n            © Copyright 1988  W. David Schwaderer");
}

#define DOS_INT_21    0x21
#define DOS_FETCH_IV  0x35

int CheckDosIVs()
{
    union  REGS  InRegs, OutRegs;
    struct SREGS SegRegs;

    InRegs.h.ah = DOS_FETCH_IV;
    InRegs.h.al = NetbiosInt5C;

    int86x(DOS_INT_21, &InRegs, &OutRegs, &SegRegs);

    switch (SegRegs.es) {

      case 0x0000 : return FAILURE;
                    break;
      case 0xF000 : return FAILURE;
                    break;
      default :     return SUCCESS;
                    break;
```

Listing 8-1. (cont.)

```
    }
}

int IssueInvalidNetbiosRequest()
{
    struct Ncb  PresenceNcb;

    ClearNcb(&PresenceNcb);

    PresenceNcb.NcbCommand = NETBIOS_INVALID_COMMAND;

    NetbiosRequest(&PresenceNcb);

    if (PresenceNcb.NcbRetCode == (USGC) 0x03)
        return SUCCESS;
    else
        return FAILURE;
}

int EditParms(argc, argv)
int    argc;
char *argv[];
{
    int ReturnFlag = SUCCESS;

    if (argc != 4) {
        printf("\n\n\x07Incorrect number of parameters...");
        return FAILURE;
    }

    if ((atoi(argv[1]) < 0) || (MAX_ADAPTER_NUMBER < atoi(argv[1]) )) {
        printf("\n\n\x07Incorrect adapter-number parameter value (%d)...",
                                                      atoi(argv[1]));
        ReturnFlag = FAILURE;
    }

    if ((atoi(argv[2]) < 0) || (MAX_SESSION_COUNT < atoi(argv[2]))) {
        printf("\n\n\x07Incorrect session-count parameter value (%d)...",
                                                      atoi(argv[2]));
        ReturnFlag = FAILURE;
    }

    if ((atoi(argv[3]) < 0) || (MAX_COMMAND_COUNT < atoi(argv[3]))) {
        printf("\n\n\x07Incorrect command-count parameter value (%d)...",
```

Listing 8-1. (cont.)

```
                                                       atoi(argv[3]));
    ReturnFlag = FAILURE;
  }


  if (ReturnFlag == FAILURE)
    return FAILURE;


  if (atoi(argv[2]) == 0) {
    printf("\n\nWarning...");
    printf("NetBIOS selects the session count value...\x07");
  }


  if (atoi(argv[3]) == 0) {
    printf("\n\nWarning...");
    printf("NetBIOS selects the command count value...\x07");
  }


  return SUCCESS;
}


void ResetAdapter(AdapterNumber, SessionCount, CommandCount)
unsigned AdapterNumber, SessionCount, CommandCount;
{
  printf("\n\nNETBIOS adapter %d reset parameters ==>", AdapterNumber);
  printf(" %d session%s and %d command%s...",
          SessionCount, (SessionCount == 1) ? "" : "s",
          CommandCount, (CommandCount == 1) ? "" : "s");


  printf("\n\nPlease wait for the adapter to reset...");


  ResetNcb.NcbCommand = NETBIOS_RESET_WAIT_ONLY; /* reset command code */


  ResetNcb.NcbLanaNum = AdapterNumber;      /* adapter number        */
  ResetNcb.NcbLsn     = SessionCount;       /* concurrent session count */
  ResetNcb.NcbNum     = CommandCount;       /* concurrent command count */


  NetbiosRequest(&ResetNcb);                /* Ncb was already zero    */


  if (!ResetNcb.NcbRetCode) {
    printf("\n\nThe return code was %x.\n", ResetNcb.NcbRetCode);
  }
  else {
    printf("\n\n\x07The return code was %x ", ResetNcb.NcbRetCode);
    AnalyzeResetError(ResetNcb.NcbRetCode);
```

Listing 8-1. (cont.)

```c
        printf("\n");
    }
}


void ClearNcb(NcbPtr)
struct Ncb *NcbPtr;
{
    int    i;
    char *CharPtr;

    CharPtr = (char *) NcbPtr;

    for ( i = 0; i < sizeof(ZeroNcb); i++ )
        *CharPtr++ = 0x00;
}


void NetbiosRequest(NcbPointer)
struct Ncb *NcbPointer;
{
 union  REGS  InRegs, OutRegs;
 struct Ncb far *NcbPtr = (struct Ncb far *) NcbPointer;

    SegRegs.es  = FP_SEG(NcbPtr);
    InRegs.x.bx = FP_OFF(NcbPtr);

    int86x(NetbiosInt5C, &InRegs, &OutRegs, &SegRegs);
}


void AnalyzeResetError(ResetErrorCode)
int ResetErrorCode;
{
        if (ResetErrorCode == 0x03) {
            printf("[invalid command code]");
            return;
        }

        if (ResetErrorCode == 0x23) {
            printf("[adapter not installed]");
            return;
        }

        if ((0x3F < ResetErrorCode) && (ResetErrorCode < 0x50)) {
            printf("[unusual network condition -or- unacceptable ring-status]");
            return;
```

Listing 8-1. (cont.)

```
     }

     if (0x4F < ResetErrorCode) {
        printf("[adapter malfunction -or- ");
        printf("Adapter/PC unusual condition/error ]");
        return;
     }

     printf("[undocumented error]\x07");
}

void Explain()
{
   printf("\n\nusage: reset adapter-number session-count command-count");
   printf("\n\n    where: 0 <= adapter-number <= %d", MAX_ADAPTER_NUMBER);
   printf("\n              0 <= session-count  <= %d",   MAX_SESSION_COUNT);
   printf("\n              0 <= command-count  <= %d",   MAX_COMMAND_COUNT);
}

void ExitNow()
{
     printf("\n\nEnding RESET because of parameter input errors...\n");
     exit(1);
}
```

Support Routines

The main( ) routine first invokes Logo( ) which displays a logo. It then calls CheckDosIVs( ) and IssueInvalidNetbiosRequest( ) to verify that NetBIOS is present. Part I discusses these tests in more detail.

If NetBIOS is not present, the program terminates after issuing an acerbic comment. Otherwise, control passes to EditParms( ) which checks the command-line parameters.

EditParms( )

The various EditParms( ) routine checks are:

1. The parameter count should be four.
2. The adapter number should have a nonnegative value of zero or a value not greater than MAX_ADAPTER_NUMBER.

3. The requested number of sessions should be less than the maximum allowable (MAX_SESSION_COUNT).

4. The requested number of maximum outstanding commands allowable should be less than the maximum allowable (MAX_COMMAND_COUNT).

If the session or command value is zero, a warning is presented to the user stating that NetBIOS will compute the parameter value.

   If the parameters are not acceptable, main( ) invokes Explain( ) to display the appropriate parameter values and then exits by invoking Exit-Now( ). Otherwise, the parameters are acceptable and main( ) invokes the ResetAdapter( ) routine to reset the adapter.

ResetAdapter( )

The ResetAdapter( ) routine first displays the adapter number, session count, and pending command count values it uses in its Reset command. Because the NetBIOS reset may take a few seconds, it issues a request for user patience. Whether it actually delays the few seconds is controlled by the IBM LAN Support Program CR parameter discussed in Part I.

   ResetAdapter( ) completes the required fields in the Ncb structure named ResetNcb located near the top of the listing, and invokes Netbios-Request( ) to issue the request. If NetBIOS is not present in the machine, the machine generally freezes at this point. Note that the symbolic value of the Reset command code (NETBIOS_RESET_WAIT_ONLY) clearly indicates that a no-wait version of the command does not exist.

   After NetBIOS returns, ResetAdapter( ) inspects the return code. If it is zero, then ResetAdapter( ) displays a success message and returns to main( ) which then exits. Alternatively, ResetAdapter( ) displays the non-zero return code and invokes AnalyzeResetError( ) to display an English explanation before it exits.

AnalyzeResetError( )

Properly analyzing error codes is a challenge because different IBM Net-BIOS implementations provide different adapter-dependent error codes. The error code analysis presented in AnalyzeResetError( ) is for errors applying to the PC Network LANA NetBIOS. Note that IBM Token-Ring 4Xh and FXh error codes reflect an unacceptable ring status and an adapter/PC unusual condition/error, respectively. Clearly, the applicability of an unacceptable ring status error code to a CSMA/CD PC Network adapter controlled by the IBM LAN Support Program is inappropriate. Thus, you must refer generally to the adapter's NetBIOS documentation before you can correctly interpret error codes.

Why Didn't ResetNcb Get Zeroed by ClearNcb( )?

Because of its position in the program, ResetNcb is located in static storage, which is always initialized to zeros. Thus, ResetNcb does not require zeroing before ResetAdapter( ) uses it. However, if ResetNcb is a Reset-Adapter( ) automatic variable or was used in a previously completed Net-BIOS command, it requires zeroing by invoking ClearNcb( ). Part I discusses the ClearNcb( ) and NetbiosRequest( ) routines in more detail.

The NetBIOS Adapter Status Sample Program

The primary challenge of any adapter status program is displaying the large amount of returned data. The job is significantly complicated because different IBM versions of NetBIOS return different data or return the same data at different displacements within the returned information.

For example, IBM LAN Support Program NetBIOS implementations return the maximum datagram packet size at offset 48 (decimal). The original LANA NetBIOS does not return this data at all and offset 48 resides within a reserved area for this NetBIOS version. Moreover, the IBM LAN Support Program returns the major NetBIOS version number at offset 06 (decimal). However, the LANA NetBIOS returns the adapter jumper settings at offset 06 and the NetBIOS major version number at offset 08.

Finally, Token-Ring adapter status data may contain extended status information, valid only for adapter status commands for local adapters. This information may also contain adapter counter information that is valid "only if no ring-status appendage is defined" according to the *Token-Ring PC Adapter Technical Reference Manual*. There is no method to determine whether such a ring-status appendage is defined. See Part IV of this book for more details.

Because the primary purpose of this book is to teach basics, the Adapter Status sample program takes the simple road and illustrates a partial NetBIOS Adapter Status command applicable to adapters controlled by the IBM LAN Support Program. A complete general program is left as a reader exercise. Note that the netbios2.h include file provides sample adapter status structures for both IBM adapter status formats. The IBM LAN Support Program format and the PC Network LANA format are Dlc-Status and LanaStatus structures, respectively. The PC Network II and II/A adapters use the DlcStatus structure.

The main( ) Function

The main( ) routine displays a simple logo and invokes EditArgs( ) to validate the single valid input parameter. Assuming the parameter passes the tests, RequestStatus( ) issues the Adapter Status command. If the command is not successful, a complaint is displayed containing the failing return code and the program ends. Otherwise, DlcStatus( ) displays the returned adapter type and permanent node name information fields. Finally, main( ) displays the number of NetBIOS names in the adapter Net-BIOS name table before exiting. Note that each name in the table requires 18 bytes and that the minimum buffer size is 60 bytes. Since the IBM LAN Support Program N parameter allows a maximum of 254 names in the NetBIOS name table, a buffer size of 4,632 bytes (60 + 18 × 254) is generally required to hold all possible returned data.

EditArgs( )

The Adapter Status sample program accepts one input parameter— the name of the adapter to provide the adapter status information. It may be a local or remote adapter.

Input Parameter Name Format
The name may be a unique name, a group name, or a permanent node name. A NetBIOS name generally consists of 16 arbitrary characters. However, the Adapter Status program does not support this because some characters (e.g., carriage return) cannot be specified on the PC-DOS command line. The permanent node name specification technique overcomes this limitation.

Parameter Processing—Special Cases
There are three special cases that are distinguished by the first character of the input parameter:

1. If the first character is a question mark (?), no name is specified and the program returns usage information before exiting.

2. If the first character is an asterisk (*), the local adapter specified in the Adapter Status command's NcbLanaNum field provides the data.

3. If the first character is a backslash (\), the parameter specifies a local or remote adapter permanent node name. The actual format of the parameter is: \x.hh.hh.hh.hh.hh.hh.

where each h represents a valid hexadecimal digit. In this case, the six specified bytes are appended to 10 bytes of binary zeros to create the actual network permanent node name. Note that the length of this type specification is exactly 20 characters. A valid 20-character parameter is converted to a six-byte value invoking sscanf( ). This should produce exactly six hexadecimal characters.

These six characters are placed in the six-element HoldNodeId character array. After zeroing the first 10 characters of the 16-element HoldNetworkName character array, these six characters are then moved into the last six characters of the HoldNetworkName character array, completing the permanent node name specification later used in the Adapter Status command. Finally, note that NetBIOS names can use special characters such as the ASCII carriage return value or a binary zero character. However, users cannot enter such characters on the PC-DOS prompt line as part of a 16-character name.

Allowing an alternate parameter length of exactly 50 characters and extending the switch statement logic permits general 16-character NetBIOS name specifications as implied above. This is left as a straight-forward reader exercise. The format of such a parameter is:

```
\x.hh.hh.hh.hh.hh.hh.hh.hh.hh.hh.hh.hh.hh.hh.hh
```

Parameter Processing—Normal Case

If the parameter is not a special-case parameter, it is treated as a normal symbolic network name and is copied directly into the 16-element HoldNetworkName character array. In this case, all characters are significant and lowercase letters are different than uppercase letters.

If the name has less than 16 characters, the remaining uninitialized HoldNetworkName array character elements are set to ASCII blanks. Warning! While some programs such as the IBM Token-Ring Network/PC Network Interconnect Program require blanks as the 16th character, arbitrarily selecting blanks as a filler character value can be a significant programming hazard. Other programs may use different filler character values resulting in name parameters that look the same on the PC-DOS command lines but have different NetBIOS name table values.

Perhaps binary zeros would be more appropriate, as a filler or even ASCII carriage returns. The important thing is to recognize that such an arbitrary decision is likely inappropriate. The only alternative is to allow a 50-character input parameter that allows users to specify the hexadecimal value of every name character.

DlcStatus( ) and DisplayNetbiosLevel( )

DlcStatus( ) in Listing 8-2 first invokes DisplayNetbiosLevel( ) to display the level of the NetBIOS supporting the target adapter. DisplayNetbios-Level( ) assumes that the IBM LAN Support Program provided the adapter status data, so it displays the NetBIOS level as well as the type of parameters used to initialize the DXMT0MOD.SYS device driver (NetBIOS) before returning to the DlcStatus routine. Note that DXMINFO.DOC contains critical information on the data format that is incorporated in the netbios2.h header file.

Like DisplayNetbiosLevel( ), DlcStatus( ) assumes the IBM LAN Support Program provides the adapter status data, and so determines and displays what type adapter has provided it, concluding its operation by displaying the permanent node name of that adapter. Note that Dlc-Status( ) could display much more data but a complete listing results in excruciatingly boring pages of printf( ) statements, so that task is left as a reader exercise.

Listing 8-2. STATUS.C

```
#define LINT_ARGS

#include <dos.h>
#include <ctype.h>
#include <stdio.h>
#include <string.h>
#include <process.h>
#include "netbios2.h"

struct SREGS SegRegs;

struct Ncb        StatusNcb;
struct DlcStatus  DlcData;      /* LAN Support Program Status Structure */

unsigned char HoldNodeId[6];
unsigned char HoldNetworkName[16];
```

Listing 8-2. (cont.)

```c
#if defined(LINT_ARGS)
extern   int main(int argc,char * *argv);
extern   unsigned char RequestStatus(void);
extern   void DisplayDlcStatus(char * *argv);
extern   void DisplayNetbiosLevel(void);
extern   void ClearNcb(struct Ncb *NcbPtr);
extern   void NetbiosRequest(struct Ncb *NcbPointer);
extern   int EditArgs(int argc,char * *argv);
extern   void Logo(void);
extern   void Explain(void);
extern   void ExitNow(void);
#endif


int main(argc, argv)
int    argc;
char *argv[];
{
    unsigned char temp;

    Logo();

    if (!EditArgs(argc, argv))
        ExitNow();

    if (temp = RequestStatus())
        printf("\n\nRequest status error %02Xh...\n", temp);
    else {
        DisplayDlcStatus(argv);

        printf("\n\nThere ");
        (DlcData.NameTableEntryCount == 1) ? printf("is") : printf("are");
        printf(" %u ", DlcData.NameTableEntryCount);
        (DlcData.NameTableEntryCount == 1) ? printf("entry") :
printf("entries");
        printf(" in the adapter Name Table.");
    }

    putchar('\n');

    return 0;
}


unsigned char RequestStatus()
```

Listing 8-2. (cont.)

```
{
   int  temp;
   char far *StatusBufferPtr = (char far *) &DlcData;

   ClearNcb(&StatusNcb);

   StatusNcb.NcbBufferOffset  = (char *)   FP_OFF(StatusBufferPtr);
   StatusNcb.NcbBufferSegment = (unsigned) FP_SEG(StatusBufferPtr);

   StatusNcb.NcbCommand      = NETBIOS_ADAPTER_STATUS;
   StatusNcb.NcbLength       = sizeof(DlcData);
   StatusNcb.NcbLanaNum      = 0;

   for (temp = 0; temp < 16; temp++)
   StatusNcb.NcbCallName[temp] =  HoldNetworkName[temp];

   NetbiosRequest(&StatusNcb);

   return StatusNcb.NcbRetCode;
}

void DisplayDlcStatus(argv)
char *argv[];
{
   int i, j;

   DisplayNetbiosLevel();

       /*----------------- Adapter Type -------------------*/

   switch (DlcData.LanAdapterType) {
      case TOKEN_RING_ADAPTER :
                              printf("Token Ring Adapter.");
                              break;
      case PC_NETWORK_ADAPTER :
                              printf("PC Network Adapter.");
                              break;
      default :
                              printf("Unknown Adapter...\x07");
                              break;
   }

       /*--------------- Permanent Node Name ---------------*/
```

Listing 8-2. (cont.)

```c
    printf("\n\nAdapter Permanent Node Name: ");

    for (i = 0; i < sizeof(DlcData.PermanentNodeName); i++)
      printf("%02X", ((unsigned char) 0xFF) & DlcData.PermanentNodeName[i]);
}


void DisplayNetbiosLevel()
{

                /*---   NETBIOS Version Information ---*/

    printf("\n\nUsing NetBIOS Version %u.%u ",
                    (DlcData.MajorVersionNumber & VERSION_MASK),
                    (DlcData.MinorVersionNumber & VERSION_MASK));

    switch (DlcData.MinorVersionNumber & PARM_MASK) {
      case OLD_PARMS :
                    printf("with \"old\"");
                    break;
      case NEW_PARMS :
                    printf("with \"new\"");
                    break;
      default   :
                    printf("?? - Undefined input parameter format\x07");
    }

    printf(" parameters on a ");
}


void ClearNcb(NcbPtr)
struct Ncb *NcbPtr;
{
    int   i;
    char *CharPtr;

    CharPtr = (char *) NcbPtr;

    for ( i = 0; i < sizeof(ZeroNcb); i++ )
      *CharPtr++ = 0x00;
}


void NetbiosRequest(NcbPointer)
struct Ncb *NcbPointer;
{
```

Listing 8-2. (cont.)

```c
union  REGS  InRegs, OutRegs;  /* defined in dos.h */
struct Ncb far *NcbPtr = (struct Ncb far *) NcbPointer;

    segread(&SegRegs);

    SegRegs.es  = FP_SEG(NcbPtr);
    InRegs.x.bx = FP_OFF(NcbPtr);

    int86x(NetbiosInt5C, &InRegs, &OutRegs, &SegRegs);
}


int EditArgs(argc, argv)
int    argc;
char *argv[];
{
    char  c;
    int   temp;
    char *NodeNamePointer;

    if (argc < 2) {
        Explain();
        return FAILURE;
    }

    if (argc > 2) {
        printf("\nToo many parameters...\n");
        Explain();
        return FAILURE;
    }

    switch (*argv[1]) {

      case '?' :
                Explain();
                return FAILURE;
                break;

      case '\\' :
                if (strlen(argv[1]) != 20) {
                    printf("\nParameter has the incorrect length.");
                    printf("\nShould be 20 characters long.");
                    return FAILURE;
                }
```

Listing 8-2. (cont.)

```
temp = sscanf(argv[1], "\\x.%2x.%2x.%2x.%2x.%2x.%2x",
                        &HoldNodeId[0], &HoldNodeId[1],
                        &HoldNodeId[2], &HoldNodeId[3],
                        &HoldNodeId[4], &HoldNodeId[5]);

if (temp != 6) {
   printf("\nscanf() problem with input parameter...");
   printf("\nplease clean up your input parameter...");
   printf("\nformat    ==> \\x.HH.HH.HH.HH.HH.HH");
   printf("\nparameter ==> %s", argv[1]);
   return FAILURE;
}


printf("\nRequesting status for network node \\x.");
printf("%02X.%02X.%02X.%02X.%02X.%02X",
    HoldNodeId[0] & 0x00FF, HoldNodeId[1] & 0x00FF,
    HoldNodeId[2] & 0x00FF, HoldNodeId[3] & 0x00FF,
    HoldNodeId[4] & 0x00FF, HoldNodeId[5] & 0x00FF);

for (temp = 0; temp < 10; temp++) {
  HoldNetworkName[temp] = 0x00;
}


for (temp = 0; temp < 10; temp++) {
  HoldNetworkName[temp+10] = HoldNodeId[temp];
}


break;

default:

if (strlen(argv[1]) > 16) {
   printf("\nParameter has the incorrect length.");
   printf("\nShould be one to sixteen characters long.");
   return FAILURE;
}
for (temp = 0, NodeNamePointer = argv[1];
    (temp <16) && (c = *NodeNamePointer);
    temp++, NodeNamePointer++)          {
        HoldNetworkName[temp] = c;
}


for ( ; temp < 16; temp++) {
  HoldNetworkName[temp] = ' ';
}
```

Listing 8-2. (cont.)

```
            if (*argv[1] == '*')
                printf("\nRequesting status for local primary adapter.");
            else
                printf("\nRequesting status for %s", argv[1]);

            break;
    }

    return SUCCESS;

}

void Logo()
{
    printf("\n         NetBIOS Adapter Status Program");
    printf("\n     © Copyright 1988 W. David Schwaderer\n");
}

void Explain()
{
    printf("\nusage: status Node-ID\n");
    printf("\n Node-ID: \\x.hh.hh.hh.hh.hh.hh  for Permanent Node ID");
    printf("\n     -or-   12345!@#$*aBcDeF  for Network Name");
    printf("\n     -or-   *  for Local Primary Adapter Status");
}

void ExitNow()
{
    printf("\n\n\x07Program ending...\n");
    exit(1);
}
```

The Adapter Reset and Adapter Status Synergy

Resetting PC Network LANA adapters with varying maximum session and pending command values determines the maximum message size packet the adapter can transmit. (Note this does not apply to other IBM LAN adapters and the maximum datagram size is always 512 bytes for PC Network LANA adapters.)

It is possible to reveal the exact undocumented effect these combined parameters have on the maximum packet size by issuing Adapter Reset commands while varying their values from 1 to 32 and by issuing intervening Adapter Status commands. The results differ for the two different levels of NetBIOS available for PC Network LANA adapters and are displayed in Figures 8-1 and 8-2.

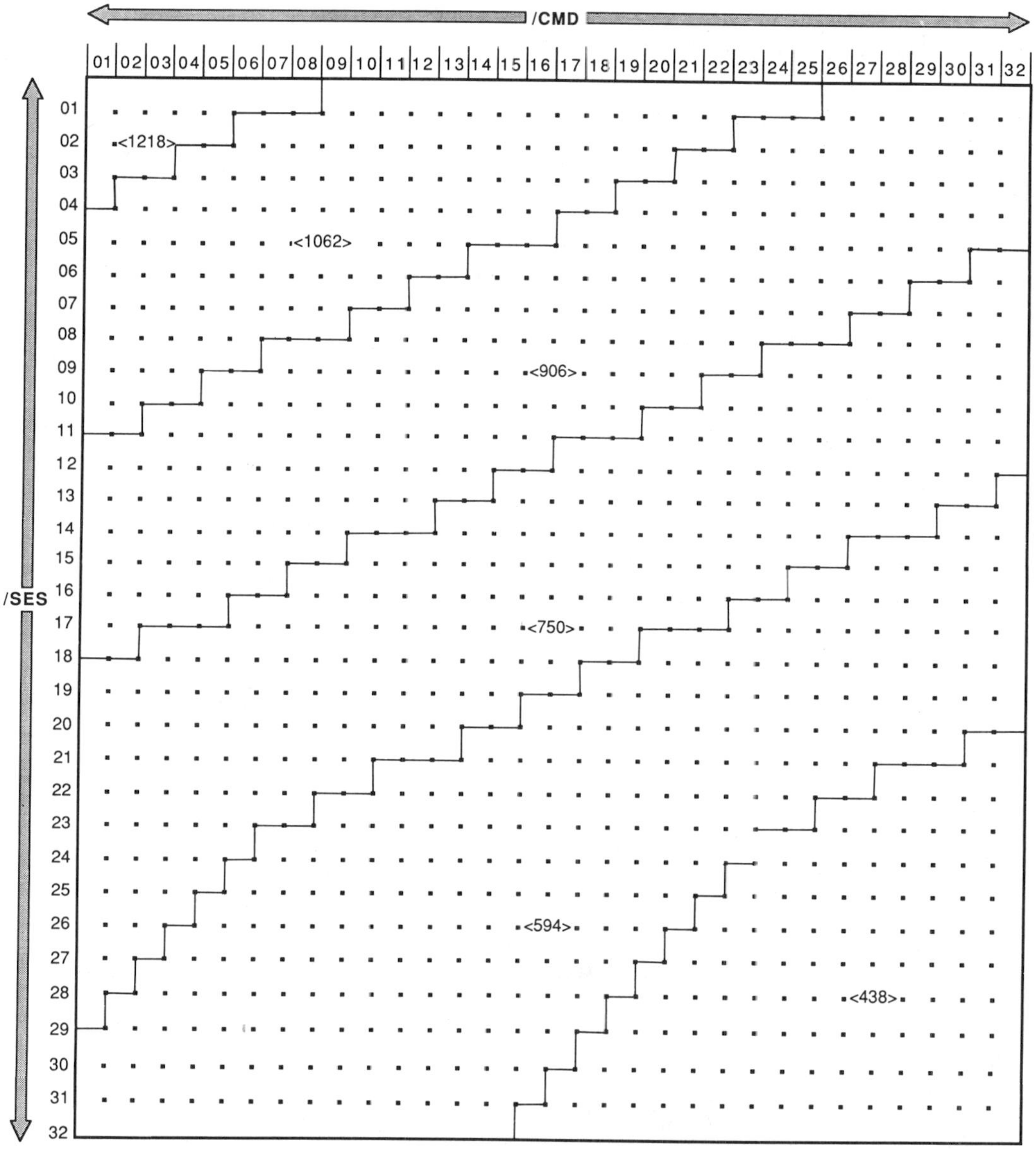

Fig. 8-1. Packet size (in bytes) as a function of /CMD and /SES for LANA protocol level 1.23.

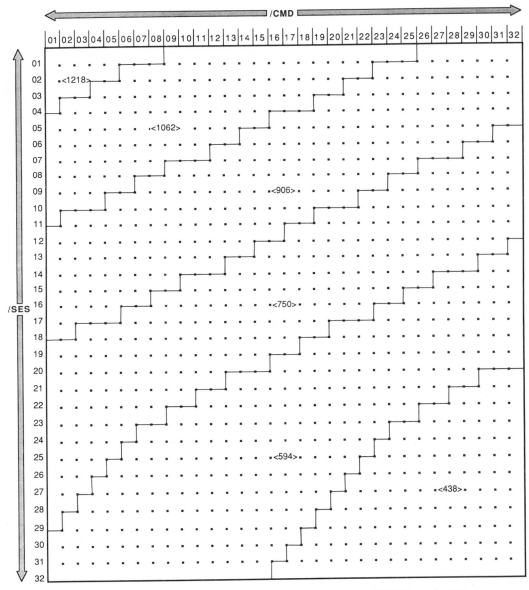

**Fig. 8-2. Packet size (in bytes) as a function of /CMD and /SES for
LANA protocol level 1.33.**

The NetBIOS Cancel Sample Program

The NetBIOS Cancel sample program in Listing 8-3 illustrates the procedure to cancel a pending Ncb command. The program begins by invok-

ing Logo( ) to display a logo. It then invokes RequestStatus( ) which
issues an Adapter Status command with a no-wait option for a network
name consisting of 16 uppercase X's. Since such a name is unlikely to
exist, the NetbiosRequest( ) routine should return before the command
completes.

Listing 8-3. CANCEL.C

```
#define LINT_ARGS

#include <dos.h>
#include <stdio.h>
#include "netbios2.h"

struct SREGS SegRegs;

struct Ncb        StatusNcb, CancelNcb;
struct DlcStatus  DlcData;

#if defined(LINT_ARGS)
extern   int main(int argc,char * *argv);
extern   void RequestStatus(void);
extern   void CancelRequestStatus(void);
extern   void AnalyzeNcbStatus(void);
extern   void ClearNcb(struct Ncb *NcbPtr);
extern   void NetbiosRequest(struct Ncb *NcbPointer);
extern   void Logo(void);
#endif

int main(argc, argv)
int    argc;
char *argv[];
{
    unsigned char temp;

    Logo();

    RequestStatus();

    CancelRequestStatus();

    AnalyzeNcbStatus();

    putchar('\n');

    return 0;
```

Listing 8-3. (cont.)

```
}

void RequestStatus()
{
    int   temp;
    char far *StatusBufferPtr = (char far *) &DlcData;

    ClearNcb(&StatusNcb);

    StatusNcb.NcbBufferOffset  = (char *)   FP_OFF(StatusBufferPtr);
    StatusNcb.NcbBufferSegment = (unsigned) FP_SEG(StatusBufferPtr);

    StatusNcb.NcbCommand       = NETBIOS_ADAPTER_STATUS + NO_WAIT;
    StatusNcb.NcbLength        = sizeof(DlcData);
    StatusNcb.NcbLanaNum       = 0;

    for (temp = 0; temp < 16; temp++)
        StatusNcb.NcbCallName[temp] =  'X';

    NetbiosRequest(&StatusNcb);
}

void CancelRequestStatus()
{
    struct Ncb far *NcbPtr = (struct Ncb far *) &StatusNcb;

    ClearNcb(&CancelNcb);

    CancelNcb.NcbBufferOffset  = (char *)   FP_OFF(NcbPtr);
    CancelNcb.NcbBufferSegment = (unsigned) FP_SEG(NcbPtr);

    CancelNcb.NcbCommand       = NETBIOS_CANCEL_WAIT_ONLY;
    CancelNcb.NcbLanaNum       = 0;

    NetbiosRequest(&CancelNcb);
}

void AnalyzeNcbStatus()
{
    printf("\nCancel NcbRetCode ==> %02Xh", CancelNcb.NcbRetCode);
    printf("\nStatus NcbRetCode ==> %02Xh", StatusNcb.NcbRetCode);
}

void ClearNcb(NcbPtr)
```

Listing 8-3. (cont.)

```c
struct Ncb *NcbPtr;
{
   int   i;
   char *CharPtr;

   CharPtr = (char *) NcbPtr;

   for ( i = 0; i < sizeof(ZeroNcb); i++ )
      *CharPtr++ = 0x00;
}


void NetbiosRequest(NcbPointer)
struct Ncb *NcbPointer;
{
 union  REGS  InRegs, OutRegs;  /* defined in dos.h */
 struct Ncb far *NcbPtr = (struct Ncb far *) NcbPointer;

    segread(&SegRegs);

    SegRegs.es  = FP_SEG(NcbPtr);
    InRegs.x.bx = FP_OFF(NcbPtr);

    int86x(NetbiosInt5C, &InRegs, &OutRegs, &SegRegs);
}


void Logo()
{
   printf("\n         NetBIOS Cancel Program");
   printf("\n © Copyright 1988 W. David Schwaderer \n");
}
```

The program invokes CancelRequestStatus( ) to cancel the presumably pending Adapter Status command. The pending command uses an Ncb named StatusNcb that has program scope, so CancelRequestStatus( ) can easily address it. Because the Cancel command has only a Wait form, its NetbiosRequest( ) returns synchronously—after the command has completed. Finally, the program invokes AnalyzeNcbStatus( ) to present the NcbRetCode values of both the Adapter Status and Cancel commands. If the program has successfully completed, these return codes should be 0Bh and 00h, respectively.

Normally, a program should never leave a command pending before exiting, though it is possible in this program for the Cancel command to fail under unusual circumstances. In this situation, the Adapter Status command completes when the adapter's system time-out expires or when the target adapter responds successfully. If the latter occurs, NetBIOS then alters the memory where the Adapter Status buffer was located. In any event, NetBIOS alters the memory where the Ncb was located. At worst, NetBIOS then detects a nonzero Post Routine field value and begins execution at some (usually) disastrous point in memory. If you execute this program and the Cancel command is not successful, you may wish to reset your adapter to clear the pending Adapter Status command.

The NetBIOS Unlink Sample Program

The NetBIOS Unlink sample program in Listing 8-4 illustrates the NetBIOS Unlink command that disconnects a client PC Network LANA adapter from an RPL server. The command is trapped by the adapter's native ROM NetBIOS and is converted to a Hang Up command that uses another Ncb.

You will likely never need to use this command, but it is supported in many versions of NetBIOS for compatibility with IBM's original NetBIOS. In any event, its utility is increasingly limited with passing time. Note that a PC Network LANA's NetBIOS virtually always returns a zero return code unless a very unusual condition occurs. Part I discusses this command in more detail.

Listing 8-4. UNLINK.C

```
#define LINT_ARGS

#include <dos.h>
#include <stdio.h>
#include "netbios2.h"

#if defined(LINT_ARGS)
extern  int main(int argc,char * *argv);
extern  void Logo(void);
extern  void UnlinkAdapterNow(void);
extern  void NetbiosRequest(struct Ncb *NcbPointer);
#endif

struct Ncb UnlinkNcb;

int main(argc, argv)
int   argc;
char *argv[];
```

Listing 8-4. (cont.)

```c
{
  Logo();
  UnlinkAdapterNow();
  return 0;
}


void Logo()
{
  printf("\n         NetBIOS Adapter Unlink Sample Program");
  printf("\n         © Copyright 1988  W. David Schwaderer");
}


void UnlinkAdapterNow()
{
    printf("\n\nAttempting to Unlink NetBIOS adapter 0...");

    UnlinkNcb.NcbCommand = NETBIOS_UNLINK_WAIT_ONLY; /* Unlink command code */

    UnlinkNcb.NcbLanaNum = 0x00;              /* unchecked, but should be zero */

    NetbiosRequest(&UnlinkNcb);

    if (!UnlinkNcb.NcbRetCode) {
       printf("\n\nAs hard-coded by NetBIOS, the return code was %x.\n",
                                              UnlinkNcb.NcbRetCode);
    }
    else {
       printf("\n\n\x07The return code was %x ", UnlinkNcb.NcbRetCode);
    }
}


void NetbiosRequest(NcbPointer)
struct Ncb *NcbPointer;
{
 union  REGS  InRegs, OutRegs;  /* defined in dos.h */
 struct SREGS SegRegs;          /* defined in dos.h */
 struct Ncb far *NcbPtr = (struct Ncb far *) NcbPointer;

    SegRegs.es  = FP_SEG(NcbPtr);
    InRegs.x.bx = FP_OFF(NcbPtr);

    int86x(NetbiosInt5C, &InRegs, &OutRegs, &SegRegs);
}
```

Chapter 9

Name Support Programming

The NetBIOS Name Activity sample program, Listing 9-1, with routines
NetbiosAddName( ) and FileNetbiosNameTable( ) illustrate how to add
and delete NetBIOS names to and from local name tables.

The NetBIOS Name Activity Sample Program

The main( ) routine begins by invoking Logo( ) which displays a logo. It
then resets the adapter insuring that the NetBIOS name table is empty
and that there are no pending commands. It then calls the NetbiosAdd-
Name( ) routine.

When NetbiosAddName( ) returns, it resets the adapter to allow
FillNetbiosNameTable to demonstrate NcbNum values beginning at 02h
after each adapter reset. It then calls FillNetbiosNameTable( ). When
FillNetbiosNameTable( ) returns, the program resets that adapter for the
last time and exits.

Listing 9-1. NAME.C

```
#define LINT_ARGS

#include <dos.h>
#include <stdio.h>
#include "netbios2.h"

#if defined(LINT_ARGS)
extern   int main(int argc,char * *argv);
extern   void AddNetbiosName(void);
extern   void DeleteNetbiosName(unsigned char NetbiosNameChar);
```

Listing 9-1. (cont.)

```c
extern  void FillNetbiosNameTable(void);
extern  void ResetAdapter(void);
extern  void Logo(void);
extern  void ClearNcb(struct Ncb *NcbPtr);
extern  void NetbiosRequest(struct Ncb *NcbPointer);
#endif

struct Ncb NameNcb;    /* automatically set to zero in static storage */

int main(argc, argv)
int    argc;
char *argv[];
{
  Logo();

  ResetAdapter();
  AddNetbiosName();

  ResetAdapter();
  FillNetbiosNameTable();

  ResetAdapter();
  putchar('\n');

  return 0;
}

void AddNetbiosName()
{
    USGC i = 0;

    printf("\n\nNetBIOS Add Name Example...");

    printf("\n  Adding the name 'A'+%02Xh+00h+...+00h.  ", i);

    ClearNcb(&NameNcb);

    NameNcb.NcbCommand  = NETBIOS_ADD_NAME;
    NameNcb.NcbName[0]  = 'A';
    NameNcb.NcbName[1]  = i;
    NameNcb.NcbLanaNum  = 0;

    NetbiosRequest(&NameNcb);
```

Listing 9-1. (cont.)

```
    printf("\n  Its NcbNum value is %02Xh.", NameNcb.NcbNum);

    DeleteNetbiosName(i);
}


void DeleteNetbiosName(NetbiosNameChar)
USGC NetbiosNameChar;
{
    struct Ncb DeleteNameNcb;

    printf("\n\nNetBIOS Delete Name Example...");

    printf("\n  Deleting the name 'A'+%02Xh+00h+...+00h.  ",
                               NetbiosNameChar);
    ClearNcb(&DeleteNameNcb);

    DeleteNameNcb.NcbCommand = NETBIOS_DELETE_NAME;
    DeleteNameNcb.NcbName[0] = 'A';
    DeleteNameNcb.NcbName[1] = NetbiosNameChar;
    DeleteNameNcb.NcbLanaNum = 0;

    NetbiosRequest(&DeleteNameNcb);

    printf("\n  The Delete Name command return code was %02Xh.",
                               DeleteNameNcb.NcbRetCode);
}

void FillNetbiosNameTable()
{
   USGC i = 1;

   printf("\n\nNetBIOS Name Table exhaustion exercise...");

   ClearNcb(&NameNcb);

   while (!NameNcb.NcbRetCode) {  /* add names until there is an error */

      printf("\n  Adding the Group Name 'A'+%02Xh+00h+...+00h now.  ", i);

      ClearNcb(&NameNcb);

      NameNcb.NcbCommand = NETBIOS_ADD_GROUP_NAME;
      NameNcb.NcbName[0] = 'A';
      NameNcb.NcbName[1] = i++;
```

Listing 9-1. (cont.)

```
      NameNcb.NcbLanaNum = 0;

      NetbiosRequest(&NameNcb);

      if (!NameNcb.NcbRetCode)
         printf("Its NcbNum value is %02Xh.", NameNcb.NcbNum);
      else
         printf("\n  The Add Group Name command failed...");
   }

   printf("\n  The failing Add Group Name command return code was %02Xh.",
                             NameNcb.NcbRetCode);

   printf("\n\nThe adapter's name table holds %u added names...",
                             i-2);

   printf("\n\nExiting the Name Table exercise.");
}

void ResetAdapter()
{
   struct Ncb ResetNcb;

   printf("\n\nResetting the adapter.  ");

   ResetNcb.NcbCommand = NETBIOS_RESET_WAIT_ONLY; /* reset command code */

   ResetNcb.NcbLanaNum = 0;        /* adapter number           */
   ResetNcb.NcbLsn     = 32;       /* concurrent session count */
   ResetNcb.NcbNum     = 32;       /* concurrent command count */

   NetbiosRequest(&ResetNcb);

   printf("The Reset command return code was %02Xh.", ResetNcb.NcbRetCode);
}

void Logo()
{
  printf("\n      NetBIOS Name Activity Sample Program");
  printf("\n      © Copyright 1988  W. David Schwaderer");
}

void ClearNcb(NcbPtr)
struct Ncb *NcbPtr;
```

Listing 9-1. (cont.)

```
{
    int    i;
    char *CharPtr;

    CharPtr = (char *) NcbPtr;

    for ( i = 0; i < sizeof(ZeroNcb); i++ )
        *CharPtr++ = 0x00;
}


void NetbiosRequest(NcbPointer)
struct Ncb *NcbPointer;
{
 union  REGS   InRegs, OutRegs;
 struct SREGS SegRegs;
 struct Ncb far *NcbPtr = (struct Ncb far *) NcbPointer;

    segread(&SegRegs);

    SegRegs.es  = FP_SEG(NcbPtr);
    InRegs.x.bx = FP_OFF(NcbPtr);

    int86x(NetbiosInt5C, &InRegs, &OutRegs, &SegRegs);
}
```

The AddNetbiosName Routine

The AddNetbiosName routine adds a unique name to the NetBIOS name table using a wait option. When the command completes, the routine displays the name's NcbNum value which should be 02h because of the previous Adapter Reset command. (AddNetbiosName( ) assumes the Add Name command successfully completed.) Before exiting, AddNetbios-Name( ) invokes DeleteNetbiosName( ) to delete the name from the Net-BIOS name table. At this point, the next NcbNum value should be 03h, but the adapter is reset by main( ) after AddNetbiosName returns.

The FillNetbiosNameTable Routine

FillNetbiosNameTable( ) is a brute force routine that determines how many names an adapter's NetBIOS name table can hold. It continues to add unlikely group names until an Add Group Name command returns a nonzero return code.

When a command is successful, FillNetbiosNameTable( ) displays the associated NcbNum which should start at 02h because of the Adapter Reset that main( ) issued immediately before calling FillNetbiosNameTable. Otherwise, the command fails and the routine displays the failing return code before exiting. Note that the return code should be 0Eh if the name table has been filled.

Finally, note that this routine may take a long time to complete if the NetBIOS name table holds many names.

Chapter 10

Datagram Support Programming

This chapter presents a simple datagram application that determines the maximum size datagram an adapter can transmit. If the IBM LAN Support program controls the adapter, the value of the maximum datagram size is available at offset 48 (decimal) in returned adapter status information. However, other NetBIOS implementations do not provide this information with an Adapter Status command, so another method is required.

The program in Listing 10-1 uses a brute force approach that begins by transmitting a one-byte datagram. If the datagram transmission is successful, the program increments the datagram size and transmits another datagram. This continues until an error occurs.

Listing 10-1. MAXDG.C

```
#define LINT_ARGS

#include <dos.h>
#include <stdio.h>
#include "netbios2.h"

struct SREGS SegRegs;

struct Ncb  DatagramNcb;

char Buffer[1];

char ClientName[16] = "WDS-Datagram";

#if defined(LINT_ARGS)
extern   int main(int argc,char * *argv);
extern   void InitDatagramNcb(void);
extern   void XmitDatagram(unsigned int Length);
```

Listing 10-1. (cont.)

```c
extern  void ClearNcb(struct Ncb *NcbPtr);
extern  void NetbiosRequest(struct Ncb *NcbPointer);
extern  void Logo(void);
#endif

int main(argc, argv)
int   argc;
char *argv[];
{
   USGC XmitError = FALSE;
   USGI LastGoodSize, SendSize = 1;

   Logo();

   printf("\n");

   InitDatagramNcb();

   while(!XmitError) {
      XmitDatagram(SendSize);
      if (DatagramNcb.NcbRetCode) {
         XmitError = TRUE;
         LastGoodSize = SendSize - 1;
      } else  {
         SendSize++;
         putchar('.');
      }
   }

   printf("\n\nDatagram Send failed; return code == %02Xh",
                                  DatagramNcb.NcbRetCode);

   printf("\n\nMaximum datagram length == %u bytes...\n",
                              LastGoodSize);

   return 0;
}

void InitDatagramNcb()
{
  USGI temp;

  char far * BufferPtrFar = (char far *) Buffer;
```

Listing 10-1. (cont.)

```c
    ClearNcb(&DatagramNcb);

    DatagramNcb.NcbCommand = NETBIOS_SEND_DATAGRAM;

    DatagramNcb.NcbBufferOffset  = (char *) FP_OFF(BufferPtrFar);
    DatagramNcb.NcbBufferSegment = (USGI)   FP_SEG(BufferPtrFar);

    DatagramNcb.NcbNum        = 0x01;  /* use Permanent Node Name NameNum */

    for (temp = 0; temp < 16; temp++)
        DatagramNcb.NcbCallName[temp] =  ClientName[temp];
}

void XmitDatagram(Length)
USGI Length;
{
  DatagramNcb.NcbLength  = Length;
  NetbiosRequest(&DatagramNcb);
}

void ClearNcb(NcbPtr)
struct Ncb *NcbPtr;
{
    int   i;
    char *CharPtr;

    CharPtr = (char *) NcbPtr;

    for ( i = 0; i < sizeof(ZeroNcb); i++ )
       *CharPtr++ = 0x00;
}

void NetbiosRequest(NcbPointer)
struct Ncb *NcbPointer;
{
 union  REGS  InRegs, OutRegs;  /* defined in dos.h */
 struct Ncb far *NcbPtr = (struct Ncb far *) NcbPointer;

    segread(&SegRegs);

    SegRegs.es  = FP_SEG(NcbPtr);
    InRegs.x.bx = FP_OFF(NcbPtr);

    int86x(NetbiosInt5C, &InRegs, &OutRegs, &SegRegs);
```

Listing 10-1. (cont.)

```
}

void Logo()
{
    printf("\n    NetBIOS Datagram Size Program");
    printf("\n © Copyright 1988 W. David Schwaderer");
}
```

The main( ) Function

The main( ) function begins by calling Logo( ) to present a logo. It then calls InitDatagramNcb( ), which initializes a Send Datagram Ncb with a wait option. After initializing the Ncb, main( ) enters a while loop which terminates when the variable XmitError becomes TRUE.

In this loop, main( ) calls XmitDatagram( ) and provides it with a datagram length. After XmitDatagram( ) returns, main( ) checks the return code for success. If it is successful, main( ) increments the datagram size, displays a period (.) to provide user feedback, and begins another execution of the loop.

Alternatively, the command fails and the loop terminates because the variable XmitError is set to TRUE. If the command fails because the size is too large, the return code is 01h (Illegal Buffer Length). Before exiting, main( ) displays the failing command's return code and the size of the last successfully transmitted datagram.

Note the program repeatedly uses the same Ncb but never reinitializes it. This is generally not advisable, but is acceptable in this instance because the command uses a wait option and the values of the Ncb fields initialized by InitDatagramNcb( ) do not vary. Most importantly, the Ncb is located in static storage and is not an automatic variable.

InitDatagramNcb( ) and XmitDatagram( )

InitDatagramNcb( ) initializes all fields required for a Send Datagram with the exception of the NcbLength field. XmitDatagram( ) initializes this field immediately before issuing the command. Since the command specifies the wait option, control returns to XmitDatagram( ) synchronously at the command's completion and XmitDatagram( ) immediately returns to main( ).

Chapter 11

Intermediate Datagram Applications

This chapter presents two datagram applications that respectively act as server and client applications. The server datagram application periodically broadcasts current date and time information to potential clients.

Using datagrams allows an unlimited number of clients to receive date and time information from an unlimited number of servers. Having multiple clients simultaneously use the same datagram economizes the LAN's transmission capability, and having more than one server provides a measure of insurance that client PCs can always receive date and time information. Neither of these advantages are easily achieved using session communication.

Client machines can subsequently use the date and time information to set their current date and time during AUTOEXEC.BAT execution. This procedure is analogous to procedures used to initialize a machine's date and time from a battery-backed clock-calendar board.

A Date and Time Server Application

The server application uses its permanent node name to beacon datagrams containing the current date and time. The program in Listing 11-1 terminates when a Ctrl-Break is struck at the keyboard. Note that the implementation of this application allows multiple date and time servers to exist simultaneously on a given network.

Listing 11-1. DATETIME.C

```
#define LINT_ARGS

#include <dos.h>
```

Listing 11-1. (cont.)

```c
#include <stdio.h>
#include "netbios2.h"

struct SREGS SegRegs;

struct Ncb  DateTimeNcb;
USGC        TimeNameNum;

struct DateTimeStruct DateTimeInfo;

char ClientName[16] = "WDS-DateTime";

#if defined(LINT_ARGS)
extern  int main(int argc,char * *argv);
extern  void FetchDateAndTime(void);
extern  void XmitDateTime(void);
extern  void ClearNcb(struct Ncb *NcbPtr);
extern  void NetbiosRequest(struct Ncb *NcbPointer);
extern  void Logo(void);
#endif

int main(argc, argv)
int    argc;
char *argv[];
{
   unsigned char temp;

   Logo();

   printf("\n");

   while(TRUE) {
       FetchDateAndTime();
       XmitDateTime();
       putchar('.');
   }

   putchar('\n');

   return 0;
}

#define DOS_INT        0x21
#define DOS_FETCH_DATE 0x2A
```

Listing 11-1. (cont.)

```c
#define DOS_FETCH_TIME 0x2C

void FetchDateAndTime()
{
    union  REGS  InRegs, OutRegs;

    InRegs.h.ah = DOS_FETCH_DATE;

    int86(DOS_INT, &InRegs, &OutRegs);

    DateTimeInfo.DateCX = OutRegs.x.cx;
    DateTimeInfo.DateDX = OutRegs.x.dx;

    InRegs.h.ah = DOS_FETCH_TIME;

    int86(DOS_INT, &InRegs, &OutRegs);

    DateTimeInfo.TimeCX = OutRegs.x.cx;
    DateTimeInfo.TimeDX = OutRegs.x.dx;
}


void XmitDateTime()
{
  USGI temp;

  char far * BufferPtrFar = (char far *) &DateTimeInfo;

  ClearNcb(&DateTimeNcb);

  DateTimeNcb.NcbCommand = NETBIOS_SEND_DATAGRAM;

  DateTimeNcb.NcbBufferOffset  = (char *) FP_OFF(BufferPtrFar);
  DateTimeNcb.NcbBufferSegment = (USGI)   FP_SEG(BufferPtrFar);

  DateTimeNcb.NcbLength  = sizeof(DateTimeInfo);
  DateTimeNcb.NcbNum     = 0x01;  /* use Permanent Node Name NameNum */

  for (temp = 0; temp < 16; temp++)
     DateTimeNcb.NcbCallName[temp] =  ClientName[temp];

  NetbiosRequest(&DateTimeNcb);
}


void ClearNcb(NcbPtr)
```

Listing 11-1. (cont.)

```c
struct Ncb *NcbPtr;
{
   int   i;
   char *CharPtr;

   CharPtr = (char *) NcbPtr;

   for ( i = 0; i < sizeof(ZeroNcb); i++ )
      *CharPtr++ = 0x00;
}

void NetbiosRequest(NcbPointer)
struct Ncb *NcbPointer;
{
 union  REGS  InRegs, OutRegs;  /* defined in dos.h */
 struct Ncb far *NcbPtr = (struct Ncb far *) NcbPointer;

    segread(&SegRegs);

    SegRegs.es  = FP_SEG(NcbPtr);
    InRegs.x.bx = FP_OFF(NcbPtr);

    int86x(NetbiosInt5C, &InRegs, &OutRegs, &SegRegs);
}

void Logo()
{
   printf("\n    NetBIOS Date/Time Server Program");
   printf("\n © Copyright 1988 W. David Schwaderer");
}
```

The main( ) Function

The main( ) function begins by calling Logo( ) to present a logo. It then enters an infinite loop which invokes FetchDateAndTime( ) and XmitDateAndTime( ), and displays a period (.) to provide user execution feedback. The loop ends when a Ctrl-Break is struck at the keyboard.

FetchDateAndTime( )

FetchDateAndTime( ) issues two PC-DOS calls that fetch the current date and time, respectively. After each respective PC-DOS call, it places the supplied information in the appropriate DateTimeInfo structure element. Appendix A presents a netbios2.h listing containing a complete structure declaration for DateTimeStruct.

XmitDateAndTime( )

XmitDateAndTime( ) initializes all required DateTimeNcb structure elements with appropriate values and invokes NetbiosRequest( ) to transmit the data. Note that it uses the permanent node NcbNum value 01h for the NcbNum value. This allows the program to transmit datagrams without adding or deleting a name to or from the NetBIOS name table.

The client name has a value of "WDS-DateTime" followed by four bytes of binary zeros. These zeros result from the ClientName character array definition's defaulting the last four characters in its specification. The C default is binary zero.

A Date and Time Client Application

The date and time client application in Listing 11-2 is more complicated than its server counterpart because it adds and deletes a name from the NetBIOS name table. Moreover, it cannot assume a server is providing date and time information. Thus, the client application issues a no-wait option Receive Datagram command allowing it to cancel the Receive Datagram if a prudent period elapses and no information is received. Note some program functions are not described because they are similar to previously described functions.

Listing 11-2. The SET_D_T.C

```
#define LINT_ARGS

#include <dos.h>
#include <time.h>
#include <stdio.h>
#include "netbios2.h"

struct SREGS SegRegs;

struct Ncb  DateTimeNcb;
USGC        TimeNameNum;
```

Listing 11-2. (cont.)

```
struct DateTimeStruct DateTimeInfo;

char ClientName[16] = "WDS-DateTime";

#if defined(LINT_ARGS)
extern  int main(int argc,char * *argv);
extern  int AddClientName(void);
extern  void IssueDateTimeRequest(void);
extern  void Delay(void);
extern  void DelayTick(void);
extern  void SetDateTimeAttempt(void);
extern  void SetDateAndTimeNow(void);
extern  void CancelDateTimeRequest(void);
extern  void DeleteClientName(void);
extern  void DisplayDateAndTime(void);
extern  void FetchDateAndTime(void);
extern  void ClearNcb(struct Ncb *NcbPtr);
extern  void NetbiosRequest(struct Ncb *NcbPointer);
extern  void Logo(void);
#endif

#define TICK_RATE    18.2
#define SECONDS       5
#define DELAY_TICK_COUNT (TICK_RATE * SECONDS)

int main(argc, argv)
int    argc;
char *argv[];
{
    unsigned char temp;

    Logo();

    if (AddClientName()) {
        IssueDateTimeRequest();
        Delay();
        SetDateTimeAttempt();
        DeleteClientName();
    } else
        printf("\n\nProgram ending because of add-name failure.");

    DisplayDateAndTime();

    putchar('\n');
```

Listing 11-2. (cont.)

```c
    return 0;
}


int AddClientName()
{
    struct Ncb AddNameNcb;

    USGI temp = 0;

    ClearNcb(&AddNameNcb);

    AddNameNcb.NcbCommand  = NETBIOS_ADD_GROUP_NAME;
    AddNameNcb.NcbLanaNum  = 0;

    for (temp = 0; temp < 16; temp++)
        AddNameNcb.NcbName[temp] =  ClientName[temp];

    printf("\n\nAdding the client name...please wait...");

    NetbiosRequest(&AddNameNcb);

    if (!AddNameNcb.NcbRetCode) {
      printf("\n  The add-name was successful...");
      printf("\n  The client's NcbNum value is %02Xh.",
                                    AddNameNcb.NcbNum);
      TimeNameNum = AddNameNcb.NcbNum;
      return SUCCESS;
    } else {
      return FAILURE;
      printf("\n   The add-rame was not successful...");
    }
}


void IssueDateTimeRequest()
{
  char far * BufferPtrFar = (char far *) &DateTimeInfo;

  ClearNcb(&DateTimeNcb);

  DateTimeNcb.NcbCommand = NETBIOS_RECEIVE_DATAGRAM + NO_WAIT;

  DateTimeNcb.NcbBufferOffset  = (char *) FP_OFF(BufferPtrFar);
  DateTimeNcb.NcbBufferSegment = (USGI)   FP_SEG(BufferPtrFar);
```

Listing 11-2. (cont.)

```
  DateTimeNcb.NcbLength  = sizeof(DateTimeInfo);
  DateTimeNcb.NcbNum     = TimeNameNum;

  NetbiosRequest(&DateTimeNcb);
}

void Delay()
{
  USGC Quit  = FALSE;
  USGI DelayedTicks = 0;

  printf("\n\nAttempting to fetch the date and time from the network...");
  printf("please wait...");

  while (!Quit) {
      if (DateTimeNcb.NcbCmdCplt != 0xFF) {
         return;
      } else {
         DelayTick();
         if (DelayedTicks++ > DELAY_TICK_COUNT)
            return;
      }
  }
}

#define DOS_INT        0x21
#define DOS_FETCH_TIME 0x2C

void DelayTick()
{
   union  REGS  InRegs, OutRegs;
   USGC EntryHundredths;

   InRegs.h.ah = DOS_FETCH_TIME;

   int86(DOS_INT, &InRegs, &OutRegs);

   EntryHundredths = OutRegs.h.dl;

   while(TRUE) {

       int86(DOS_INT, &InRegs, &OutRegs);
```

Listing 11-2. (cont.)

```c
        if (EntryHundredths != OutRegs.h.dl)
            break;
    }

    return;
}


void SetDateTimeAttempt()
{
    if ((DateTimeNcb.NcbCmdCplt != 0xFF) &&
        (DateTimeNcb.NcbCmdCplt == 0x00)    ) {
        SetDateAndTimeNow();
    } else {
        printf("\n\nNo network response...");
        printf("\n  Canceling the pending receive datagram...");
        CancelDateTimeRequest();
    }
}


#define DOS_SET_DATE 0x2B
#define DOS_SET_TIME 0x2D

void SetDateAndTimeNow()
{
    union  REGS  InRegs, OutRegs;

    printf("\n\nSetting date and time from the network...");

    InRegs.h.ah = DOS_SET_DATE;
    InRegs.x.cx = DateTimeInfo.DateCX;
    InRegs.x.dx = DateTimeInfo.DateDX;

    int86(DOS_INT, &InRegs, &OutRegs);

    InRegs.h.ah = DOS_SET_TIME;
    InRegs.x.cx = DateTimeInfo.TimeCX;
    InRegs.x.dx = DateTimeInfo.TimeDX;

    int86(DOS_INT, &InRegs, &OutRegs);
}


void CancelDateTimeRequest()
{
    struct Ncb CancelNcb;
```

Listing 11-2. (cont.)

```
    struct Ncb far *NcbPtr = (struct Ncb far *) &DateTimeNcb;

    ClearNcb(&CancelNcb);

    CancelNcb.NcbBufferOffset  = (char *)   FP_OFF(NcbPtr);
    CancelNcb.NcbBufferSegment = (unsigned) FP_SEG(NcbPtr);

    CancelNcb.NcbCommand       = NETBIOS_CANCEL_WAIT_ONLY;
    CancelNcb.NcbLanaNum       = 0;

    NetbiosRequest(&CancelNcb);

    if (!CancelNcb.NcbRetCode) {
      printf("\n  The cancel was successful...");
    } else {
      printf("\n  The cancel was not successful...");
    }
}

void DeleteClientName()
{
    struct Ncb DeleteNameNcb;
    USGI temp;

    printf("\n\nDeleting client name...");

    ClearNcb(&DeleteNameNcb);

    DeleteNameNcb.NcbCommand = NETBIOS_DELETE_NAME;
    DeleteNameNcb.NcbLanaNum = 0;

  for (temp = 0; temp < 16; temp++)
    DeleteNameNcb.NcbName[temp] =  ClientName[temp];

    NetbiosRequest(&DeleteNameNcb);

    if (!DeleteNameNcb.NcbRetCode)
        printf("\n  The delete-name was successful...");
    else {
        printf("\n  The delete-name was not successful...");
        printf("\n  The return code was %02Xh.",
                            DeleteNameNcb.NcbRetCode);
    }
```

Listing 11-2. (cont.)

```
}

void DisplayDateAndTime()
{
    FetchDateAndTime();

    printf("\n\nThe current date is %02u-%02u-%04u...",
                        (USGC) (DateTimeInfo.DateDX >> 8),
                        (USGC) (DateTimeInfo.DateDX),
                        (USGI) (DateTimeInfo.DateCX)        );

    printf("\n\nThe current time is %02u:%02u:%02u...",
                        (USGC) (DateTimeInfo.TimeCX >> 8),
                        (USGC) (DateTimeInfo.TimeCX),
                        (USGC) (DateTimeInfo.TimeDX >> 8)  );
}


#define DOS_FETCH_DATE 0x2A
#define DOS_FETCH_TIME 0x2C

void FetchDateAndTime()
{
    union  REGS  InRegs, OutRegs;

    InRegs.h.ah = DOS_FETCH_DATE;

    int86(DOS_INT, &InRegs, &OutRegs);

    DateTimeInfo.DateCX = OutRegs.x.cx;
    DateTimeInfo.DateDX = OutRegs.x.dx;

    InRegs.h.ah = DOS_FETCH_TIME;

    int86(DOS_INT, &InRegs, &OutRegs);

    DateTimeInfo.TimeCX = OutRegs.x.cx;
    DateTimeInfo.TimeDX = OutRegs.x.dx;
}

void ClearNcb(NcbPtr)
struct Ncb *NcbPtr;
{
    int  i;
    char *CharPtr;
```

Listing 11-2. (cont.)

```c
    CharPtr = (char *) NcbPtr;

    for ( i = 0; i < sizeof(ZeroNcb); i++ )
        *CharPtr++ = 0x00;
}

void NetbiosRequest(NcbPointer)
struct Ncb *NcbPointer;
{
 union  REGS  InRegs, OutRegs;  /* defined in dos.h */
 struct Ncb far *NcbPtr = (struct Ncb far *) NcbPointer;

    segread(&SegRegs);

    SegRegs.es  = FP_SEG(NcbPtr);
    InRegs.x.bx = FP_OFF(NcbPtr);

    int86x(NetbiosInt5C, &InRegs, &OutRegs, &SegRegs);
}

void Logo()
{
    printf("\n    NetBIOS Date/Time Client Program");
    printf("\n © Copyright 1988 W. David Schwaderer");
}
```

The main( ) Function

The main( ) function begins by calling Logo( ) to present a logo. It then calls AddClientName( ) which attempts to add the client name as a group name. If the Add Group Name is successful then the NcbNum value of the client name is saved in TimeNameNum, and AddClientName( ) returns to main( ) with a successful return code indication. Then, main( ) calls IssueDateTimeRequest( ) to issue the Receive Datagram request which uses the TimeNameNum value.

After the Receive Datagram command is issued, main( ) calls Delay( ) to pause for an appropriate amount of time before calling SetDateTimeAttempt( ) which tries to set the date and time. The program ends after displaying the machine's current date and time, which may not be accurate if date and time information was not received.

Delay( )

Delay( ) displays a message that informs the user it is attempting to fetch the date and time from the network. It then enters a while loop that terminates when the variable Quit becomes TRUE.

In this loop, Delay( ) repeatedly checks the NcbCmdCplt field to see if it has changed from a command-pending state. If it has, the variable Quit becomes TRUE and Delay( ) returns to main( ). Otherwise, Delay( ) calls DelayTick( ) which waits a machine tick (18.2 ticks per second) before returning to Delay( ). DelayTick( ) senses a tick has occurred by repeatedly fetching the current time from PC-DOS and watching for a change in the DL register.

Delay( ) keeps track of how many ticks have occurred while the NcbCmdCplt remains in a command-pending state. After a number of ticks greater than DELAY_TICK_COUNT have occurred, Delay( ) returns to IssueDateTimeRequest( ) even though the Receive Datagram may still be pending.

SetDateTimeAttempt( )

SetDateTimeAttempt( ) inspects the NcbCmdCplt field for a command-pending status. If the command is still pending, SetDateTimeAttempt( ) invokes CancelDateTimeRequest( ) to cancel the Receive Datagram command and returns to main( ). Otherwise, SetDateTimeAttempt( ) calls SetDateAndTimeNow( ) which uses the received information to set the date and time with respective PC-DOS calls.

DisplayDateAndTime( )

DisplayDateAndTime( ) invokes FetchDateAndTime( ) which fetches the current date and time with respective PC-DOS calls. FetchDateAndTime( ) places this current date and time information in appropriate DateTimeInfo structure elements before returning to DisplayDateAndTime( ). Subsequently, DisplayDateAndTime( ) displays this information before returning to main( ).

Chapter 12

Real-Time LAN Conferencing Application

This chapter presents a datagram application providing a real-time LAN-conferencing capability. The program in Listing 12-1 allows several users to communicate with one another within a given conference, with each user seeing what the other users have entered from their keyboards. Multiple conferences can also simultaneously exist, but input from one is not received by any other conference.

Listing 12-1. CB.C

```
#define   LINT_ARGS

#include  <dos.h>
#include  <conio.h>
#include  <stdio.h>
#include  "netbios2.h"

#define   BIOS_VIDEO_REQUEST    0x10
#define   CB_NAME_TERMINATOR    0x80
#define   COLUMN_1              00
#define   COLUMN_80            79
#define   ENTIRE_SCREEN        00
#define   ESC                  0x1B
#define   FETCH_CURSOR_POSITION 0x03
#define   GROUP_NAME            2
#define   MAX_KEYBOARD_MSG      60
#define   MAX_NCBS              5
#define   NAME_SIZE            16
#define   NORMAL_ATTRIBUTE     07
#define   ONE_LINE             01
#define   PAGE_ZERO            00
#define   RETURN               0x0D
```

Listing 12-1. (cont.)

```
#define    ROW_1                  00
#define    ROW_2                  01
#define    ROW_24                 23
#define    ROW_25                 24
#define    SCROLL_UP              06
#define    SET_CURSOR_POSITION    0x02
#define    UNIQUE_NAME            1

#if defined(LINT_ARGS)
extern   int main(int argc,char * *argv);
extern   void Participate(void);
extern   void IssueReceiveDatagramRequests(void);
extern   void ServiceDatagramNcbs(void);
extern   void ProcessReceivedDatagram(unsigned int Index);
extern   void CancelReceiveDatagrams(void);
extern   void InitializeKeyboardInputArea(void);
extern   void SetupInputLine(void);
extern   void ServiceKeyboard(void);
extern   void ApplyKeystroke(unsigned char Keystroke);
extern   void SendKeyboardMsg(char *Message);
extern   void EmitUserStatusMsg(char *AppendMsg);
extern   int AddConferenceName(void);
extern   void DeleteConferenceName(void);
extern   unsigned char AddUserName(void);
extern   void DeleteUserName(void);
extern   void ClearNcb(struct Ncb *NcbPtr);
extern   unsigned char NetbiosAddName(char *Name,int NameType);
extern   void NetbiosDeleteName(char *Name);
extern   void NetbiosSendDatagram(struct Ncb *NcbPtr,
                                  struct DgStruct *BufferPtrNear,
                                  unsigned int BufferSize);
extern   void NetbiosReceiveDatagram(struct Ncb *NcbPtr,
                                     struct DgStruct *BufferPtrNear,
                                     unsigned int BufferSize);
extern   void NetbiosCancelNcb(struct Ncb *NcbPtrNear);
extern   void NetbiosRequest(struct Ncb *NcbPtrNear);
extern   void Logo(void);
extern   int EditArgs(int argc,char * *argv);
extern   void Explain(void);
extern   void ExitNow(void);
extern   void Cls(void);
extern   void ScrollScreen(unsigned int BeginRow,
                           unsigned int EndRow,
                           unsigned int RowCount);
```

Listing 12-1. (cont.)

```c
extern  void FetchCursorPosition(void);
extern  void SetPreviousCursorPosition(void);
extern  void SetCursorPosition(unsigned int Row,
                                unsigned int Column);
#endif

/*------------------------------------------------------------*/

struct Ncb InDgNcb[MAX_NCBS], OutDatagramNcb;

struct DgStruct { char OriginName[NAME_SIZE];
                  char Text[MAX_KEYBOARD_MSG];
                };

struct DgStruct OutDatagram, InDg[MAX_NCBS];

#define DATAGRAM_MSG_SIZE sizeof(OutDatagram)

char *ConferenceNamePtr, *UserNamePtr;
USGC  ConferenceNameNum,  UserNameNum;
USGI  CurrentRow, CurrentColumn;

/*------------------------------------------------------------*/

int main(argc,argv)
int  argc;
char *argv[];
{
    Logo();

    if (!EditArgs(argc, argv))
        ExitNow();

    ConferenceNamePtr = argv[1];
    UserNamePtr       = argv[2];

    if (AddConferenceName())   {
        if (AddUserName())   {
            Participate();
            Cls();
            printf("\n\nOnline program ending at user request...\n");
            CancelReceiveDatagrams();
            DeleteUserName();
        }
        DeleteConferenceName();
    }
```

Listing 12-1. (cont.)

```c
    putchar('\n');

    return 0;
}

/*---------------------------------------------------------*/

USGI Participating = TRUE;

char EnterAppend[]  = " has joined the conference...";
char DepartAppend[] = " has left the conference...";

void Participate()
{
    printf("\n\n\n*-- Online as user ");
    printf("\"%s\" in conference \"%s\"...",
            UserNamePtr,   ConferenceNamePtr);

    IssueReceiveDatagramRequests();

    EmitUserStatusMsg(EnterAppend);

    SetupInputLine();

    while(Participating) {
        ServiceDatagramNcbs();
        ServiceKeyboard();
    }

    EmitUserStatusMsg(DepartAppend);

    while (OutDatagramNcb.NcbCmdCplt == COMMAND_PENDING)
        ;    /* spin until complete */
}

/*------------------- Datagram Processing ----------------*/

void IssueReceiveDatagramRequests()
{
    USGI i;

    for (i = 0; i < MAX_NCBS; i++)
        NetbiosReceiveDatagram(&InDgNcb[i],
                                &InDg[i],
                                sizeof(InDg[i]));
}
```

Listing 12-1. (cont.)

```c
#define TARGET_NCB ((StartingNcb + index) % MAX_NCBS)

void ServiceDatagramNcbs()
{
  static USGI StartingNcb = 0; /* must be static */
         USGI index = 0;

  while (InDgNcb[TARGET_NCB].NcbCmdCplt != COMMAND_PENDING) {
      ProcessReceivedDatagram(TARGET_NCB);
      NetbiosReceiveDatagram(&InDgNcb[TARGET_NCB],
                        &InDg[TARGET_NCB],
                        sizeof(InDg[TARGET_NCB]));
      index++;
    }

    StartingNcb = TARGET_NCB;
}

void ProcessReceivedDatagram(Index)
USGI Index;
{
    USGI i;

    if (!InDgNcb[Index].NcbRetCode)  {

        FetchCursorPosition();

        ScrollScreen(ROW_2, ROW_24, 1);
        SetCursorPosition(ROW_24, 0);

        printf("%s => %s", InDg[Index].OriginName,
                        InDg[Index].Text);

        SetPreviousCursorPcsition();
    }
}

void CancelReceiveDatagrams()
{
    USGI i;

    for (i = 0; i < MAX_NCBS; i++)  {

        if (InDgNcb[i].NcbCmdCplt == COMMAND_PENDING)

            NetbiosCancelNcb(&InDgNcb[i]);
```

Listing 12-1. (cont.)

```
    }
}

/*-------------------- Keyboard Handling ----------------*/

char  *KeyboardInputPtr, KeyboardInput[MAX_KEYBOARD_MSG];
USGI   KeyboardInputLength;

void InitializeKeyboardInputArea()
{
    int i;

    for (i = 1; i < MAX_KEYBOARD_MSG; i++)
        KeyboardInput[i] = '\x00';

    KeyboardInputPtr = KeyboardInput;

    KeyboardInputLength = 0;
}

void SetupInputLine()
{
    int i;

    SetCursorPosition(ROW_25,COLUMN_1);

    for (i = 1; i < 79; i++)
        putchar(' ');

    SetCursorPosition(ROW_25,COLUMN_1);

    printf("%s => ",UserNamePtr);

    InitializeKeyboardInputArea();
}

void ServiceKeyboard()
{

    USGC Keystroke;

    if (kbhit()) {

        switch (Keystroke = (USGC) getch()) {

            case 0x00 :                    /* function key */
                    Keystroke = (USGC) getch();
```

Listing 12-1. (cont.)

```
                            break;

                    case 0x08 :
                            if (KeyboardInputLength > 0) {
                                printf("\x08 \x08");
                                  --KeyboardInputLength;
                                *(--KeyboardInputPtr) = '\x00';
                            }
                            break;

                    case ESC:                        /* quit indicator */
                            Participating = FALSE;
                            break;

                    case RETURN:              /* send indicator */
                            SendKeyboardMsg(KeyboardInput);
                            break;

                    default :
                            ApplyKeystroke(Keystroke);
                            break;
            }
        }
}

void ApplyKeystroke(Keystroke)
USGC Keystroke;
{
    if ((KeyboardInputLength+1) >= MAX_KEYBOARD_MSG)  {
        putchar('\x07');
        return;
    }

    if ((Keystroke >= ' ') && (Keystroke < 128)) {
        KeyboardInputLength++;
        *(KeyboardInputPtr++) = (char) Keystroke;
        putchar(Keystroke);
        return;
    }
}

void SendKeyboardMsg(Message)
char *Message;
{
    USGI Index;
```

Listing 12-1. (cont.)

```c
    if (KeyboardInputLength == 0)
        return;

    for (Index = 0; Index < NAME_SIZE; Index++)
        OutDatagram.OriginName[Index] = '\x00';

    strncpy(OutDatagram.OriginName, UserNamePtr, NAME_SIZE);

    for (Index = 0; Index < MAX_KEYBOARD_MSG; Index++)
        OutDatagram.Text[Index] = '\x00';

    strncpy(OutDatagram.Text, Message, MAX_KEYBOARD_MSG);

    NetbiosSendDatagram(&OutDatagramNcb,
                        &OutDatagram,
                         DATAGRAM_MSG_SIZE);

    SetupInputLine();
}

/*-------------------- Sign On/Off ----------------------*/

char MONITOR[] = "MONITOR!\x07";

void EmitUserStatusMsg(AppendMsg)
char *AppendMsg;
{
    strncpy(OutDatagram.OriginName,
            MONITOR,
            strlen(MONITOR)+1);

    strncpy(OutDatagram.Text,
            UserNamePtr,
            strlen(UserNamePtr)+1);

    strncat(OutDatagram.Text, AppendMsg);

    NetbiosSendDatagram(&OutDatagramNcb,
                        &OutDatagram,
                         DATAGRAM_MSG_SIZE);
}

/*----------------- Name Addition/Deletion ---------------*/

int AddConferenceName()
{
```

Listing 12-1. (cont.)

```
    USGC Temp;

    printf("\n\n\nChecking the Conference Name \"%s\"...",
                                    ConferenceNamePtr);

    Temp = NetbiosAddName(ConferenceNamePtr, GROUP_NAME);

    if (Temp == ILLEGAL_NAME_NUM)
        return FAILURE;
    else {
        ConferenceNameNum = Temp;
        return SUCCESS;
    }
}

void DeleteConferenceName()
{
    printf("\n\nDeleting the conference name...");
    NetbiosDeleteName(ConferenceNamePtr);
}

USGC AddUserName()
{
    USGC Temp;

    printf("\n\n\nChecking the User Name \"%s\"...",
                                    UserNamePtr);

    Temp = NetbiosAddName(UserNamePtr, UNIQUE_NAME);

    if (Temp == ILLEGAL_NAME_NUM)
        return FAILURE;
    else  {
        UserNameNum = Temp;
        return SUCCESS;
    }
}

void DeleteUserName()
{
    printf("\n\nDeleting your user name...");
    NetbiosDeleteName(UserNamePtr);
}

/*------------------ Netbios Requests ------------------*/
```

Listing 12-1. (cont.)

```
struct SREGS SegRegs;  /* defined in dos.h */

void ClearNcb(NcbPtr)
struct Ncb *NcbPtr;
{
    int   i;
    char *CharPtr = (char *) NcbPtr;

    for ( i = 0; i < sizeof(ZeroNcb); i++ )
        *CharPtr++ = '\x00';
}

USGC NetbiosAddName(Name, NameType)
char *Name;
int   NameType;
{
    struct Ncb AddNameNcb;

    NetbiosDeleteName(Name);

    ClearNcb(&AddNameNcb);

    if (NameType == UNIQUE_NAME)
        AddNameNcb.NcbCommand = NETBIOS_ADD_NAME;
    else
        AddNameNcb.NcbCommand = NETBIOS_ADD_GROUP_NAME;

    strncpy(AddNameNcb.NcbName,  Name, strlen(Name));
    AddNameNcb.NcbName[15] = CB_NAME_TERMINATOR;

    NetbiosRequest(&AddNameNcb);

    if (!AddNameNcb.NcbRetCode)
        return AddNameNcb.NcbNum;
    else {
        printf("\n\n0x%02X error with add name...",
                AddNameNcb.NcbRetCode);

        return ILLEGAL_NAME_NUM;
    }
}

void NetbiosDeleteName(Name)
char *Name;
{
    struct Ncb DeleteNameNcb;
```

Listing 12-1. (cont.)

```
    ClearNcb(&DeleteNameNcb);

    DeleteNameNcb.NcbCommand = NETBIOS_DELETE_NAME;

    strncpy(DeleteNameNcb.NcbName, Name, strlen(Name));
    DeleteNameNcb.NcbName[15] = CB_NAME_TERMINATOR;

    NetbiosRequest(&DeleteNameNcb);
}

void NetbiosSendDatagram(NcbPtr, BufferPtrNear, BufferSize)
struct Ncb      *NcbPtr;
struct DgStruct *BufferPtrNear;
USGI            BufferSize;
{
  struct DgStruct far *BufferPtrFar;

  while (NcbPtr->NcbCmdCplt == COMMAND_PENDING)
        ;                       /* spin here for completion! */

  ClearNcb(NcbPtr);

  NcbPtr->NcbCommand = NETBIOS_SEND_DATAGRAM + NO_WAIT;

  BufferPtrFar = (struct DgStruct far *) BufferPtrNear;

  NcbPtr->NcbBufferOffset  = (char *) FP_OFF(BufferPtrFar);
  NcbPtr->NcbBufferSegment = (USGI)   FP_SEG(BufferPtrFar);

  NcbPtr->NcbLength  = DATAGRAM_MSG_SIZE;
  NcbPtr->NcbNum     = UserNameNum;

  strncpy(NcbPtr->NcbCallName, ConferenceNamePtr, NAME_SIZE);
  NcbPtr->NcbCallName[15] = CB_NAME_TERMINATOR;

  NetbiosRequest(NcbPtr);
}

void NetbiosReceiveDatagram(NcbPtr,BufferPtrNear,BufferSize)
struct Ncb      *NcbPtr;
struct DgStruct *BufferPtrNear;
USGI            BufferSize;
{
  struct DgStruct far *BufferPtrFar;

  ClearNcb(NcbPtr);
```

Listing 12-1. (cont.)

```c
    NcbPtr->NcbCommand = NETBIOS_RECEIVE_DATAGRAM + NO_WAIT;

    BufferPtrFar = (struct DgStruct far *) BufferPtrNear;

    NcbPtr->NcbBufferOffset  = (char *) FP_OFF(BufferPtrFar);
    NcbPtr->NcbBufferSegment = (USGI)   FP_SEG(BufferPtrFar);

    NcbPtr->NcbLength = BufferSize;
    NcbPtr->NcbNum    = ConferenceNameNum;

    NetbiosRequest(NcbPtr);
}

void NetbiosCancelNcb(NcbPtrNear)
struct Ncb *NcbPtrNear;
{
  struct Ncb     CancelNcb;
  struct Ncb far *NcbPtrFar = (struct Ncb far *) NcbPtrNear;

  if (NcbPtrNear->NcbCmdCplt == COMMAND_PENDING) {

     ClearNcb(&CancelNcb);

     CancelNcb.NcbCommand = NETBIOS_CANCEL_WAIT_ONLY;

     CancelNcb.NcbBufferOffset  = (char *) FP_OFF(NcbPtrFar);
     CancelNcb.NcbBufferSegment = (USGI)   FP_SEG(NcbPtrFar);

     NetbiosRequest(&CancelNcb);
  }
}

void NetbiosRequest(NcbPtrNear)
struct Ncb *NcbPtrNear;
{
 union  REGS  InRegs, OutRegs;
 struct Ncb far *NcbPtrFar = (struct Ncb far *) NcbPtrNear;

    NcbPtrNear->NcbLanaNum = 0;   /* force to adapter zero */

    segread(&SegRegs);            /* init the segment regs */

    SegRegs.es = FP_SEG(NcbPtrFar);
    InRegs.x.bx = FP_OFF(NcbPtrFar);

    int86x(NetbiosInt5C, &InRegs, &OutRegs, &SegRegs);
```

Listing 12-1. (cont.)

```c
}


/*----------------- Perfunctory Routines ----------------*/

void Logo()
{
    Cls();
    printf("*- NETBIOS Online Conference");
    printf("  © Copyright 1988 W. David Schwaderer -*\n");
}

int EditArgs(argc, argv)
int   argc;
char *argv[];
{
    if (argc != 3) {
        Explain();
        printf("\n\nIncorrect number of parameters...");
        return FAILURE;
    }

    if (strlen(argv[1]) > 15) {
        Explain();
        printf("\n\nConference name \"%s\" is too long...",
                                    argv[1]);
        return FAILURE;
    }

    if (!strcmp(argv[2], "MONITOR!")) {
        printf("\n\nNo no...try another handle please...");
        return FAILURE;
    }

    if (strlen(argv[2]) > 15) {
        Explain();
        printf("\n\nHandle \"%s\" is too long...",
                          argv[2]);
        return FAILURE;
    }

    return SUCCESS;
}

void Explain()
{
```

Listing 12-1. (cont.)

```
    printf("\nusage : cb conference handle");
    printf("\n\t\tconference: The conference name...");
    printf("\n\t\thandle:    Your personal pseudonym...");
}

void ExitNow()
{
    printf("\n\n\x07Program ending because of errors...\n");
    exit(1);
}


/*-------------------- BIOS Requests --------------------*/

void Cls()
{
    ScrollScreen(ROW_1, ROW_25, ENTIRE_SCREEN);
    SetCursorPosition(ROW_1, COLUMN_1);
}

void ScrollScreen(BeginRow, EndRow, RowCount)
USGI BeginRow, EndRow, RowCount;
{
    union  REGS  InRegs, OutRegs;    /* defined in dos.h   */

    InRegs.h.ah = SCROLL_UP;         /* scroll up request  */
    InRegs.h.al = RowCount;          /* how many lines     */

    InRegs.h.ch = BeginRow;          /* top left corner    */
    InRegs.h.cl = COLUMN_1;

    InRegs.h.dh = EndRow;            /* lower right corner */
    InRegs.h.dl = COLUMN_80;

    InRegs.h.bh = NORMAL_ATTRIBUTE;  /* fill attribute     */

    int86(BIOS_VIDEO_REQUEST, &InRegs, &OutRegs);
}

void FetchCursorPosition()
{
    union  REGS  InRegs, OutRegs;    /* defined in dos.h  */

    InRegs.h.ah = FETCH_CURSOR_POSITION; /* set cursor    */
    InRegs.h.bh = PAGE_ZERO;             /* page number   */

    int86(BIOS_VIDEO_REQUEST, &InRegs, &OutRegs);
```

Listing 12-1. (cont.)

```
    CurrentRow = OutRegs.h.dh;          /* set row      */
    CurrentColumn = OutRegs.h.dl;       /* set column   */
}

void SetPreviousCursorPosition()
{
    SetCursorPosition(CurrentRow, CurrentColumn);
}

void SetCursorPosition(Row,Column)
USGI Row, Column;
{
    union  REGS  InRegs, OutRegs;       /* defined in dos.h */

    InRegs.h.ah = SET_CURSOR_POSITION;  /* set cursor   */

    InRegs.h.bh = PAGE_ZERO;            /* page number  */

    InRegs.h.dh = Row;                  /* set row      */
    InRegs.h.dl = Column;               /* set column   */

    int86(BIOS_VIDEO_REQUEST, &InRegs, &OutRegs);
}
```

The program is not only fun to use but exhibits techniques required by datagram applications. Because it is lengthy, only significant portions will be described. The remaining portions should closely resemble previously described programs.

The main( ) Function

The main( ) function begins by invoking Logo( ) which clears the screen and presents a logo on the first display line. Then, main( ) calls EditArgs( ) to validate the input parameters. If they are not acceptable, main( ) exits by invoking ExitNow( ). Otherwise, it initializes the global variables ConferenceNamePtr and UserNamePtr.

Next, main( ) calls AddConferenceName( ) which adds the conference name (the first command-line parameter) as a group name. If the Add Group Name command is successful, main( ) calls AddUserName( ) which adds the requested user's name (the second command-line parameter) with an Add Name command. A unique name is useful here in an attempt to prevent conference imposters. (Note that user pseudonyms such as RocketMan and RedRooster may significantly add to the LAN conferencing experience.)

Users are allowed to participate in the conference when main( ) invokes the primary processing routine Participate( ). When the user eventually depresses the ESC key, Participate( ) exits back to main( ) which clears the screen, cancels any pending Receive Datagrams, and deletes both the conference and user name before ending execution.

EditArgs( )

EditArgs( ) expects two command-line arguments, each of which is 15 characters or less. In addition, EditArgs does not allow the user name to be "MONITOR!." This character string is reserved by the program for supervisory use in announcing entries into and departures from conferences by individual users. Note that all 15 characters are significant.

NetBIOS Add Name Processing Routines

AddConferenceName( ) and AddUserName( ) both invoke NetbiosAddName( ) to add the requested conference and user names, respectively. Unlike the previous NetBIOS Add Name routine, NetbiosAddName contains two formal parameter declarations, when the second parameter indicating whether the name is a group or unique name. If there is a problem adding any name, NetbiosAddName returns an illegal NcbNum (00h), indicating there has been an error.

Participate( )

Participate( ) begins by displaying the requested user and conference names. It then invokes IssueReceiveDatagramRequests( ) which uses each Ncb in the InDgNcb array to issue a Receive Datagram request. Each Ncb in this array has its receive buffer in the corresponding InDg structure array.

Participate( ) then calls EmitUserStatusMsg( ) and passes a parameter causing each existing participant within the selected conference to receive notification that a new participant has joined the conference. Because newly joining participants have previously issued conference Receive Datagrams, they receive the message as well (no conference lurkers here!).

Participate( ) calls SetUpInputLine( ) which clears display line 25 and initializes the program's keystroke-accumulation buffer. It then enters the primary program-processing loop which terminates only when the variable Participating becomes FALSE (when ESC is depressed by the user). Within this loop, the program constantly flips between processing received datagrams from the other conference participants and processing the keyboard.

When the user finally depresses the ESC key, the loop ends and Participate( ) calls EmitUserStatusMsg( ), passing a parameter causing each participant within the selected conference to receive notification that the user has departed the conference. Participate( ) spins on the transmission of the departure message until it completes to avoid leaving a Send Datagram command pending after program termination.

ServiceDatagramNcbs( )

ServiceDatagramNcbs( ) checks the InDgNcb array to see if any Receive Datagram commands have completed. NetBIOS conveniently completes these Ncbs in the order they were used (IssueReceiveDatagramRequests( ) issued the Receive Datagrams using Ncb elements InDgNcb[0], InDgNcb[1], . . . InDgNcb[MAX__NCBS]), so the routine needs only to check the first Ncb it discovered was not complete the last time it checked.

This InDgNcb array element-checking is all done modulo MAX __NCBS. The variable StartingNcb is defined as a static variable so that the current starting point is remembered between routine entries and the entire process is assisted by the TARGET__NCB preprocessor definition.

If an Ncb has completed, ServiceDatagramNcbs( ) invokes ProcessReceivedDatagram( ) to display the message. ServiceDatagramNcbs( ) then reuses the Ncb to issue another Receive Datagram command before checking the next Ncb for completion. This process continues until a pending Ncb is found, the StartingNcb variable is updated, and the routine returns to Participate( ).

Note it is possible for all Ncbs to be completed at a given workstation when another conference workstation transmits a datagram. In this case, the datagram is not received by the lethargic workstation. The only possible solution is to increase the number of Ncbs in the InDgNcb array for that workstation. However, even this may not work because of restrictions on the maximum number of outstanding commands, among other reasons.

In the final analysis, datagram communication works well in relatively light message-rate situations. Its flexibility comes at the price of data integrity problems in the general case.

ProcessReceivedDatagram( )

ProcessReceivedDatagram( ) checks the return code of the Ncb that requires processing. If the return code is not zero, ProcessReceived-Datagram( ) returns without attempting to process the received datagram. Otherwise, ProcessReceivedDatagram( ) calls FetchCursorPosition( ) to save the current screen cursor position and scrolls the screen from line 1 (the second line) to line 24. It then displays the name of the user that transmitted the message and the user's message.

Before exiting, ProcessReceivedDatagram( ) calls SetPreviousCursorPosition( ) to restore the screen cursor to the position it had when ProcessReceivedDatagram( ) was entered.

ServiceKeyboard( )

ServiceKeyboard( ) checks to see if there have been any keystrokes since it was last invoked. If not, it exits. Otherwise, it reads the keystroke and examines it for significance:

- If a function key has been pressed or some other combination keystroke results in a BIOS extended keystroke (e.g., Alt-1), the keystroke is ignored. Note that this requires clearing the associated second keystroke value with another keyboard read.
- If the backspace key was pressed, the last displayed keystroke character is erased and the accumulated keystroke buffer and buffer length are adjusted appropriately.
- If the ESC key was pressed, the Participating variable is set to FALSE.
- If the ENTER key was depressed, the accumulated keystrokes are sent as a message by calling SendKeyboardMsg( ).

- Otherwise, the keystroke value is given to ApplyKeystroke( ) for processing (accumulation).

SendKeyboardMsg( )

SendKeyboardMsg( ) clears out the Send Datagram buffer area before copying the user name and message into the buffer. It then calls Netbios-SendDatagram( ) to send the conference datagram. Finally, before exiting, it calls SetUpInputLine( ) to initialize the program keystroke accumulation buffer.

Note that SendKeyboardMsg( ) does not check to see if the last Send Datagram command is still pending. Since all Send Datagram commands in this program use the same Ncb, this could be a serious program error. However, NetbiosSendDatagram( ) does this at entry. In addition, Netbi-osSendDatagram( ) also uses other logic not used in previous discussions, so you may wish to examine it a bit closer than other functions.

ApplyKeystroke( )

ApplyKeystroke( ) first checks to see that the maximum number of key-strokes have not been accumulated. If they have, ApplyKeyStroke( ) beeps the workstation and returns. Otherwise, it checks to see that the character is a valid displayable ASCII character. If so, ApplyKeystroke( ) appends that keystroke to the accumulated ones and displays the character before returning.

C File Transfer Applications

This chapter discusses two applications that provide file transfer capability via a NetBIOS session. One application, SEND.C in Listing 13-1, transmits a file. The other, RECEIVE.C in Listing 13-2 receives the file. While the programs only allow one file transmission before they both end execution, they are not difficult to extend to provide multiple-file transfers within a session, perhaps using PC-DOS wildcard file specifications. But that topic is beyond the scope of this discussion and is left as a reader exercise.

Listing 13-1. SEND.C

```
#define   LINT_ARGS

#include  <dos.h>
#include  <stdio.h>
#include  "netbios2.h"

#if defined(LINT_ARGS)
extern   int main(int argc,char * *argv);
extern   int AddSessionName(char *NamePtr);
extern   int CreateSession(void);
extern   void ProcessFile(void);
extern   void TransmitFile(struct _iobuf *FilePtr);
extern   void TerminateSession(void);
extern   void DeleteSessionName(char *NamePtr);
extern   void ClearNcb(struct Ncb *NcbPtr);
extern   unsigned char NetbiosAddName(char *Name);
extern   void NetbiosCall(struct Ncb *NcbPtr);
extern   void NetbiosDeleteName(char *Name);
extern   void NetbiosHangUp(struct Ncb *NcbPtr,unsigned char TargetLsn);
```

Listing 13-1. (cont.)

```
extern  void NetbiosSend(struct Ncb *NcbPtr);
extern  void NetbiosRequest(struct Ncb *NcbPtrNear);
extern  void Logo(void);
#endif

#define SESSION_NAME_TERMINATOR 0x88

USGC  SessionLsn;

struct Ncb ControlNcb, XmitNcb;

struct SessionMsg XmitBlock;

              /* 1234567890123 */
char SendName[] = "WDS-Send-File";
char RecvName[] = "WDS-Recv-File";

int main(argc,argv)
int  argc;
char *argv[];
{
   Logo();

   if (AddSessionName(SendName)) {

      if (CreateSession()) {
         ProcessFile();
         TerminateSession();
      }

      DeleteSessionName(SendName);
   }

   printf("\n\nProgram ending...\n");

   return 0;
}

int AddSessionName(NamePtr)
char *NamePtr;
{
   printf("\n\nAdding the session name %s...", NamePtr);

   if (NetbiosAddName(NamePtr) == ILLEGAL_NAME_NUM)
```

Listing 13-1. (cont.)

```
         return FAILURE;
    else
         return SUCCESS;
}



int CreateSession()
{
    printf("\n\nCalling to create the session...");

    NetbiosCall(&ControlNcb);

    if (!ControlNcb.NcbRetCode) {
       printf("session successfully created...");
       SessionLsn = ControlNcb.NcbLsn;
       return SUCCESS;
    } else {
       printf("session not created...error 0x%02X...",
                                 ControlNcb.NcbRetCode);
       return FAILURE;
    }
}

void ProcessFile()
{
    FILE *FilePtr;
    char  FileName[100];

    printf("\n\nPlease enter the file name to send ==> ");

    gets(FileName);

    if (FilePtr  = fopen(FileName, "rb")) {
        TransmitFile(FilePtr);
        fclose(FilePtr);
    }
}

void TransmitFile(FilePtr)
FILE *FilePtr;
{
    USGI ReadCount, ProcessFlag = TRUE, Count = 0;
    USGL TransmissionSize = 0;
```

Listing 13-1. (cont.)

```
    printf("\nFile Transfer beginning...\n");

    while (ProcessFlag == TRUE) {

        ReadCount = fread( XmitBlock.Text, sizeof(char),
                           sizeof(XmitBlock.Text), FilePtr);

        if (!ferror(FilePtr)) {

            if ((XmitBlock.TextLength = ReadCount) != 0) {

                printf("\nTransmitting block %3u...size = %u",
                                ++Count, XmitBlock.TextLength);

                NetbiosSend(&XmitNcb);

                if (XmitNcb.NcbRetCode) {
                    printf("\n\nSend error %02X...",
                                    XmitNcb.NcbRetCode);
                    ProcessFlag = FALSE;
                } else {
                    TransmissionSize += XmitBlock.TextLength;
                }
            }

            if (feof(FilePtr))         {
                printf("\n\nFile Transmitted...");
                ProcessFlag = FALSE;
            }

        } else {
            printf("\n\nError reading file...");
            ProcessFlag = FALSE;
        }
    }

    printf("\n\nTotal transmission size = %lu bytes...",
                            TransmissionSize);
}

void TerminateSession()
{
    printf("\n\nHanging Up on the session...");
```

Listing 13-1. (cont.)

```c
    NetbiosHangUp(&ControlNcb, SessionLsn);

    if (!ControlNcb.NcbRetCode)
        printf("the Hang Up was successful..");
    else
        printf("the Hang Up was not successful..");
}


void DeleteSessionName(NamePtr)
char *NamePtr;
{
    printf("\n\nDeleting the session name %s...", NamePtr);
    NetbiosDeleteName(NamePtr);
}


/*------------------- Netbios Requests -------------------*/

struct SREGS SegRegs;   /* defined in dos.h */

void ClearNcb(NcbPtr)
struct Ncb *NcbPtr;
{
    int   i;
    char *CharPtr = (char *) NcbPtr;

    for ( i = 0; i < sizeof(ZeroNcb); i++ )
        *CharPtr++ = '\x00';
}


USGC NetbiosAddName(Name)
char *Name;
{
    struct Ncb AddNameNcb;

    ClearNcb(&AddNameNcb);

    AddNameNcb.NcbCommand = NETBIOS_ADD_NAME;

    strncpy(AddNameNcb.NcbName,  Name, strlen(Name));
    AddNameNcb.NcbName[15] = SESSION_NAME_TERMINATOR;

    NetbiosRequest(&AddNameNcb);

    if (!AddNameNcb.NcbRetCode) {
```

Listing 13-1. (cont.)

```c
        printf("...the add-name was successful...");
        return AddNameNcb.NcbNum;
    } else {
        printf("...unsuccessful add-name...error %02X...",
                                        AddNameNcb.NcbRetCode);

        return ILLEGAL_NAME_NUM;
    }
}


void NetbiosCall(NcbPtr)
struct Ncb *NcbPtr;
{
    ClearNcb(NcbPtr);

    NcbPtr->NcbCommand = NETBIOS_CALL;

    strncpy(NcbPtr->NcbCallName,  RecvName, strlen(RecvName));
    NcbPtr->NcbCallName[15] = SESSION_NAME_TERMINATOR;

    strncpy(NcbPtr->NcbName,  SendName, strlen(SendName));
    NcbPtr->NcbName[15] = SESSION_NAME_TERMINATOR;

    NcbPtr->NcbSto = 30;      /* 15 second time out */
    NcbPtr->NcbRto = 30;      /* 15 second time out */

    NetbiosRequest(NcbPtr);
}

void NetbiosDeleteName(Name)
char *Name;
{
    struct Ncb DeleteNameNcb;

    ClearNcb(&DeleteNameNcb);

    DeleteNameNcb.NcbCommand = NETBIOS_DELETE_NAME;

    strncpy(DeleteNameNcb.NcbName, Name, strlen(Name));
    DeleteNameNcb.NcbName[15] = SESSION_NAME_TERMINATOR;

    NetbiosRequest(&DeleteNameNcb);
}
```

Listing 13-1. (cont.)

```c
void  NetbiosHangUp(NcbPtr, TargetLsn)
struct Ncb *NcbPtr;
USGC        TargetLsn;
{
    ClearNcb(NcbPtr);

    NcbPtr->NcbCommand = NETBIOS_HANG_UP;

    NcbPtr->NcbLsn = TargetLsn;

    NetbiosRequest(NcbPtr);
}


void NetbiosSend(NcbPtr)
struct Ncb        *NcbPtr;
{
    struct SessionMsg far *BufferPtrFar;

    ClearNcb(NcbPtr);

    NcbPtr->NcbCommand = NETBIOS_SEND;

    NcbPtr->NcbLsn      = SessionLsn;

    BufferPtrFar = (struct SessionMsg far *) &XmitBlock;

    NcbPtr->NcbBufferOffset  = (char *) FP_OFF(BufferPtrFar);
    NcbPtr->NcbBufferSegment = (USGI)   FP_SEG(BufferPtrFar);

    NcbPtr->NcbLength  = sizeof(XmitBlock);

    NetbiosRequest(NcbPtr);
}


void NetbiosRequest(NcbPtrNear)
struct Ncb *NcbPtrNear;
{
 union  REGS  InRegs, OutRegs;
 struct Ncb far *NcbPtrFar = (struct Ncb far *) NcbPtrNear;

    NcbPtrNear->NcbLanaNum = 0;   /* force to adapter zero */

    segread(&SegRegs);              /* init the segment regs */
```

Listing 13-1. (cont.)

```
    SegRegs.es  = FP_SEG(NcbPtrFar);
    InRegs.x.bx = FP_OFF(NcbPtrFar);

    int86x(NetbiosInt5C, &InRegs, &OutRegs, &SegRegs);
}


void Logo()
{
    printf("\nNETBIOS Sample Send Program");
    printf("  © Copyright 1988 W. David Schwaderer");
}
```

Listing 13-2. RECEIVE.C

```
#define   LINT_ARGS

#include  <dos.h>
#include  <stdio.h>
#include  "netbios2.h"

#if defined(LINT_ARGS)
extern  int   main(int argc,char * *argv);
extern  int   AddSessionName(char *NamePtr);
extern  int   CreateSession(void);
extern  void  ProcessFile(void);
extern  void  ReceiveFile(FILE *FilePtr);
extern  void  DeleteSessionName(char *NamePtr);
extern  void  TerminateSession(void);
extern  void  ClearNcb(struct Ncb *NcbPtr);
extern  USGC  NetbiosAddName(char *Name);
extern  void  NetbiosListen(struct Ncb *NcbPtr);
extern  void  NetbiosDeleteName(char *Name);
extern  void  NetbiosHangUp(struct Ncb *NcbPtr, USGC TargetLsn);
extern  void  NetbiosReceive(struct Ncb *NcbPtr);
extern  void  NetbiosRequest(struct Ncb *NcbPtrNear);
extern  void  Logo(void);
#endif

#define SESSION_NAME_TERMINATOR 0x88

USGC  SessionLsn;

struct Ncb ControlNcb, XmitNcb;

struct SessionMsg XmitBlock;
```

Listing 13-2. (cont.)

```c
              /* 1234567890123 */
char SendName[] = "WDS-Send-File";
char RecvName[] = "WDS-Recv-File";

int main(argc,argv)
int  argc;
char *argv[];
{
   Logo();

   if (AddSessionName(RecvName)) {

      if (CreateSession())
         ProcessFile();

      DeleteSessionName(RecvName);
   }

   printf("\n\nProgram ending...\n");

   return 0;
}


int AddSessionName(NamePtr)
char *NamePtr;
{
   printf("\n\nAdding the session name %s...", NamePtr);

   if (NetbiosAddName(NamePtr) == ILLEGAL_NAME_NUM)
      return FAILURE;
   else
      return SUCCESS;
}


int CreateSession()
{
   printf("\n\nListening to create the session...");

   NetbiosListen(&ControlNcb);

   if (!ControlNcb.NcbRetCode) {
      printf("session successfully created...");
      SessionLsn = ControlNcb.NcbLsn;
```

Listing 13-2. (cont.)

```
        return SUCCESS;
    } else {
        printf("session not created...error 0x%02X...",
                                    ControlNcb.NcbRetCode);
        return FAILURE;
    }
}


void ProcessFile()
{
    FILE *FilePtr;
    char  FileName[100];

    printf("\n\nPlease enter the file name to receive ==> ");

    gets(FileName);

    if (FilePtr  = fopen(FileName, "wb")) {
        ReceiveFile(FilePtr);
        fclose(FilePtr);
    }
}


void ReceiveFile(FilePtr)
FILE *FilePtr;
{
    USGI WriteCount, ProcessFlag = TRUE, Count = 0;
    USGL TransmissionSize = 0;

    printf("\nFile transfer beginning...\n");

    while (ProcessFlag == TRUE) {

        NetbiosReceive(&XmitNcb);

        if (XmitNcb.NcbRetCode) {
            printf("\n\nReceive error %02X...", XmitNcb.NcbRetCode);
            TerminateSession();
            ProcessFlag = FALSE;
        } else  {

            printf("\nSuccessfully received block %3u...size = %u",
                                ++Count, XmitBlock.TextLength);
```

Listing 13-2. (cont.)

```
        WriteCount = fwrite(XmitBlock.Text,          sizeof(char),
                               XmitBlock.TextLength, FilePtr);

        if (WriteCount != XmitBlock.TextLength)
            printf("...but only wrote %u bytes!\x07",
                                        WriteCount);

        TransmissionSize += XmitBlock.TextLength;
      }
   }

   printf("\n\nTotal transmission size = %lu bytes...",
                              TransmissionSize);
}

void DeleteSessionName(NamePtr)
char *NamePtr;
{
   printf("\n\nDeleting the session name %s...", NamePtr);
   NetbiosDeleteName(NamePtr);
}

void TerminateSession()
{
   printf("\n\nHanging Up on the session...");

   NetbiosHangUp(&ControlNcb, SessionLsn);

   if (!ControlNcb.NcbRetCode)
       printf("the Hang Up was successful..");
   else
       printf("the Hang Up was not successful..");
}

/*------------------- Netbios Requests -------------------*/

struct SREGS SegRegs;  /* defined in dos.h */

void ClearNcb(NcbPtr)
struct Ncb *NcbPtr;
{
    int   i;
   char *CharPtr = (char *) NcbPtr;
```

Listing 13-2. (cont.)

```c
    for ( i = 0; i < sizeof(ZeroNcb); i++ )
        *CharPtr++ = '\x00';
}


USGC NetbiosAddName(Name)
char *Name;
{
    struct Ncb AddNameNcb;

    ClearNcb(&AddNameNcb);

    AddNameNcb.NcbCommand = NETBIOS_ADD_NAME;

    strncpy(AddNameNcb.NcbName,  Name, strlen(Name));
    AddNameNcb.NcbName[15] = SESSION_NAME_TERMINATOR;

    NetbiosRequest(&AddNameNcb);

    if (!AddNameNcb.NcbRetCode) {
        printf("...the add-name was successful...");
        return AddNameNcb.NcbNum;
    } else {
        printf("...unsuccessful add-name...error %02X...",
                                    AddNameNcb.NcbRetCode);

        return ILLEGAL_NAME_NUM;
    }
}


void  NetbiosHangUp(NcbPtr, TargetLsn)
struct Ncb *NcbPtr;
USGC        TargetLsn;
{
    ClearNcb(NcbPtr);

    NcbPtr->NcbCommand = NETBIOS_HANG_UP;

    NcbPtr->NcbLsn = TargetLsn;

    NetbiosRequest(NcbPtr);
}


void NetbiosListen(NcbPtr)
struct Ncb *NcbPtr;
```

Listing 13-2. (cont.)

```c
{
   ClearNcb(NcbPtr);

   NcbPtr->NcbCommand = NETBIOS_LISTEN;

   strncpy(NcbPtr->NcbCallName, SendName, strlen(SendName));
   NcbPtr->NcbCallName[15] = SESSION_NAME_TERMINATOR;

   strncpy(NcbPtr->NcbName, RecvName, strlen(RecvName));
   NcbPtr->NcbName[15] = SESSION_NAME_TERMINATOR;

   NcbPtr->NcbSto = 30;      /* 15 second time out */
   NcbPtr->NcbRto = 30;      /* 15 second time out */

   NetbiosRequest(NcbPtr);
}

void NetbiosDeleteName(Name)
char *Name;
{
   struct Ncb DeleteNameNcb;

   ClearNcb(&DeleteNameNcb);

   DeleteNameNcb.NcbCommand = NETBIOS_DELETE_NAME;

   strncpy(DeleteNameNcb.NcbName, Name, strlen(Name));
   DeleteNameNcb.NcbName[15] = SESSION_NAME_TERMINATOR;

   NetbiosRequest(&DeleteNameNcb);
}

void NetbiosReceive(NcbPtr)
struct Ncb        *NcbPtr;
{
   struct SessionMsg far *BufferPtrFar;

   ClearNcb(NcbPtr);

   NcbPtr->NcbCommand = NETBIOS_RECEIVE;

   NcbPtr->NcbLsn     = SessionLsn;

   BufferPtrFar = (struct SessionMsg far *) &XmitBlock;
```

Listing 13-2. (cont.)

```
    NcbPtr->NcbBufferOffset  = (char *) FP_OFF(BufferPtrFar);
    NcbPtr->NcbBufferSegment = (USGI)   FP_SEG(BufferPtrFar);

    NcbPtr->NcbLength  = sizeof(XmitBlock);

    NetbiosRequest(NcbPtr);
}

void NetbiosRequest(NcbPtrNear)
struct Ncb *NcbPtrNear;
{
 union  REGS  InRegs, OutRegs;
 struct Ncb far *NcbPtrFar = (struct Ncb far *) NcbPtrNear;

    NcbPtrNear->NcbLanaNum = 0;    /* force to adapter zero */

    segread(&SegRegs);             /* init the segment regs */

    SegRegs.es  = FP_SEG(NcbPtrFar);
    InRegs.x.bx = FP_OFF(NcbPtrFar);

    int86x(NetbiosInt5C, &InRegs, &OutRegs, &SegRegs);
}

void Logo()
{
    printf("\nNETBIOS Sample Receive Program");
    printf("  © Copyright 1988 W. David Schwaderer");
}
```

Application Overview

SEND.C and RECEIVE.C work in tandem to transfer files. They both begin by adding unique names to their NetBIOS name table. SEND.C uses the name WDS-Send-File; RECEIVE uses the name WDS-Recv-File. Both names are terminated in the 16th position with a nonzero value, guaranteeing their uniqueness from IBM reserved names.

If the Add Name commands are successful, both applications attempt to establish a session with the other. RECEIVE.C initiates its side of Net-BIOS session with a Listen command specifying its unique name as well as the unique name SEND.C uses. The Listen command must be pending before the Call command issued by SEND.C times-out.

The Listen command uses a no-wait option so SEND.C must connect to it or the machine executing RECEIVE.C must eventually be rebooted. If the SEND.C Call command times-out, simply execute SEND.C again to establish the session. After this is done, SEND.C and RECEIVE.C prompt their users for the file that is respectively transmitted and received. After the users reply to their prompts, perhaps using different names, the data transfer begins. Note that each side of the session specifies a 15-second time-out in its Listen and Call commands for session Receive and Send commands, so users should not wait too long to respond to prompts after the other user responds or the session will abort. If it does abort, simply run the programs again.

If any error is detected by a session partner during the transmission session, that partner aborts the session using a Hang Up command and the other session partner's Send or Receive command subsequently completes with a "Session Aborted" return code. Otherwise, the session continues transferring data using a C structure that contains both data and a value indicating how much data actually resides in the area reserved for it. This structure is defined in the netbios2.h header file.

When SEND.C eventually has no more data to transfer, it issues a Hang Up command to terminate the session. When RECEIVE.C's pending Receive command completes with an error, it attempts to abort the session which no longer exists. The Hang Up command subsequently fails with a "Session Closed" error code.

Everything considered, NetBIOS session communication is very easy as Listings 13-1 and 13-2 illustrate. In fact, the program logic to read and write the files is nearly as difficult as the actual NetBIOS session logic. The sample programs are laced with printf( ) statements that provide user feedback as the session continues. These statements also considerably reduce any mystery within the programs' logic, though experienced users may find their unnecessarily chatty nature somewhat offensive. As much logic as possible is shared between the programs to reduce the programming effort even further. Have fun and happy file transfers.

Chapter 14

Medialess Workstations, RPL, and Redirectors

Medialess workstations, RPL, and redirectors share two common attributes:

- Each involves the transfer of data requests (e.g., read, write, etc.) from one workstation to another for resolution.
- Because the data request is performed elsewhere, the possibility exists that the data is being used by many other machines, thereby causing potential data sharing problems.

Clients and Servers

In such situations, requesting machines, referred to as clients, obtain data storage and management services from cooperating machines, referred to as servers. Usually, clients and servers communicate via a LAN connection. Depending on the LAN and the number of clients, it is often possible for data requests to be processed faster and more economically using a high-performance server rather than slower local storage devices at client machines.

Medialess Workstations

Medialess workstations are client machines that have no local diskette or disk storage. The primary advantage of these machines is their lower cost and the natural data security provided by not being able to copy data onto a diskette that may enter or leave the establishment.

Remote Program Load (RPL)

Medialess workstations typically use RPL to load their operating systems into memory. Once loaded, the operating system initializes the workstation normally, oblivious to the absence of local disk and diskette devices. Subsequent applications similarly execute, unaware of the absence of local storage devices.

Redirectors

Redirectors are components that intercept local data requests and redirect (transfer) them to server machines. In contrast to RPL, which initially operates with no operating system present, redirectors operate as system extensions.

Examples of popular redirectors are Microsoft Corporation's redirector in the Microsoft Networks (MS-NET) product and REDIR.EXE used in IBM's PC LAN Program (PCLP). In the OS/2 arena, Microsoft provides a redirector in its Microsoft LAN Manager product and IBM includes the OS/2 LAN Requestor function in the IBM OS/2 Extended Edition version 1.1.

Data Layers

Figure 14-1 depicts a conceptual representation of the layers that resolve data requests within popular PC-DOS machines. This figure clearly illustrates that data requests can be captured at any of three points in their processing:

> the INT 21 PC-DOS Interface
> the Block Device Driver Call Interface
> the INT 13 BIOS Interface

The INT 21 PC-DOS Interface

The INT 21 PC-DOS interface provides a variety of machine services including data services at the file level. These services open, close, create, modify, and erase files based on application program requests.

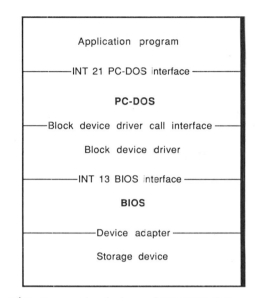

**Fig. 14-1. Conceptual view of PC-DOS data request
processing layers.**

Applications load registers and initialize various data fields with values that indicate the type of service requested and which particular file or files the request relates to. The application then issues an INT 21 request which is intercepted by PC-DOS and acted on. PC-DOS eventually returns after performing the task to the best of its ability.

The Block Device Driver Call Interface

PC-DOS device drivers are modules that control specific devices. Their primary advantage is that they allow programmers to create operating systems that are independent of any particular device-specific considerations. Thus, when a new device replaces another, typically only the specific device driver needs to change—not the operating systems that support the device.

There are two types of PC-DOS device drivers: character device drivers and block device drivers. A common misconception is that character device drivers can only handle one-character-at-a-time requests while block device drivers can handle blocks of data at a time.

Character device drivers control the operation of devices such as printers, keyboards, displays, etc. Using operating system services such as I/O redirection, these devices can be regarded as filelike devices.

Block device drivers control the operation of devices such as disks, diskette drives, CD-ROM devices, etc. These types of devices support file systems. Thus, the primary distinction between character and block device drivers is independent of an ability to process blocks of data with a single request.

PC-DOS invokes device driver services using a program-call interface that is documented in the *PC-DOS Technical Reference Manual*. This interface can be involved, depending on the device, and is beyond the scope of this book. For further information on device drivers, consult the *Manual* or *Writing MS-DOS Device Drivers* (Lai 1987).

The INT 13 BIOS Interface

The INT 13 BIOS interface provides the lowest level data service interface. After loading registers with values that specify the type of request, PC-DOS block device drivers issue an INT 13 interrupt request. The registers and the significance of their contents are listed in Table 14-1.

Table 14-1. Interrupt Registers

Register	Meaning
AH	Request type (reset, read, write, format track, etc.)
CH	Cylinder number
CL	Sector number
DH	Head number
DL	Drive Number (0x00 ==〉 A:, 0x01 ==〉 B:, etc.)
ES :BX	Address of buffer for reads/writes

After the BIOS performs the requested operation, it follows the following steps:

1. placing the operation final status in the AH register
2. placing requested device information (if any) in the CX and DX registers
3. setting the carry flag (CY) to zero or one, respectively, indicating request success or failure
4. returning via a FAR RET 2 instruction that preserves the existing flag settings

The module that issued the request resumes execution and subsequently analyzes the results.

A Redirector Implementation

The REDIR.EXE redirector has a set of private interfaces allowing it to determine which servers to establish NetBIOS sessions with, and to identify which client devices should have their requests forwarded to a server. More than one client device can be serviced by a single redirector.

REDIR.EXE operates at the INT 21 PC-DOS interface by trapping INT 21 PC-DOS requests and inspecting them. If a request is not for a device the redirector is handling, the request is passed on to PC-DOS for local processing. Otherwise, the redirector transmits the request to the server using the Server/Redirector protocol via a Server Message Block (SMB). The *May 1985 IBM Personal Computer Seminar Proceedings* (volume 2, number 8-1) document describes this protocol, which is beyond the scope of this discussion.

The primary advantage of a redirector implementation is that it allows servers to provide extensive services for clients because client requests are intercepted at a very high level. As an example, the REDIR.EXE redirector provides a variety of data sharing support. However, redirector implementations typically require significant programming efforts and you must have a very intimate knowledge of PC-DOS before you can write implementations that function transparently to applications.

A Block Device Driver Implementation

Block device drivers allow client workstations to specify disk requests for a specific virtual drive to be passed to the device driver for forwarding to, and processing by, a server. The target server and device are specified during the installation of the device driver. The installation process should also establish a communication session between the client and server workstation. The disk space provided by the server to the client is referred to as a Remote Virtual Disk (RVD).

In contrast to a redirector, a block device driver can typically service requests only for a single device. Data sharing facilities are also limited but can be crudely implemented by returning a "Media Changed" result to client PC-DOS Media Check function calls whenever the server indicates data has changed at the server. Client machines receiving such a signal flush their buffers and reread the device to obtain the correct information. (See Lai (1987) and the *PC-DOS Technical Reference Manual*.)

The INT 13 BIOS Interface

The INT 13 BIOS interface presents data requests at the lowest possible interface—the BIOS interface. Because all local device requests result in INT 13 calls, modules that operate at this level can forward requests for several devices to one or more servers using preestablished NetBIOS sessions. These modules may be PC terminate-and-stay-resident (TSR) programs or adapter RPL logic. These modules have virtually no knowledge of why a given request is being issued because the accompanying information is too scanty to make a determination. For example, is a sector-read request part of a sequential read for a fragmented data file on the server disk, or is it simply a read for a sector in another data file? While a redirector can easily determine this, modules operating at the INT 13 level cannot.

A module operating at the INT 13 level *can* make very informed decisions regarding which server disk sectors should be cached locally because it can monitor the media access patterns. On the other hand, a redirector operates at too high a level to enjoy this degree of media access visibility.

A NetBIOS RPL Implementation—Or How Does PC-DOS Get in There?

The original PC Network (LANA) card provides the only NetBIOS RPL capability within the IBM LAN product line. All other adapters provide RPL services at the DLC level. However, the process is necessarily similar for all RPL machines.

The LANA adapter BIOS is entered during the final phase of the PC BIOS initialization process. Before returning to BIOS, the adapter BIOS

1. initializes the adapter protocol logic
2. saves the current ROM BASIC interrupt vector (INT 18) value

3. replaces the ROM BASIC interrupt vector with a new value that points inside the adapter's BIOS

Eventually, BIOS attempts to load a boot sector from the A: diskette drive. If the attempt fails, it attempts to load one from the C: disk drive. If that fails, BIOS issues an INT 18 request in an attempt to invoke ROM BASIC, which causes the microprocessor to begin executing the adapter BIOS's RPL logic.

Entering the RPL Logic

The RPL logic first restores the ROM BASIC interrupt vector to the value it previously saved. Next, the adapter allocates the top 1K of memory for its use and builds an Ncb there. It then issues an Adapter Status command to fetch the permanent node name. Finally, it checks to see if the LANA's W1 jumper has been removed. If not, the adapter issues the ROM BASIC interrupt, permanently giving control to ROM BASIC.

If jumper W1 has been removed on the LANA card, the logic issues a NetBIOS Reset command, specifying 32 sessions and 32 pending commands. Next, it issues a NetBIOS Call command to the network name IBMNETBOOT (ten contiguous capital letters followed by six binary zeros) using its own permanent node name and NcbSto and NcbRto values of 240 (120 seconds).

If the Call command is not successful, the logic issues the ROM BASIC interrupt, permanently giving control to ROM BASIC. Otherwise, a boot server exists on the network that should be able to help the client machine boot. Thus, the client adapter saves the current setting of the INT 13 interrupt vector and replaces it with another vector that points at its INT 13 redirection logic and sets an indicator that RPL is active.

The Initial INT 13 Reset Command

Next, the RPL logic issues an INT 13 Reset command for some undetermined drive number (DL is not set). This drives the adapter redirection logic that first checks to see that the request code in the AH register does not have a value of 0x05, 0x06, 0x07, 0x0A, or 0x0B.

If the command is one of the unwanted commands, a value of 0x01 is loaded into the AL register and the carry flag is set indicating failure. Otherwise, the logic checks to see if redirection is active. If not, the request is passed to the original INT 13 entry point whose value was previously saved. Since a reset request command has an AH value of 0x00, and RPL is active for the sake of this discussion, the logic builds a message from the register settings and sends it to the RPL server using the existing Ncb in high memory over the previously created session (the NcbLsn must necessarily have a value of one).

Request Message Format

This message is eleven bytes long and has the following format:

```
-------------------------------
¦ AX ¦ CX ¦ DX ¦ ES ¦ BX ¦ ?? ¦
-------------------------------
+0    +2    +4    +6    +8    +10
Displacement
```

The eleventh byte (byte 10) is uninitialized and provides an area to hold the returning carry flag indicator that the server must return.

Write Requests (AH == 0x03)

At this point, the redirection logic inspects the AH register's request code. If it specifies a write, the redirection logic computes the size of the data from the register settings (assuming 512 bytes per sector) and sends the data beginning at the memory location pointed at by the ES :BX register pair with a Send command. It then issues a Receive for 11 bytes to obtain the register values returned by the server.

Read Requests (AH == 0x02)

If the request specifies a read, the logic issues a Receive command for an 11-byte message. This returning message contains the returned registers from the server. If the read operation was successful at the server, the data was transmitted appended to the registers. This means the Receive must complete with an error code of 0x06 (message incomplete) if the read operation was successful at the server.

The logic computes the size of the remaining message from the original registers and issues another receive for the pending data. The data buffer is specified by the ES:BX register. Otherwise, the read operation was unsuccessful at the server and no data is forthcoming.

Other Requests

Because the request was for a reset, the redirection logic simply issues a Receive command for 11 bytes to obtain the register values the server must always return. Thus, regardless of the command, the redirection logic always receives register values before returning to the RPL logic.

Returning from the Redirection Logic

Before returning to the RPL logic, the redirection code loads the correct registers from the register values returned by the server. Next, it sets the carry flag based on the contents of the 11th byte (byte 10). If this byte has a value of 0x00, the carry flag is cleared. Otherwise, the carry flag is set indicating a problem with the request. Finally, the redirection logic returns via a FAR RET 2 instruction that preserves the flag settings.

Loading the Boot Record

Remembering that the redirection logic was originally entered as a result of the RPL logic's issuing a BIOS INT 13 reset command, control returns to the RPL logic. The RPL logic then issues an INT 13 request after setting the register values listed in Table 14-2. This request specifies that the server send a boot record. However, the server only needs to have a data file created from a bootable diskette. This type of data file is referred to as a diskette image.

Table 14-2. Interrupt Register Values

Register	Value	Meaning
AH	0x02	Read request specified
AL	0x01	Read one sector
CH	0x00	Read cylinder (track) number zero
CL	0x01	Read sector number one
DH	0x0000	Use head number zero
DL	0x0000	Use Drive A:
ES:BX	0x0000:0x7C00	Put the data at 0000 7C00

Using the register settings that arrive from the client, the server only needs to calculate a displacement into the diskette image data file to find the correct 512 bytes to send. Once located, the data is transmitted to the client, appended to the 11-byte header that contains the returning register values.

Booting Up

Once the boot record arrives safely, the client machine jumps to location 0000 :7C00 and begins executing the boot record. If the server is slightly sophisticated, the boot record it initially transmits could actually be a small program that contains a short list of diskette images the client can select to actually boot from.

The program can present the list as a menu and allow the user to select the appropriate image. After selection, the bogus boot record can relocate some of its logic to a different area of memory. This logic sends the selection to the server and issues another request for a boot record. Since the server knows which diskette image to use, it transmits the actual boot record from the selected diskette image.

The standard boot process now occurs:

1. The boot record begins issuing read requests to load PC-DOS. These requests are intercepted by the adapter redirection logic and forwarded to the server for processing.
2. The diskette image's CONFIG.SYS is processed.
3. The diskette image's AUTOEXEC.BAT is executed.

Eventually, the client machine can execute a program such as the IBM PC LAN Program that allows it to access network servers. After doing so, it is probably appropriate to end the session with the RPL server so the server can reuse the session table entry for another client machine. (Note that a slightly sophisticated RPL server can service many client machines simultaneously, each using its own diskette image.)

Unlinking from an RPL Server

Since an RPL session must have an NcbLsn value of one at a client machine, it would be easy to issue a Hang Up command specifying an NcbLsn value of one. However, the redirection logic would indicate that RPL was still active.

If the client machine actually had an A: diskette drive, it would not be able to use it because the redirection logic would continue to attempt to redirect all INT 13 requests over the nonexistent session. To avoid this problem, NetBIOS provides the Unlink command.

The Unlink Command

The Unlink command is trapped by the NetBIOS interface and passed to special logic if RPL is still active. Otherwise, the command is ignored but returns with a zero return code. The special logic

- issues a Hang Up command for the RPL session
- releases the memory that was allocated at the beginning of the RPL logic execution
- resets the RPL active indicator to indicate that RPL is not active

However, all INT 13 requests must continue to enter the redirection logic because the INT 13 interrupt vector cannot be reset to its original BIOS setting in case other TSRs may have captured the vector during the boot process. The redirection logic continues to be driven even though it no longer performs any useful function. It simply passes the requests to the original INT 13 routines when it detects that RPL is no longer active. Finally, because the Unlink is tied to the LANA NetBIOS RPL, it is easy to see that most NetBIOS coders will never have a requirement to use the command. However, most NetBIOS implementations honor the command as a compatibility legacy.

The *PC Network Technical Reference Manual* has sample programs that illustrate an RPL server program and provide a utility to build diskette images. Since the programs are provided as assembly listings, they provide an educational way to learn the RPL process.

Part III

A Cyclic Redundancy Check (CRC) Treatise

Chapter 15

CRC Fundamentals

LAN adapters typically provide transmission techniques to verify that messages traverse the LAN's media without error. However, not all LAN nodes and their adapters have the necessary hardware to guarantee that messages are transferred between the LAN adapter and the node's memory without error.

For example, many LAN adapters do not have parity checking on the memory that buffers their messages. Hence, sensitive applications may require transmitter and receiver applications to provide end-to-end data integrity checking on all LAN messages.

The Need for CRC Checking

Cyclic Redundancy Checking (CRC) processing is a powerful error checking technique, but is often misunderstood because of its complexity. Consequently, many popular CRC "implementations" do not implement CRC checking to observe existing popular conventions, and so do not generally interact correctly outside of limited environments.

With a message CRC technique, various data fields within a message are used to produce a value, called a CRC, which is included as the final message field. When a message arrives at its destination, the receiving machine uses an identical process to calculate a CRC and compares its independently calculated CRC with the one that arrived with the message. If the two CRCs do not match, an error occurred and the communication session proceeds under the protocol's error recovery provisions. However, if the two CRCs do match, chances are "good" that the message arrived without mishap. In truth, using a CRC does not guarantee

100% error detection, but it can significantly improve the chances of detecting errors without the cost of trying to achieve perfect detection. How "good" the chances are depends on the CRC method used. Some are clearly more effective than others.

The XMODEM Check Sum

Ward Christensen's XMODEM protocol computes a CRC-like value (technically a check-sum) for each message by adding together the binary values of message characters and dividing the sum by 256. The one-byte remainder value is transmitted to, and used by, a receiving machine in much the same manner as a CRC.

Statistical calculations indicate that XMODEM's approach detects about 95% of all potential transmission errors for XMODEM's 128-byte character messages, making its data transmission sessions typically successful.

As an example of an error that XMODEM does not detect, consider one that reverses the position of two adjacent bytes within a message. Here, "carp" may erroneously become "crap." Since the sum of the binary values of the characters is the same, the error goes undetected with curious and unpredictable social consequences. Because a 5% chance for an error to slip through is too large for many applications, CRC techniques are available to replace XMODEM's check-sum approach.

CRC Mathematics

Protocols that use CRC checking often transmit messages consisting of a header field followed by a text field. Within a typical message (Figure 15-1), the beginning of the header portion is indicated by an SOH character (Start of Header, 0x01).

The text field begins with an STX character (Start of TeXt, 0x02), which also terminates the header field. The text field is terminated by an ETX (End of TeXt, 0x03) or ETB (End of Text Block, 0x17). The CRC field follows the ETX/B character. The particular message fields used to generate the CRC vary by specific protocol and are not addressed here.

Before discussing how CRC values are computed, let's review some elementary concepts.

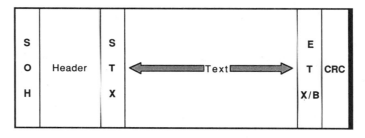

Fig. 15-1. Format of a typical message.

Algebraic Polynomial Division

Recall the many pleasures of polynomial division. In this procedure, one algebraic polynomial divides another to yield a quotient polynomial and a remainder polynomial. For example, suppose you had the following:

$$F(x) = x^5 + 9x^3 + x^2 + 1$$

$$P(x) = x^2 - 1$$

Dividing F(x) by P(x) yields a quotient polynomial Q(x) of

$$Q(x) = x^3 + 10x + 1$$

and a remainder R(x) polynomial of

$$R(x) = 10x + 2$$

Figure 15-2 has the mathematics for the division. Adding R(x) to the product of P(x) by Q(x) returns F(x) as a final result. That is, the process is reversible.

In Figure 15-2, every polynomial has a numeric degree determined by the value of the highest power of x found in a term that is nonzero. In this example, the degree of P(x) is two; the degree of F(x) is five. When one polynomial divides another, the remainder R(x) always has a degree less than the degree of the divisor polynomial, P(x). Thus, the remainder polynomial always has equal to or fewer terms than the degree of the di-

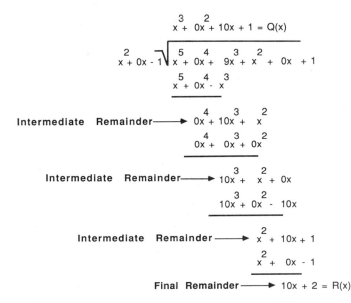

Fig. 15-2. Algebraic polynomial division.

visor polynomial. In the figure, R(x) has two terms and its degree is one, which is less than the degree of P(x).

The last two terms of F(x) (0x + 1) are not divided by P(x) because they have a smaller degree than the divisor. Their presence is reflected in the remainder R(x), but not the quotient Q(x). Stated differently, the divisor polynomial was not directly applied to the low-order terms of F(x).

All arithmetic in this example uses normal decimal arithmetic within standard polynomial division procedures, which produce intermediate remainders used in the next step of the division process.

When subtracting or adding one term from or to another, borrowing or carrying from an adjacent term is not permitted because the terms are independent.

Now consider Figure 15-3 which uses a shorthand method to summarize the steps in this example.

Modulo Two Arithmetic and Polynomial Division

Modulo two arithmetic is easy to confuse with base-two (binary) arithmetic because both types allow only digits having a value of zero or one. However, in base-two arithmetic, 1 + 1 equals 10 and in modulo two arithmetic, 1 + 1 equals zero.

```
                    1   0  10   1
                 _____
       1  0  -1 √ 1   0   9   1   0   1
                  1   0  -1
                  _____
                      0  10   1
                      0   0   0
                      _____
                         10   1   0
                         10   0  -10
                         _____
                              1  10   1
                              1   0  -1
                              _____
                                 10   2
```

Fig. 15-3. Algebraic polynomial division, shorthand form.

Table 15-1 has the complete addition and subtraction tables for modulo two computing, as well a corresponding exclusive-OR table. Clearly, there is no difference between the modulo two arithmetic operations and the exclusive-OR operation.

Table 15-1. Modulo Two Arithmetic vs. Exclusive-OR

First Value	Second Value	Sum of Values	Difference of Values	Exclusive-OR of Values
0	0	0	0	0
0	1	1	1	1
1	0	1	1	1
1	1	0	0	0

Thus, if we have two polynomials,

$$P(x) = x^2 + 1$$

$$F(x) = x^5 + x^3 + 1$$

dividing F(x) by P(x) using modulo two arithmetic yields

$$Q(x) = x^3 \text{ and } R(x) = 1$$

See Figure 15-4 for the details.

$$x^3 = Q(x) \; == \; 1 \; 0 \; 0 \; 0$$

$$P(x) = x^2 + 1 \; == \; 1 \; 0 \; 1 \; \overline{\big)\; 1 \; 0 \; 1 \; 0 \; 0 \; 1} \; == \; F(x) = x^5 + x^3 + 1$$

```
                                          1 0 1
          Intermediate  Remainder ──────▶  0 0 0
                                           0 0 0
          Intermediate  Remainder ──────▶  0 0 0
                                           0 0 0
                Final  Remainder ──────▶   0 0 1 == 1 = R(x)
```

Fig. 15-4. Modulo two division, shorthand form.

Adding R(x) to the product of P(x) and Q(x) recovers the original P(x):

$$P(x) \; [x] \; Q(x) + R(x) = F(x)$$

Since modulo two subtraction is equivalent to an exclusive-OR operation,

$$P(x) \; [x] \; Q(x) = F(x) - R(x) = F(x) + R(x) = F(x) \text{ exclusive-OR } R(x)$$

Thus, under modulo two arithmetic rules, dividing a dividend polynomial F(x) by a polynomial Q(x) produces a remainder polynomial R(x). Then, the sum of F(x) and R(x) is evenly divisible by Q(X). Finally, in all cases, the coefficients of all polynomial terms is zero or one.

CRC Calculation

In CRC calculations, a message's bit pattern is treated as a shorthand representation of a corresponding polynomial's coefficients. Assuming eight bits per message byte, a given ten-byte message would have 80 bits that uniquely define an 80-term polynomial (having terms with degree 79 through zero). By definition, these polynomial term coefficients all have a value of zero or one.

To compute a message CRC, a selected polynomial (P(x)) divides a polynomial (F(x)) derived from the message using the rules of modulo two arithmetic. This yields a remainder polynomial (R(x)) whose coefficients have the same shorthand representation as the bits of the message's CRC value.

Message Bit Patterns

Suppose a message consists of three data characters: A, B, and C (Figure 15-5). To transmit the message, the first byte (A) is transmitted, then the second (B), followed by the last (C). However, because the bits of a byte are traditionally transmitted low-order bit first, the bits must be reversed on a byte-by-byte basis to obtain the corresponding polynomial actually representing the message's bit pattern.*

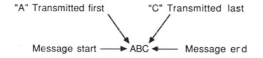

Fig. 15-5. Message byte transmission order.

Thus, the ASCII character, A, equivalent to a binary 01000001, is bitwise reversed to become 10000010. This new value corresponds to the polynomial

$$1X^7 + 0X^6 + 0X^5 + 0X^4 + 0X^3 + 0X^2 + 1X^1 + 0X^0$$

CRC Preconditioning

Once a message's bit pattern is determined, a number of binary digits typically having the same value (all zeros or ones) and equal in number to the degree of the polynomial divisor are prepended to the message bit pattern (Figure 15-6). This introduces an initial intermediate value remainder for the subsequent CRC division.

---

*One exception to the low-order bit-first transmission rule is the ANSI/IEEE 802.5 Standard observed by IBM's Token-Ring adapters. However, since LAN adapters traditionally provide CRC checking on the LAN media, all programs in this book assume that the low-order bit first convention will be observed. This allows the programs to be useful in other telecommunication environments as well as in LAN environments.

PP . . . PMM . . . MZZ . . . Z

Legend: P → Prepended bit values
M → Message bits
Z → Appended binary zeros

Fig. 15-6. Prepending a CRC preconditioning value.

Binary Zero Padding

Next, a number of binary zeros, equal in number to the degree of the polynomial divisor, are appended to the message bit pattern. This allows the divisor polynomial to be applied against every bit position of the original message polynomial.

Modulo Two Division

The polynomial created by the original message bit pattern and the prepending and padding steps is divided using a selected CRC divisor polynomial under modulo two arithmetic division rules.

CRC Postconditioning

The resulting quotient is discarded and the remainder is subject to further processing under the rules of the CRC generation procedures. Typically, the value is left alone or is, at most, subject to a bitwise inversion where all binary zeros are transformed to binary ones and vice versa.

CRC Transmission Procedure

The calculated CRC value is transmitted immediately following transmission of the original message. The CRC is transmitted high-order bit first as a single unit, even if it consists of more than eight bits. All the CRC bits are transmitted, even high-order zero bit(s).

Transmitting the CRC after the original message characters has the effect of subtracting the calculated CRC value from the polynomial created by the prepending, message bit reversal, and padding steps (Figure 15-7). Prepending CRC bits to the message bit stream has the same effect as subtracting the CRC value from the message bit stream appended with binary zeros.

```
MM ... MZZ ... Z
      - CC ... C
```
```
MM ... MCC ... C
```

Legend: C → CRC bit values
         M → Message bits
         Z → Appended binary zeros

Fig. 15-7. Appending CRC bits to the message bit stream.

Message Receipt Procedure

The receiving machine calculates the CRC on the arriving data characters
and includes the arriving CRC characters as though they were part of the
original message. It also omits the CRC postconditioning procedure.

Processing the original message bytes and the CRC bytes in this manner results in a value called a residue. Because the receiving machine
does not perform a CRC postconditioning procedure, the final value is a
residue and not a CRC. Each CRC implementation expects a specific residue value for a successful message reception. If the calculated residue
differs from the expected value, an error occurred during the transfer.

Prevalent CRC Polynomials

The mathematical theory involved in selecting effective divisor polynomials for CRC computations is beyond most graduate mathematics
courses. It involves mathematical field theory at levels that make all but
the most dedicated math aficionados blanch in bewilderment. Luckily,
we can present the results of the mathematics without understanding the
process used to derive them.

The most commonly used CRC polynomials, their associated preconditioning values and postconditioning procedures, and receiving sta-
tion-specific final remainders are indicated in Table 15-2.

Because the remainder for degree 16 divisor polynomials is degree 15
or less, using one of the first two polynomials (CRC-16 or CRC-CCITT)
results in a 16-bit remainder. This allows detection of all errors spanning
16 bits or less and about 99.995% of the others.

Table 15-2. Popular CRC Values

Polynomial	Polynomial Name	Preconditioning Value	Postconditioning Procedure	Final Residue
$x^{16} + x^{15} + x^2 + 1$	CRC-16	0x0000	None	0x0000
$x^{16} + x^{12} + x^5 + 1$	CRC-CCITT (SDLC/HDLC)	0xFFFF	Bit Inversion	0xF0B8
$x^{32} + x^{26} + x^{23} + x^{22} + x^{16} + x^{12} + x^{11} + x^{10} + x^8 + x^7 + x^5 + x^4 + x^2 + x + 1$	CRC-32	0xFFFFFFFF	Bit Inversion	0xDEBB20E3

Which Polynomial Should You Use?

Statistical analysis shows that the SDLC/HDLC polynomial is slightly better suited to some communication environments. This advantage is primarily due to the data link layers associated with this polynomial that typically use bit-stuffing techniques to guarantee the absence of SDLC/HDLC frame flag bytes within messages. So, if you are not doing bit-stuffing, the CRC-16 and CRC-CCITT polynomials are virtually equivalent in their ability to detect errors.

For messages less than 4,000 characters, either the CRC-16 or CRC-CCITT polynomials are excellent. However, the 99.995% error detection rate for the 16-bit CRC polynomials decreases as the message size becomes larger than 4,000 bytes. So, if you are sending large messages or want an extra measure of data integrity, use the CRC-32 polynomial.

The CRC-16 and the CRC-CCITT polynomials have reversed forms. The reversed form of CRC-16 is

$$x^{16} + x^{14} + x + 1$$

and of CRC-CCITT is the following:

$$x^{16} + x^{11} + x^4 + 1$$

Chapter 16

CRC-16 and CRC General Mechanics

Suppose we wish to compute the CRC-16 CRC for a message consisting of the three characters "ABC." Remembering the bit reversal on a byte-by-byte basis, the CRC preconditioning step, and padding of 16 binary zero bits forced by division by a polynomial of degree 16, the division is set up as illustrated in Figure 16-1. Note that the prepending step can be omitted for CRC-16 because it only prepends binary zeros.

```
"A" = 01000001  →  100000010

"B" = 01000010  →  010000010

"C" = 01000011  →  110000010
```

```
1 10000000  00000101√ 00000000  00000000  100000010  010000010  110000010 00000000  00000000
|◄— CRC-16  divisor —►| |◄———16 zeros———►| |◄—A—►| |◄—B—►| |◄—C—►| |◄———16 zeros———►|
        (preconditioning)         Bitwise    Bitwise    Bitwise     (padding)
                                  Reversed   Reversed   Reversed
```

Fig. 16-1. Sample CRC-16 division setup.

For those interested in performing the computation, the division remainder is 0x4521 or binary 0100010100100001. If the result is not obvious, don't worry—it isn't. Although the *task* of hand-computing the remainder of a 4,000-character message is formidable, the *thought* is completely unnerving!

A C function that performs the individual bit reversals and related computations is illustrated without further comment in Listing 16-1. While looking at this program, you might well imagine the computational pressure on the engine to produce CRCs with all the bit selection, shifting, and exclusive-ORing involved that occurs for each message byte. Moreover, the CRC itself must be reversed bitwise before transmitting (not illustrated). Surely there must be a better way, and there is. However, many programs continue to use the slow, inefficient method despite the existence of superior approaches.

Listing 16-1. Bit-Oriented CRC Calculation

```
unsigned CrcAccum;               /* keep intermediate remainders here...    */

WdsCrcCalc2(NewChar)             /* inefficient, traditional CRC-16 routine */
unsigned char NewChar;           /* this is the next character to compute on */
{
    int  i;
    long x;
    unsigned char ReversedChar;

    ReversedChar = ReverseChar(NewChar);        /* reverse the byte's bits */

    x = ( (long) CrcAccum << 8) + ReversedChar;       /* append byte to
                                                intermediate remainder */

    for ( i = 0; i < 8; i++) {                            /* loop here */

        x <<= 1;                              /* stage up the high-order bit  */

        if ( x &  0x01000000 )                /* high-order bit a one?        */
            x ^= 0x01102100;                  /* if so,  subtract the divisor */
    }

    CrcAccum =  ((( x & 0x00FFFF00) >> 8 )); /* eliminate debris and save */
}


unsigned ReverseChar(c)
unsigned char c;
{
    unsigned i, ShiftRight, ShiftLeft;
    unsigned char ReversedC;

    ReversedC = 0;
    ShiftRight = 0x0080;     /* beware, below right-shifting isn't portable */
    ShiftLeft  = 0x0001;

    for (i = 0; i < 8; ShiftLeft <<= 1, ShiftRight >>= 1, i++) {

        if( c & ShiftRight)                     /* found a one-bit?       */
```

Listing 16-1. (cont.)

```
        ReversedC |= ShiftLeft;                  /* if so, set it reversed */
    }


    return(ReversedC);
}
```

CRC Hardware

Because CRC approaches existed before the widespread availability of microprocessors, CRC computation was usually accomplished in hardware. A preliminary representation of hardware circuitry necessary to produce CRC-16 CRCs is illustrated in Figure 16-2. Note the bits are ordered differently in the *data* and *intermediate remainder registers.*

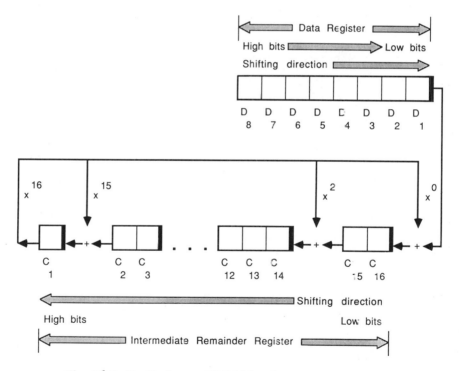

Fig. 16-2. Preliminary CRC-16 hardware arrangement.

At the beginning of each message, the intermediate remainder register is initialized to the appropriate preconditioning value (0x0000 for

CRC-16). Each message data byte is sequentially placed in the data register, which shifts from left to right. For each byte, the illustrated circuitry emulates the CRC-16 modulo two polynomial division process by using the value of the intermediate remainder register's high-order bit ($C[1]$) to subtract the lower order terms of the divisor polynomial, when appropriate ($x**15$, $x**2$, and $x**0$), and create new intermediate remainders.

The subtraction is accomplished by exclusive-OR gates on the intermediate remainder's lower order bits. They are moved from right to left as the high-order bit rotates out of the intermediate remainder shift register circuitry.

Each nonzero divisor polynomial term requires an exclusive-OR gate, which is situated so that adding the value of the subscript of the bit intermediate remainder register immediately to the left of the OR gate to the exponent of the corresponding polynomial divisor term produces a sum of sixteen. (Here, 1 plus 15, 14 plus 2, and 16 plus 0 all equal 16.)

If the current intermediate remainder register high-order bit ($C[1]$) is a zero bit, then the lower order bits are promoted untouched and a subtraction of all zero bits results. If the intermediate remainder register high-order bit is a one bit, the lower order bits of the divisor polynomial are exclusive-ORed at the appropriate positions as the bits are promoted to the next bit position.

Each time the current high-order bit shifts out of the intermediate remainder register, the current low-order bit in the data register shifts into the low-order bit of the intermediate remainder register, perhaps being modified by the value of the latter's high-order bit in the process. This emulates the polynomial division process which introduces new bits into the current intermediate remainders by having them drop down from the dividend.

When the data register has shifted eight times (assuming eight bits to a byte), the next sequential message data byte is placed in the data register. When there are no more data bytes to transmit, two bytes of zeros are sequentially placed in the data register to achieve the necessary padding of binary zeros for a 16th-order CRC divisor polynomial. Since there is no postconditioning step, this completes the CRC calculation process and the 16-bit CRC value can be transmitted. However, the 16-bit value must be transmitted high-order bit first as a contiguous unit (e.g., as bits $C[1]$, $C[2]$, . . . , $C[16]$). This requires a bit reversal of the CRC value to compensate for the transmission circuitry's transmitting the low-order bit first. Rather than do this in hardware, the circuitry can compute the entire CRC in a bit-reversed manner. This is illustrated in Figure 16-3 and explains why the register bit positions were numbered differently in Figure 16-2.

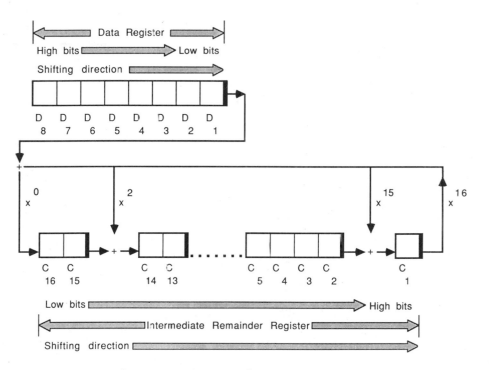

Fig. 16-3. Improved CRC-16 hardware arrangement.

Note, the two final binary zero padding bytes have the effect of multiplying the message polynomial by $2^{**}16$, but advancing the introduction of the data bits by 16 positions has the same effect. So, using the popular circuitry illustrated in Figure 16-4 eliminates the requirement to process the final two bytes of binary zeros and accelerates the CRC calculation in the process. In this scheme, the right-most bits of both registers are exclusive-ORed together to produce an intermediate bit value of either a zero or one. (In the case of the data register, the right-most bit is the low-order bit; in the case of the intermediate remainder register, it is actually the high-order bit.) The registers are then shifted to the right one bit position.

During the shift, the intermediate bit value is also exclusive-ORed with the bits leaving CRC register bit positions 15 and 2. The results of these operations are then placed in positions 14 and 1, respectively. In addition, the intermediate bit value is placed in the intermediate remainder's register bit position 16. Finally, the data register is shifted right one position to present the next bit for processing.

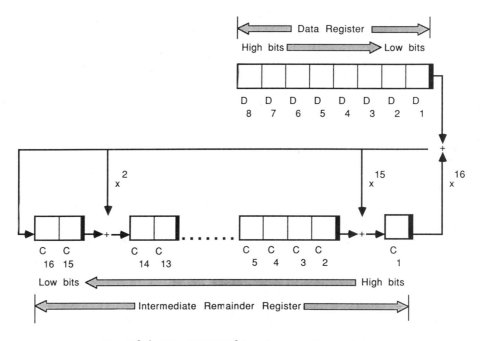

Fig. 16-4. Final CRC-16 hardware arrangement.

Observations

All data bits are naturally processed in reverse order on a byte-by-byte basis, so bit-reversal provisions are not required in this method. In addition, inserting data bits at the new position eliminates processing the two bytes of zero padding. Finally, the CRC register is arranged so that it can be right-shifted as a unit for proper transmission. This is done by transmitting the right-most byte first followed by the left-most byte.

If it seems a bit mysterious, it really isn't. Let's shift a byte through a CRC-16 generator by hand. The data byte is binary 00000001.

```
----------------------------------------------------------------------

Start :                        Data = 0000000   1
                                                 ¦
                                                 ¦
                                                 V
                     --------------------- +       Intermediate value = 1
                     ¦    ¦            ¦  ¦ ^
                     ¦    ¦            ¦  ¦ ¦
                     ¦    V            V  ¦ ¦
                     ->00 + 0000000000000 + 0
```

```
--------------------------------------------------------------------------

Result after shift 1          Data = X000000   0
                                               |
                                               V
                       ---------------------- + New Irtermediate value = 1
                       |     |             | ^
                       |     V             V |
                       ->10 + 1000000000000 + 1


--------------------------------------------------------------------------

Result after shift 2          Data = XX00000   0
                                               |
                                               V
                       ---------------------- + New Intermediate value = 1
                       |     |             | ^
                       |     V             V |
                       ->11 + 1100000000000 + 1


--------------------------------------------------------------------------

Result after shift 3          Data = XXX0000   0
                                               |
                                               V
                       ---------------------- + New Intermediate value = 1
                       |     |             | ^
                       |     V             V |
                       ->11 + 0110000000000 + 1


--------------------------------------------------------------------------

Result after shift 4          Data = XXXX000   0
                                               |
                                               V
                       ---------------------- + New Intermediate value = 1
                       |     |             | ^
                       |     V             V |
                       ->11 + 0011000000000 + 1


--------------------------------------------------------------------------
```

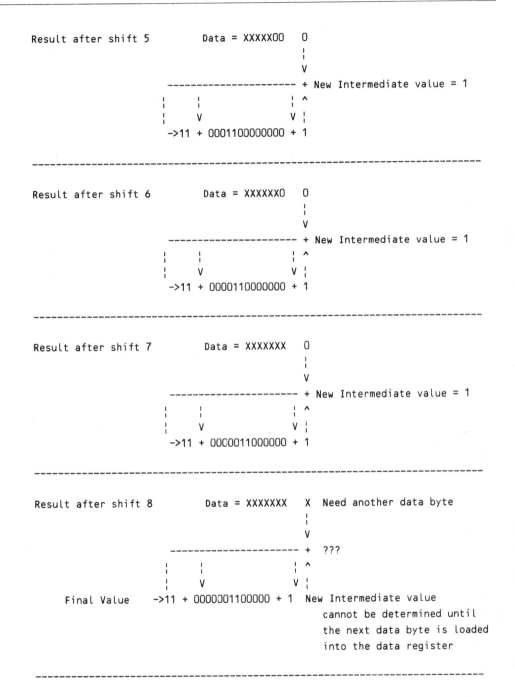

```
Result after shift 5         Data = XXXXX00    0
                                               |
                                               V
                   ------------------- + New Intermediate value = 1
                   |      |          | ^
                   |      V          V |
                   ->11 + 0001100000000 + 1
```

```
Result after shift 6         Data = XXXXXX0    0
                                               |
                                               V
                   ------------------- + New Intermediate value = 1
                   |      |          | ^
                   |      V          V |
                   ->11 + 0000110000000 + 1
```

```
Result after shift 7         Data = XXXXXXX    0
                                               |
                                               V
                   ------------------- + New Intermediate value = 1
                   |      |          | ^
                   |      V          V |
                   ->11 + 0000011000000 + 1
```

```
Result after shift 8         Data = XXXXXXX    X  Need another data byte
                                               |
                                               V
                   ------------------- + ???
                   |      |          | ^
                   |      V          V |
   Final Value     ->11 + 0000001100000 + 1  New Intermediate value
                                              cannot be determined until
                                              the next data byte is loaded
                                              into the data register
```

When manually computing the CRC for this byte using modulo two polynomial division, be sure to perform the necessary bit reversal and bit padding of the dividend value.

Because CRC-16 has no postconditioning, the CRC-16 value for this operation is equal to the value that is left in the intermediate remainder register. This value is subsequently transmitted and processed as though it were a single value spanning two data bytes.

If the receiving station has the same CRC value in its CRC register (as it is on a successful transmission), it receives the right-most CRC byte first. Thus, the intermediate bit value produced by the exclusive-ORing process during the receipt of the inbound CRC-16 CRC value is always a zero bit. Similarly, the intermediate values produced by processing the left-most byte of the CRC-16 CRC value should always yield an intermediate bit value of binary zero at each step. Thus, when the receiving station completes processing the incoming CRC bytes, there should always be a zero value in the receiving station's intermediate CRC-16 register.

This is the test for a successful transmission using CRC-16 and corresponds to our observation that there should be no remainder because

$$P(x) \ [x] \ Q(x) = F(x) - R(x) = F(x) \ \text{Exclusive-OR} \ R(x) = F(x) + R(x)$$

Here, $F(x)$ is the message polynomial multiplied by $X**16$ (padded with two bytes of binary zeros). In other words, transmitting the CRC and processing it as part of the inbound message is equivalent to adding it to a message that has been right-shifted 16 bits resulting in an evenly divisible polynomial.

The zero residue test does not hold for all CRCs, however. Because the CRC-CCITT calculation process has a bit-inverting postconditioning step, the remainder is not transmitted—only its inverse. This means the inbound data stream is guaranteed not to be evenly divisible and always leaves a nonzero residue after processing. This is clear because, during receipt of the inbound CRC-CCITT CRC value, the bit inversion step always forces the intermediate bit values to have a value of one.

One small problem remains. The programming to achieve this approach is no faster or easier than for the preceding polynomial division discussion example. What is needed is an approach that is fast and easy to code.

Generalized CRC-16 Shifting

Suppose that you want to calculate the CRC-16 of an arbitrary byte for an arbitrary value in the intermediate remainder register. Assume the following layout:

```
                        High                    Low
           Data Byte: D8 D7 D6 D5 D4 D3 D2 D1


  Low                                                High
¦<--------- Intermediate Remainder Register --------->¦
  C16 C15 C14 C13 C12 C11 C10 C9 C8 C7 C6 C5 C4 C3 C2 C1
```

Using the procedure outlined above, we can apply the arbitrary byte to the arbitrary CRC value. As before, D1 and C1 are exclusive-ORed together. The result is exclusive-ORed to bits C15 and C2 as they shift to the left and the result of exclusive-ORing D1 and C1 is placed in C16. The data byte and intermediate remainder register look like this:

```
           Data Byte: X   D8 D7 D6 D5 D4 D3 D2

¦<--------- Intermediate Remainder Register --------->¦
  0   C16 C15 C14 C13 C12 C11 C10 C9 C8 C7 C6 C5 C4 C3 C2
 V1        V1                                        V1
```

where $V1 = D1 + C1$ and all values within a CRC intermediate register column are exclusive-ORed together to provide the bit value for that bit position within the register. In general, let $Vi = Di + Ci$.

After processing two bits, the data byte and intermediate remainder register look like this:

```
           Data Byte:   X   X   D7 D6 D5 D4 D3

¦<--------- Intermediate Remainder Register --------->¦
  0   0   C16 C15 C14 C13 C12 C11 C10 C9 C8 C7 C6 C5 C4 C3
      V1        V1                                      V1
  V2      V2                                            V2
```

After processing three bits, the data byte and intermediate remainder register look like this:

```
           Data Byte:   X   X   X   D7 D6 D5 D4

¦<---------- Intermediate Remainder Register --------->¦
  0   0   0   C16 C15 C14 C13 C12 C11 C10 C9 C8 C7 C6 C5 C4
          V1        V1                                    V1
      V2      V2                                          V2
  V3      V3                                              V3
```

After processing four bits, the data byte and intermediate remainder register look like this:

```
                 Data Byte: X   X   X   X  D7 D6 D5

¦<---------- Intermediate Remainder Register --------->¦
0   0   0   0  C16 C15 C14 C13 C12 C11 C10 C9 C8 C7 C6 C5
            V1      V1                              V1
        V2      V2                                  V2
     V3      V3                                     V3
  V4      V4                                        V4
```

After processing 8 bits, elimination of canceling instances of the same bits involved in a bit position's exclusive-OR calculation, and rearrangement of values, the data byte and CRC register look like this:

```
               Data Byte:  X  X  X  X  X  X  X  X

¦<------------ Intermediate Remainder Register ------------->¦
0   0   0   0   0   0   0   0  C16 C15 C14 C13 C12 C11 C10 C9
V1  V1  V7  V6  V5  V4  V3  V2  V1  V1                      V1
V2  V2  V8  V7  V6  V5  V4  V3  V2                          V2
V3  V3                                                     V3
V4  V4                                                     V4
V5  V5                                                     V5
V6  V6                                                     V6
V7  V7                                                     V7
V8                                                         V8
```

This is equivalent to the following diagram:

```
               Data Byte:  X  X  X  X  X  X  X  X

¦<------------ Intermediate Remainder Register ------------->¦
0   0   0   0   0   0   0   0  C16 C15 C14 C13 C12 C11 C10 C9
V1  V1  V8  V7  V6  V5  V4  V3  V2  V1                      V1
V2  V2                                                     V2
V3  V3                                                     V3
V4  V4                                                     V4
V5  V5                                                     V5
V6  V6                                                     V6
V7  V7                                                     V7
V8  V8                                                     V8
    V8  V7  V6  V5  V4  V3  V2  V1
```

Noting that $P = V1 + V2 + V3 + V4 + V5 + V6 + V7 + V8$ is simply the parity of the data byte (even or odd), the figure collapses to

```
                   Data Byte:  X  X  X  X  X  X  X  X

|<-------------- Intermediate Remainder Register ------------->|
0  0   0   0   0   0   0   0  C16 C15 C14 C13 C12 C11 C10 C9
       V8  V7  V6  V5  V4  V3  V2  V1
   V8  V7  V6  V5  V4  V3  V2  V1
P  P                                                        P
```

which provides an ultrahigh-performance CRC-16 computation approach for assembly language programs on machines providing parity values for data characters.

Table Look-Up Schemes

These diagrams all indicate that the new intermediate remainder of a CRC-16 calculation is computable from the initial values of the data byte and the intermediate remainder register. Specifically, if you create an intermediate byte value V that is the exclusive-OR of the left-most byte of the existing CRC intermediate remainder and the new data byte, the new CRC intermediate remainder is created by right-shifting by eight bits (with zero filling in the high-order positions) the existing CRC intermediate remainder, and exclusive-ORing a value that can be derived from the various bits of V. Since V can only have 256 values, it is possible to construct a table that holds the 256 unsigned integer values. Then, the value corresponding to a particular value of V is quickly located, using V as an index.

The CRC-16 calculation algorithm now becomes:

1. At the beginning of each message, set the intermediate remainder register to zero (the CRC-16 preconditioning step).
2. Fetch the first byte of the message.
3. Exclusive-OR the fetched byte with the low-order byte of the intermediate remainder to obtain a byte V.
4. Right-shift the intermediate remainder eight bits with the high-order bits (being zero) filling in the process.
5. Using V as an index, fetch a 16-bit unsigned integer value from the

CRC table and exclusive-OR it to the shifted intermediate remainder.

6. The result of the exclusive-OR operation is the new value of the intermediate remainder.

7. For each unprocessed byte in the message, sequentially fetch the byte and go to step 3.

8. The intermediate remainder is transmitted left-most byte first, followed by the right-most byte.

This approach processes entire bytes of data using a look-up table. Hence the popular name *Bytewise Table Look-up CRC*.

The C program in Listing 16-2 computes the CRC-16 look-up table and shows how to use it. The first CRC-16 computation is on the binary value 0x0100 which produces a bitwise-reversed CRC value of 0x9001. The second example calculates the CRC-16 of 0x0100 followed by its bytewise-reversed CRC (0x0190). In this case, the CRC is zero as it should be.

The third example illustrates that a string's CRC calculation should not include the terminating NULL character. In general, the C function strlen cannot be used to compute the length of a message because the message may contain NULL characters, which cause the strlen function to return an incorrect (shorter) message length.

Listing 16-2. CRC16.C

```
/*-----------------------------------------------------------*/
/*      High Performance CRC-16 Computation Routine          */
/*                                                           */
/*          Copyright 1988 W. David Schwaderer                */
/*                All rights reserved                        */
/*                                                           */
/*        Warning...this program uses bit fields!             */
/*          For warnings on bit field hazards see:            */
/*                                                           */
/*          C Wizard's Programming Reference                  */
/*                W. David Schwaderer                         */
/*                Wiley Press, 1985                           */
/*                                                           */
/*-----------------------------------------------------------*/

#define LINT_ARGS

#include <stdio.h>
#include "netbios2.h"
```

Listing 16-2. (cont.)

```c
#if defined(LINT_ARGS)
extern  int main(int argc,char * *argv);
extern  void GenerateTable(void);
extern  void PrintTable(void);
extern  unsigned int GenerateCRC(unsigned int Length,char *TextPtr);
extern  void Logo(void);
#endif

USGI crc_table[256];     /*   globally accessible */


main(argc, argv)
int    argc;
char *argv[];
{
  USGI length, crc;

                        /* crc = 0x9001 */
  static char TestArray1[] = { '\x01', '\x00'};

  static char TestArray2[] = { '\x01', '\x00', '\x01', '\x90'};
                              /* bytewise         bytewise */
                              /* unreversed       reversed */


  static char TestMsg[] = "This is a test message.";

  Logo();

  GenerateTable();                 /* compute the crc_table  */

  PrintTable();                    /* display the table      */

  length = sizeof(TestArray1);     /* example 1              */
  crc   = GenerateCRC(length, TestArray1); /* calculate CRC  */
  printf("\n\n\nTestArray1 CRC = 0x%04X", crc);

  length = sizeof(TestArray2);     /* example 2              */
  crc   = GenerateCRC(length, TestArray2); /* calculate CRC */
  printf("\n\n\nTestArray2 CRC = 0x%04X", crc);

                                   /* example 3              */
  length = sizeof(TestMsg) - 1;    /* avoid terminating NUL  */
  crc   = GenerateCRC(length, TestMsg); /* calculate a CRC   */
  printf("\n\n\nText = [%s]\nCRC = %04X\n\n", TestMsg, crc);
```

Listing 16-2. (cont.)

```
  return 0;
}


void GenerateTable()    /* generate the look-up table */
{
  int temp;
  union { int i;
        struct {
                    USGI i1  :1;  /* low order bit  */
                    USGI i2  :1;
                    USGI i3  :1;
                    USGI i4  :1;
                    USGI i5  :1;
                    USGI i6  :1;
                    USGI i7  :1;
                    USGI i8  :1;  /* high order bit */
                    USGI     :8;  /* unused byte    */
           } Bit;
        } iUn;


  union {  USGI  Entry;
        struct {
                    USGI b1  :1;  /* low order bit  */
                    USGI b2  :1;
                    USGI b3  :1;
                    USGI b4  :1;
                    USGI b5  :1;
                    USGI b6  :1;
                    USGI b7  :1;
                    USGI b8  :1;
                    USGI b9  :1;
                    USGI b10 :1;
                    USGI b11 :1;
                    USGI b12 :1;
                    USGI b13 :1;
                    USGI b14 :1;
                    USGI b15 :1;
                    USGI b16 :1;  /* high order bit */
                 } EntryBit;
        } EntryUn;

  for (iUn.i = 0; iUn.i < 256; iUn.i++) {

    EntryUn.Entry = 0; /* bits 2 thru 6 zeroed out now */
```

Listing 16-2. (cont.)

```
    temp = (iUn.Bit.i7 ^ iUn.Bit.i6 ^ iUn.Bit.i5 ^
            iUn.Bit.i4 ^ iUn.Bit.i3 ^ iUn.Bit.i2 ^
            iUn.Bit.i1);

    EntryUn.EntryBit.b16 = (iUn.Bit.i8 ^ temp);
    EntryUn.EntryBit.b15 = (temp);
    EntryUn.EntryBit.b14 = (iUn.Bit.i8 ^ iUn.Bit.i7);
    EntryUn.EntryBit.b13 = (iUn.Bit.i7 ^ iUn.Bit.i6);
    EntryUn.EntryBit.b12 = (iUn.Bit.i6 ^ iUn.Bit.i5);
    EntryUn.EntryBit.b11 = (iUn.Bit.i5 ^ iUn.Bit.i4);
    EntryUn.EntryBit.b10 = (iUn.Bit.i4 ^ iUn.Bit.i3);
    EntryUn.EntryBit.b9  = (iUn.Bit.i3 ^ iUn.Bit.i2);
    EntryUn.EntryBit.b8  = (iUn.Bit.i2 ^ iUn.Bit.i1);
    EntryUn.EntryBit.b7  = (iUn.Bit.i1);
    EntryUn.EntryBit.b1  = (iUn.Bit.i8 ^ temp);

    crc_table[iUn.i] = EntryUn.Entry;

  }

}

void PrintTable()        /* print out the look-up table */
{
  int i;

  for (i = 0; i < 256; i++) {
    if ( !(i % 8) )
      printf("\n 0x%02X  -  %04X", i, crc_table[i]);
    else
      printf("  %04X", crc_table[i]);
  }
}

USGI GenerateCRC(Length, TextPtr)
  USGI  Length;
  char     *TextPtr;
{
  int i, index;
  USGI crc;

  crc = 0;      /* crc starts at zero for each message */
```

Listing 16-2. (cont.)

```
  for (i = 0; i < Length; i++, TextPtr++) {
    index = ( (crc ^ *TextPtr) & 0x00FF);
    crc = ( (crc >> 8) & 0x00FF) ^ crc_table[index];
  }


  return crc;


}


void Logo()
{
    printf("\n\n    High Performance CRC-16 Computation Routine");
    printf("\n        Copyright 1988 W. David Schwaderer\n\n");
}


/* *-------------------- Program Output --------------------*
```

0x00	-	0000	C0C1	C181	0140	C301	03C0	0280	C241
0x08	-	C601	06C0	0780	C741	0500	C5C1	C481	0440
0x10	-	CC01	0CC0	0D80	CD41	0F00	CFC1	CE81	0E40
0x18	-	0A00	CAC1	CB81	0B40	C901	09C0	0880	C841
0x20	-	D801	18C0	1980	D941	1B00	DBC1	DA81	1A40
0x28	-	1E00	DEC1	DF81	1F40	DD01	1DC0	1C80	DC41
0x30	-	1400	D4C1	D581	1540	D701	17C0	1680	D641
0x38	-	D201	12C0	1380	D341	1100	D1C1	D081	1040
0x40	-	F001	30C0	3180	F141	3300	F3C1	F281	3240
0x48	-	3600	F6C1	F781	3740	F501	35C0	3480	F441
0x50	-	3C00	FCC1	FD81	3D40	FF01	3FC0	3E80	FE41
0x58	-	FA01	3AC0	3B80	FB41	3900	F9C1	F881	3840
0x60	-	2800	E8C1	E981	2940	EB01	2BC0	2A80	EA41
0x68	-	EE01	2EC0	2F80	EF41	2D00	EDC1	EC81	2C40
0x70	-	E401	24C0	2580	E541	2700	E7C1	E681	2640
0x78	-	2200	E2C1	E381	2340	E101	21C0	2080	E041
0x80	-	A001	60C0	6180	A141	6300	A3C1	A281	6240
0x88	-	6600	A6C1	A781	6740	A501	65C0	6480	A441
0x90	-	6C00	ACC1	AD81	6D40	AF01	6FC0	6E80	AE41
0x98	-	AA01	6AC0	6B80	AB41	6900	A9C1	A881	6840
0xA0	-	7800	B8C1	B981	7940	BB01	7BC0	7A80	BA41
0xA8	-	BE01	7EC0	7F80	BF41	7D00	BDC1	BC81	7C40
0xB0	-	B401	74C0	7580	B541	7700	B7C1	B681	7640
0xB8	-	7200	B2C1	B381	7340	B101	71C0	7080	B041
0xC0	-	5000	90C1	9181	5140	9301	53C0	5280	9241
0xC8	-	9601	56C0	5780	9741	5500	95C1	9481	5440
0xD0	-	9C01	5CC0	5D80	9D41	5F00	9FC1	9E81	5E40

Listing 16-2. (cont.)

```
0xD8  -  5A00  9AC1  9B81  5B40  9901  59C0  5880  9841
0xE0  -  8801  48C0  4980  8941  4B00  8BC1  8A81  4A40
0xE8  -  4E00  8EC1  8F81  4F40  8D01  4DC0  4C80  8C41
0xF0  -  4400  84C1  8581  4540  8701  47C0  4680  8641
0xF8  -  8201  42C0  4380  8341  4100  81C1  8081  4040


TestArray1 CRC = 0x9001


TestArray2 CRC = 0x0000


Text = [This is a test message.]
CRC = 9D6A
*/
```

CRC Compatibility Caveats

A number of "CRC implementations" exist that do not provide the results the example CRC programs in this book provide. Typically, the differences in the other implementations are a consequence of their ignoring one or more of the following conventions:

- the bit reversal legacy of message characters
- the convention of transmitting a CRC in a contiguous bit-reversed manner, high-order bit first
- international preconditioning and postconditioning standards for different CRC computation approaches

The CRC example programs in this book operate correctly in a variety of hardware and software environments. Ignoring data communication legacies, arcane as they may be, precludes the other "CRC implementations" from successfully operating in the same environments, though the other implementations can operate with each other when each ignores the identical conventions.

Each of the CRC programs in this section builds a table and then uses it. Clearly a more efficient approach is to define the table as an array of constants so that it does not have to be generated each time the program executes.

Chapter 17

CRC-CCITT and Minimum Look-Up Table Sizes

The CRC-CCITT polynomial is:

$$x^{16} + x^{12} + x^5 + 1$$

Using the discussion in Chapter 16 as a reference, the appropriate CRC-CCITT generation hardware is illustrated in Figure 17-1.

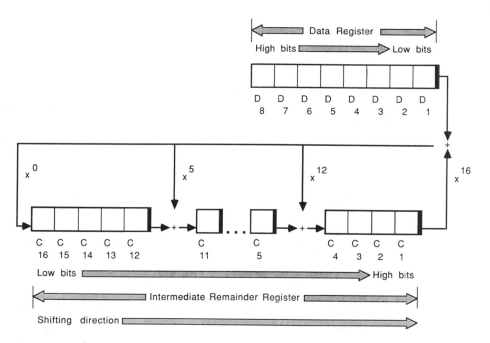

Fig. 17-1. Typical CRC-CCITT hardware representation.

After processing 1 bit, the intermediate remainder register value is:

```
0   C16 C15 C14 C13 C12 C11 C10 C09 C08 C07 C06 C05 C04 C03 C02
V01                 V01                     V01
```

After processing 2 bits, the intermediate remainder register value is:

```
0    0  C16 C15 C14 C13 C12 C11 C10 C09 C08 C07 C06 C05 C04 C03
V02 V01             V02 V01                 V02 V01
```

After processing 3 bits, the intermediate remainder register value is:

```
0    0    0  C16 C15 C14 C13 C12 C11 C10 C09 C08 C07 C06 C05 C04
V03 V02 V01         V03 V02 V01             V03 V02 V01
```

After processing 4 bits, the intermediate remainder register value is:

```
0    0    0    0  C16 C15 C14 C13 C12 C11 C10 C09 C08 C07 C06 C05
V04 V03 V02 V01     V04 V03 V02 V01         V04 V03 V02 V01
```

After processing 8 bits, the intermediate remainder register value is:

```
0    0    0    0    0    0    0    0  C16 C15 C14 C13 C12 C11 C10 C09
V08 V07 V06 V05 V04 V03 V02 V01     V04 V03 V02 V01
V04 V03 V02 V01     V08 V07 V06 V05                 V08 V07 V06 V05
                V04 V03 V02 V01                 V04 V03 V02 V01
```

The Table Look-Up Approach

If a C program uses a CRC-CCITT bytewise table look-up approach, the table requires an array of 256 unsigned integers occupying 512 bytes of memory for a typical machine. Thus, there would be no space savings. However, a program processes each byte's nibbles independently, just as it processes each message byte independently. Reexamining the CRC-CCITT intermediate register after processing four bits indicates this is very easy to do.

This approach only requires 16 unsigned integers that occupy a mere 32 bytes in a typical machine. The only requirement is that two table look-ups are required for each byte instead of one table look-up. Clearly this is a classic trade-off between storage conservation versus conservation of machine cycles.

A program can also process two bits at a time, requiring four table look-ups using a table having four entries and requiring a total of 8 bytes. However, the program instructions to achieve the four passes for each byte may take more memory than the 24 bytes saved by using a four-entry table instead of a larger 16-entry table.

The program in Listing 17-1 uses a *nibblewise table look-up* approach to compute CRC-CCITT values. Its structure is similar to the CRC-16 sample program, so it is presented without much discussion. The primary differences are:

- It illustrates the compact table-generation principles.
- It illustrates the proper CRC-CCITT postconditioning step.
- It illustrates the proper CRC-CCITT preconditioning step.
- It demonstrates that the CRC-CCITT residue, computed by processing a message and its CRC-CCITT bytes, has a value of 0xF0B8.

The only catch is that the program's GenerateCRC( ) routine always inverts its computed values before returning them. That is not appropriate when computing a CRC residue, so there is a nonintuitive value inversion to undo the unwanted inversion performed by the CRC calculation routine.

Listing 17-1. CRC-CCITT

```
/*------------------------------------------------------------*/
/*           High Performance Compact                 */
/*          CRC-CCITT Computation Routine             */
/*                                                    */
/*        Copyright 1988 W. David Schwaderer          */
/*              All rights reserved                   */
/*                                                    */
/*      Warning...this program uses bit fields!       */
/*       For warnings on bit field hazards see:       */
/*                                                    */
/*         C Wizard's Programming Reference           */
/*              W. David Schwaderer                   */
/*                Wiley Press, 1985                   */
/*                                                    */
/*------------------------------------------------------------*/

#define LINT_ARGS

#include <stdio.h>
#include "netbios2.h"
```

Listing 17-1. (cont.)

```c
#if defined(LINT_ARGS)
extern  int main(int argc,char * *argv);
extern  void GenerateTable(void);
extern  void PrintTable(void);
extern  unsigned int GenerateCRC(unsigned int Length,
                              unsigned char *TextPtr);
extern  void Logo(void);
#endif

USGI crc_table[16];                 /* what a tiny table! */

char TestArray1[] = { 'X', 'Y', 'Z' };  /* crc = 0x7ADD  */

char TestArray2[] = { 'X', 'Y', 'Z', '\xDD', '\x7A'};
                      /*  bytewise         bytewise */
                      /*  unreversed       reversed */

main(argc, argv)
int   argc;
char *argv[];
{
  USGI length, crc, residue;

  Logo();

  GenerateTable();                          /* compute the crc_table */

  PrintTable();                             /* display the table */

  length = sizeof(TestArray1);              /* example 1     */
  crc    = GenerateCRC(length, TestArray1); /* calculate CRC */
  printf("\n\nTestArray1 CRC = 0x%04X", crc);   /* display the CRC */

  length  = sizeof(TestArray2);             /* example 2     */
  residue = GenerateCRC(length, TestArray2);  /* calculate residue */

  /*-- To display the residue you must invert the returned "crc"! --*/
  /*------ The residue must always be 0xF0B8 for CRC-CCITT... ------*/

  printf("\n\nTestArray2 residue = 0x%04X\n", ~residue); /* invert! */

  return 0;
}

void GenerateTable()    /* generate the look-up table */
{
```

Listing 17-1. (cont.)

```
USGI  temp;
union { USGI i;
       struct {
                    USGI i1  :1;   /* low order bit  */
                    USGI i2  :1;
                    USGI i3  :1;
                    USGI i4  :1;
                    USGI i5  :1;
                    USGI i6  :1;
                    USGI i7  :1;
                    USGI i8  :1;   /* high order bit */
                    USGI     :8;   /* unused byte    */
              } Bit;
       } iUn;

union {  USGI  Entry;
       struct {
                    USGI b1  :1;   /* low order bit  */
                    USGI b2  :1;
                    USGI b3  :1;
                    USGI b4  :1;
                    USGI b5  :1;
                    USGI b6  :1;
                    USGI b7  :1;
                    USGI b8  :1;
                    USGI b9  :1;
                    USGI b10 :1;
                    USGI b11 :1;
                    USGI b12 :1;
                    USGI b13 :1;
                    USGI b14 :1;
                    USGI b15 :1;
                    USGI b16 :1;   /* high order bit */
              } EntryBit;
       } EntryUn;

for (iUn.i = 0; iUn.i < 16; iUn.i++) {     /* only 16 entries! */

   EntryUn.Entry = 0;             /* zeros out unreferenced bits */

   EntryUn.EntryBit.b16 =
   EntryUn.EntryBit.b11 =
   EntryUn.EntryBit.b4  =  iUn.Bit.i4;

   EntryUn.EntryBit.b15 =
```

Listing 17-1. (cont.)

```
    EntryUn.EntryBit.b10 =
    EntryUn.EntryBit.b3  =  iUn.Bit.i3;

    EntryUn.EntryBit.b14 =
    EntryUn.EntryBit.b9  =
    EntryUn.EntryBit.b2  =  iUn.Bit.i2;

    EntryUn.EntryBit.b13 =
    EntryUn.EntryBit.b8  =
    EntryUn.EntryBit.b1  =  iUn.Bit.i1;

    crc_table[iUn.i] = EntryUn.Entry;    /* save the computed value */
  }
}

void PrintTable()        /* print out the look-up table */
{
  USGI i;

  printf("\n\n    Look at this Tiny CRC-CCITT Look-Up Table...\n");

  for (i = 0; i < 16; i++) {
    if ( !(i % 8) )
      printf("\n 0x%02X  -  %04X", i, crc_table[i]);
    else
      printf("  %04X", crc_table[i]);
  }
}

USGI GenerateCRC(Length, TextPtr)
  USGI  Length;
  USGC *TextPtr;
{
  USGC TempChar;
  USGI i, index, CrcTemp;

  CrcTemp = 0xFFFF;                    /* CRC-CCITT preconditioning ==> 0xFFFF */

  for (i = 0; i < Length; i++, TextPtr++) {

    TempChar = *TextPtr;

    index = ((CrcTemp ^ TempChar) & 0x000F);  /* isolate low-order nibble */
    CrcTemp = ((CrcTemp >> 4) & 0x0FFF) ^ crc_table[index];   /* apply it */

    TempChar >>= 4;                           /* stage the next four bits */
```

Listing 17-1. (cont.)

```
    index = ((CrcTemp ^ TempChar) & 0x000F);  /* isolate low-order nibble */
    CrcTemp = ((CrcTemp >> 4) & 0x0FFF) ^ crc_table[index]; /* 2nd nibble */

  }

  return ~CrcTemp;          /* CRC-CCITT post conditioning ==> bit inversion */
}

void Logo()
{
    printf("\n\n           High Performance Compact");
    printf("\n         CRC-CCITT Computation Routine");
    printf("\n      Copyright 1988 W. David Schwaderer");
}


/* ---------------- End of Program Logic -------------------*

/*


              16   12    5
  polynomial = x  + x   + x  + 1


  After 4-bit processing cycles...

  b16 b15 b14 b13 b12 b11 b10  b9  b8  b7  b6  b5  b4  b3  b2  b1
  --- --- --- --- --- --- --- --- --- --- --- --- --- --- --- ---
   0   0   0   0  C16 C15 C14 C13 C12 C11 C10 C09 C08 C07 C06 C05
  VO4 VO3 VO2 VO1  -  VO4 VO3 VO2 VO1  -   -   -  VO4 VJ3 VO2 VO1


  Each 4-bit processing phase is independent of any other...

  *---------------- Program Output --------------------*

    Look at this Tiny CRC-CCITT Look-Up Table...

0x00 -  0000  1081  2102  3183  4204  5285  6306  7387
0x08 -  8408  9489  A50A  B58B  C60C  D68D  E70E  F78F

TestArray1 CRC = 0x7ADD

TestArray2 residue = 0xF0B8

*/
```

Chapter 18

CRC-32—Token-Ring, PC Network, and Ethernet

The CRC-32 polynomial is the CRC divisor in IBM Token-Ring, IBM PC Network and a variety of other CSMA/CD LANs including Ethernet. Unlike the SDLC/HDLC polynomial, CRC-32 provides a 32-bit CRC value that is useful to the receipt of messages that are too large for the SDLC/HDLC CRC, though it uses a similar preconditioning and postconditioning process.

The CRC-32 preconditioning process loads the intermediate remainder register with 0xFFFFFFFF. The postconditioning process inverts the final remainder to produce the 32-bit CRC which is transmitted high-order bit first as a contiguous 32-bit sequence. The appropriate CRC-32 residual value is 0xDEBB20E3L.

Using this discussion as a backdrop, the derivation of a CRC-32 generation program is essentially trivial. The following diagrams should be obvious at this point in the book:

```
                                                                D08 D07 D06 D05 D04 D03 D02 D01 -->

                                                                                                |
                        Initial State Before Shifting                                           |

                                                                                                |
                                                                                                V

 <----<----<----<----<----<----<----<----<----<----<----<----<----<----<----<----<----<----<----<----<--- +
 0  1  2  3  4  5  6  7  8  9  10 11 12 13 14 15 16 17 18 19 20 21 22 23 24 25 26 27 28 29 30 31 32 ^
 |  |  |     |  |     |  |     |  |  |              |                 |  |        |                    |
 |  |  |     |  |     |  |     |  |  |              |                 |  |        |                    |
 V  V  V     V  V     V  V     V  V  V              V                 V  V        V                    |
 C32 C31 C30 C29 C28 C27 C26 C25 C24 C23 C22 C21 C20 C19 C18 C17 C16 C15 C14 C13 C12 C11 C10 C09 C08 C07 C06 C05 C04 C03 C02 C01-->
```

```
                              After Shift 1                    X   D08 D07 D06 D05 D04 D03 D02

 0  C32 C31 C30 C29 C28 C27 C26 C25 C24 C23 C22 C21 C20 C19 C18 C17 C16 C15 C14 C13 C12 C11 C10 C09 C08 C07 C06 C05 C04 C03 C02
V01 V01 V01     V01 V01     V01 V01     V01 V01 V01             V01                 V01 V01         V01


                              After Shift 2                    X   X   D08 D07 D06 D05 D04 D03

 0   0  C32 C31 C30 C29 C28 C27 C26 C25 C24 C23 C22 C21 C20 C19 C18 C17 C16 C15 C14 C13 C12 C11 C10 C09 C08 C07 C06 C05 C04 C03
    V01 V01 V01     V01 V01     V01 V01     V01 V01 V01             V01                 V01 V01         V01
V02 V02 V02     V02 V02     V02 V02     V02 V02 V02             V02                 V02 V02         V02


                              After Shift 3                    X   X   X   D08 D07 D06 D05 D04

 0   0   0  C32 C31 C30 C29 C28 C27 C26 C25 C24 C23 C22 C21 C20 C19 C18 C17 C16 C15 C14 C13 C12 C11 C10 C09 C08 C07 C06 C05 C04
        V01 V01 V01     V01 V01     V01 V01     V01 V01 V01             V01                 V01 V01         V01
    V02 V02 V02     V02 V02     V02 V02     V02 V02 V02             V02                 V02 V02         V02
V03 V03 V03     V03 V03     V03 V03     V03 V03 V03             V03                 V03 V03         V03


                              After Shift 4                    X   X   X   X   D08 D07 D06 D05

 0   0   0   0  C32 C31 C30 C29 C28 C27 C26 C25 C24 C23 C22 C21 C20 C19 C18 C17 C16 C15 C14 C13 C12 C11 C10 C09 C08 C07 C06 C05
            V01 V01 V01     V01 V01     V01 V01     V01 V01 V01             V01                 V01 V01         V01
        V02 V02 V02     V02 V02     V02 V02     V02 V02 V02             V02                 V02 V02         V02
    V03 V03 V03     V03 V03     V03 V03     V03 V03 V03             V03                 V03 V03         V03
V04 V04 V04     V04 V04     V04 V04     V04 V04 V04             V04                 V04 V04         V04


                              After Shift 8 (Final Shift)      X   X   X   X   X   X   X   X

 0   0   0   0   0   0   0   0  C32 C31 C30 C29 C28 C27 C26 C25 C24 C23 C22 C21 C20 C19 C18 C17 C16 C15 C14 C13 C12 C11 C10 C09
                        V01 V01 V01     V01 V01     V01 V01     V01 V01 V01             V01                 V01 V01
                    V02 V02 V02     V02 V02     V02 V02     V02 V02 V02             V02                 V02 V02
                V03 V03 V03     V03 V03     V03 V03     V03 V03 V03             V03                 V03 V03         V03
            V04 V04 V04     V04 V04     V04 V04     V04 V04 V04             V04                 V04 V04         V04
        V05 V05 V05     V05 V05     V05 V05     V05 V05 V05             V05                 V05 V05         V05
    V06 V06 V06     V06 V06     V06 V06     V06 V06 V06             V06                 V06 V06         V06
V07 V07 V07     V07 V07     V07 V07     V07 V07 V07             V07                 V07 V07         V07
V08 V08 V08     V08 V08     V08 V08     V08 V08 V08             V08                 V08 V08         V08
V01 V01 V01     V01 V01     V01 V01     V01 V01 V01             V01                 V01 V01         V01
V02 V02 V02     V02 V02     V02 V02     V02 V02 V02             V02                 V02 V02         V02
```

The program in Listing 18-1 illustrates a bytewise table look-up to generate CRC-32 values. Note that the look-up table occupies 1,024 bytes of memory in a typical machine (256 entries, each requiring four bytes), and a nibblewise look-up approach only requires a 64-byte table (16 entries, each requiring four bytes). Clearly, a nibblewise table look-up approach can provide a substantial advantage in many environments. The creation of a nibblewise look-up table approach is left as a trivial exercise for the reader.

Listing 18-1. CRC32.C

```
/*-------------------------------------------------------*/
/*      High Performance CRC-32 Computation Routine      */
/*                                                       */
/*          Copyright 1988 W. David Schwaderer           */
/*              All rights reserved                      */
/*                                                       */
/*      Warning...this program uses bit fields!          */
/*      For warnings on bit field hazards see:           */
/*                                                       */
/*      The C Wizard's Programming Reference             */
/*              W. David Schwaderer                      */
/*                Wiley Press, 1985                      */
/*                                                       */
/*-------------------------------------------------------*/

#include <stdio.h>
#include "netbios2.h"


#define GOOD_CRC32_RESIDUAL   0xDEBB20E3L


#define LINT_ARGS


#if defined(LINT_ARGS)
extern   int main(int argc,char * *argv);
extern   unsigned long GenerateCRC32(unsigned int Length,char *TextPtr);
extern   void GenerateTable(void);
extern   void PrintTable(void);
extern   void Logo(void);
#endif


USGC TestArray1[] = {'T', 'e', 's', 't'};  /* Crc == 0x78.4D.D1.32 */


USGC TestArray2[] = {'T', 'e', 's', 't',    0x32, 0xD1, 0x4D, 0x78};
                    /*  byte-wise                 byte-wise      */
                    /*  unreversed                reversed       */
                    /*  message                   msg Crc        */
```

Listing 18-1. (cont.)

```
char TestMsg[] = "This is a test message.";

USGL CrcTable[256];          /*    globally accessible */

                 /* ====================================== */

int main(argc, argv)
int    argc;
char *argv[];
{
  USGL Crc;
  USGI i, Length;

  Logo();

  GenerateTable();                                 /* fill in the CrcTable   */

  PrintTable();                                    /* display the table      */

  Length = sizeof(TestArray1);            /* can't generally use strlen */
  Crc = GenerateCRC32(Length, TestArray1);         /* calculate CRC-32       */
  printf("\n\nTestArray1 CRC == 0x%08lX", Crc);

  Length = sizeof(TestArray2);
  Crc = GenerateCRC32(Length, TestArray2);         /* calculate CRC-32       */

  Crc = ~Crc;        /* we want the actual CRC residue, not its complement */
  printf("\n\nReversed CRC32 of TestArray1+its CRC == 0x%08lX", Crc);

  if (Crc == GOOD_CRC32_RESIDUAL)
     printf("\n\nThe CRC-32 Calculation is correct...");
  else
     printf("\n\nThe CRC-32 Calculation is NOT correct...");

  printf("\n\n(TestArray1 + its CRC) Residual as Un-reversed Binary:\n==> ");

  for (i = 0; i < 32; i++) {

     if ((i > 0) && (!(i % 8)))
        printf(" ");
     else if ((i > 0) && (!(i % 4)))
             printf(".");

     if ( ((long) 0x01 << i) & Crc)
```

Listing 18-1. (cont.)

```
          printf("1");
        else
            printf("0");
  }


  printf(" <==\n");

  Length = sizeof(TestMsg) - 1; /* avoid terminating NUL  */
  Crc = GenerateCRC32(Length, TestMsg); /* calculate a CRC  */
  printf("\n\n\nText = [%s]\nCRC = %08lX\n\n", TestMsg, Crc);

  return 0;         /* end now........... */

}


              /* ===================================== */

USGL GenerateCRC32(Length, TextPtr)
             USGI Length;
             char *TextPtr;
{
  int i, index;
  USGL Crc;

  Crc = 0xFFFFFFFFL;      /* CRC starts as all Fs for each message */

  for (i = 0; i < Length; i++, TextPtr++) {
    index = ( (Crc ^ *TextPtr) & 0x000000FFL);
    Crc = ((Crc >> 8) & 0x00FFFFFFL) ^ CrcTable[index];
  }


  return ~Crc;       /* return a 1's complement */
}

              /* ===================================== */

void GenerateTable()    /* generate the look-up table */
{
  union { USGI i;
          struct {
                  USGI i1  :1;  /* MSC low order bit  */
                  USGI i2  :1;
                  USGI i3  :1;
                  USGI i4  :1;
```

Listing 18-1. (cont.)

```
                USGI i5  :1;
                USGI i6  :1;
                USGI i7  :1;
                USGI i8  :1;  /* MSC high order bit */
                USGI     :8;  /* unused bits        */
            } Bit;
        } iUn;


    union {    USGL  Entry;
           struct {
                USGI b1  :1;  /* MSC low order bit  */
                USGI b2  :1;
                USGI b3  :1;
                USGI b4  :1;
                USGI b5  :1;
                USGI b6  :1;
                USGI b7  :1;
                USGI b8  :1;
                USGI b9  :1;
                USGI b10 :1;
                USGI b11 :1;
                USGI b12 :1;
                USGI b13 :1;
                USGI b14 :1;
                USGI b15 :1;
                USGI b16 :1;
                USGI b17 :1;
                USGI b18 :1;
                USGI b19 :1;
                USGI b20 :1;
                USGI b21 :1;
                USGI b22 :1;
                USGI b23 :1;
                USGI b24 :1;
                USGI b25 :1;
                USGI b26 :1;
                USGI b27 :1;
                USGI b28 :1;
                USGI b29 :1;
                USGI b30 :1;
                USGI b31 :1;
                USGI b32 :1;  /* MSC high order bit */
           } EntryBit;
        } EntryUn;
```

Listing 18-1. (cont.)

```
for (iUn.i = 0; iUn.i < 256; iUn.i++) {

    EntryUn.Entry = 0;       /* zero out the value */

    EntryUn.EntryBit.b32 = (iUn.Bit.i2  ^  iUn.Bit.i8);
    EntryUn.EntryBit.b31 = (iUn.Bit.i1  ^  iUn.Bit.i2  ^
                            iUn.Bit.i7  ^  iUn.Bit.i8);
    EntryUn.EntryBit.b30 = (iUn.Bit.i1  ^  iUn.Bit.i2  ^
                            iUn.Bit.i6  ^  iUn.Bit.i7  ^
                            iUn.Bit.i8);
    EntryUn.EntryBit.b29 = (iUn.Bit.i1  ^  iUn.Bit.i5  ^
                            iUn.Bit.i6  ^  iUn.Bit.i7);

    EntryUn.EntryBit.b28 = (iUn.Bit.i2  ^  iUn.Bit.i4  ^
                            iUn.Bit.i5  ^  iUn.Bit.i6  ^
                            iUn.Bit.i8);
    EntryUn.EntryBit.b27 = (iUn.Bit.i1  ^  iUn.Bit.i2  ^
                            iUn.Bit.i3  ^  iUn.Bit.i4  ^
                            iUn.Bit.i5  ^  iUn.Bit.i7  ^
                            iUn.Bit.i8);
    EntryUn.EntryBit.b26 = (iUn.Bit.i1  ^  iUn.Bit.i2  ^
                            iUn.Bit.i3  ^  iUn.Bit.i4  ^
                            iUn.Bit.i6  ^  iUn.Bit.i7);
    EntryUn.EntryBit.b25 = (iUn.Bit.i1  ^  iUn.Bit.i3  ^
                            iUn.Bit.i5  ^  iUn.Bit.i6  ^
                            iUn.Bit.i8);

    EntryUn.EntryBit.b24 = (iUn.Bit.i4  ^  iUn.Bit.i5  ^
                            iUn.Bit.i7  ^  iUn.Bit.i8);
    EntryUn.EntryBit.b23 = (iUn.Bit.i3  ^  iUn.Bit.i4  ^
                            iUn.Bit.i6  ^  iUn.Bit.i7);
    EntryUn.EntryBit.b22 = (iUn.Bit.i3  ^  iUn.Bit.i5  ^
                            iUn.Bit.i6  ^  iUn.Bit.i8);
    EntryUn.EntryBit.b21 = (iUn.Bit.i4  ^  iUn.Bit.i5  ^
                            iUn.Bit.i7  ^  iUn.Bit.i8);

    EntryUn.EntryBit.b20 = (iUn.Bit.i2  ^  iUn.Bit.i3  ^
                            iUn.Bit.i4  ^  iUn.Bit.i6  ^
                            iUn.Bit.i7  ^  iUn.Bit.i8);
    EntryUn.EntryBit.b19 = (iUn.Bit.i1  ^  iUn.Bit.i2  ^
                            iUn.Bit.i3  ^  iUn.Bit.i5  ^
                            iUn.Bit.i6  ^  iUn.Bit.i7);
    EntryUn.EntryBit.b18 = (iUn.Bit.i1  ^  iUn.Bit.i2  ^
```

Listing 18-1. (cont.)

```
                              iUn.Bit.i4  ^  iUn.Bit.i5  ^
                              iUn.Bit.i6);
        EntryUn.EntryBit.b17 = (iUn.Bit.i1  ^  iUn.Bit.i3  ^
                              iUn.Bit.i4  ^  iUn.Bit.i5);


        EntryUn.EntryBit.b16 = (iUn.Bit.i3  ^  iUn.Bit.i4  ^
                              iUn.Bit.i8);
        EntryUn.EntryBit.b15 = (iUn.Bit.i2  ^  iUn.Bit.i3  ^
                              iUn.Bit.i7);
        EntryUn.EntryBit.b14 = (iUn.Bit.i1  ^  iUn.Bit.i2  ^
                              iUn.Bit.i6);
        EntryUn.EntryBit.b13 = (iUn.Bit.i1  ^
                              iUn.Bit.i5);


        EntryUn.EntryBit.b12 = (iUn.Bit.i4);
        EntryUn.EntryBit.b11 = (iUn.Bit.i3);
        EntryUn.EntryBit.b10 = (iUn.Bit.i8);
        EntryUn.EntryBit.b9  = (iUn.Bit.i2  ^  iUn.Bit.i7  ^
                              iUn.Bit.i8);


        EntryUn.EntryBit.b8  = (iUn.Bit.i1  ^  iUn.Bit.i6  ^
                              iUn.Bit.i7);
        EntryUn.EntryBit.b7  = (iUn.Bit.i5  ^  iUn.Bit.i6);
        EntryUn.EntryBit.b6  = (iUn.Bit.i2  ^  iUn.Bit.i4  ^
                              iUn.Bit.i5  ^  iUn.Bit.i8);
        EntryUn.EntryBit.b5  = (iUn.Bit.i1  ^  iUn.Bit.i3  ^
                              iUn.Bit.i4  ^  iUn.Bit.i7);


        EntryUn.EntryBit.b4  = (iUn.Bit.i2  ^  iUn.Bit.i3  ^
                              iUn.Bit.i6);
        EntryUn.EntryBit.b3  = (iUn.Bit.i1  ^  iUn.Bit.i2  ^
                              iUn.Bit.i5);
        EntryUn.EntryBit.b2  = (iUn.Bit.i1  ^  iUn.Bit.i4);
        EntryUn.EntryBit.b1  = (iUn.Bit.i3);


      CrcTable[iUn.i] = EntryUn.Entry;
    }
  }


              /* ====================================== */

void PrintTable()        /* print out the look-up table */
{
  int i;
```

Listing 18-1. (cont.)

```c
   for (i = 0; i < 256; i++) {
     if ( !(i % 4) )
       printf("\n %02X  -  %08lX", i, CrcTable[i]);
     else
       printf("  %08lX", CrcTable[i]);
   }
}


void Logo()
{
     printf("\n\n   High Performance CRC-32 Computation Routine");
     printf("\n          Copyright 1988 W. David Schwaderer\n\n");
}


/*=================== End of Program Logic ======================*/

/*

   *--------- Program Output Start ---------*

   00  -  00000000  77073096  EE0E612C  990951BA
   04  -  076DC419  706AF48F  E963A535  9E6495A3
   08  -  0EDB8832  79DCB8A4  E0D5E91E  97D2D988
   0C  -  09B64C2B  7EB17CBD  E7B82D07  90BF1D91
   10  -  1DB71064  6AB020F2  F3B97148  84BE41DE
   14  -  1ADAD47D  6DDDE4EB  F4D4B551  83D385C7
   18  -  136C9856  646BA8C0  FD62F97A  8A65C9EC
   1C  -  14015C4F  63066CD9  FA0F3D63  8D080DF5
   20  -  3B6E20C8  4C69105E  D56041E4  A2677172
   24  -  3C03E4D1  4B04D447  D20D85FD  A50AB56B
   28  -  35B5A8FA  42B2986C  DBBBC9D6  ACBCF940
   2C  -  32D86CE3  45DF5C75  DCD60DCF  ABD13D59
   30  -  26D930AC  51DE003A  C8D75180  BFD06116
   34  -  21B4F4B5  56B3C423  CFBA9599  B8BDA50F
   38  -  2802B89E  5F058808  C60CD9B2  B10BE924
   3C  -  2F6F7C87  58684C11  C1611DAB  B6662D3D
   40  -  76DC4190  01DB7106  98D220BC  EFD5102A
   44  -  71B18589  06B6B51F  9FBFE4A5  E8B8D433
   48  -  7807C9A2  0F00F934  9609A88E  E10E9818
   4C  -  7F6A0DBB  086D3D2D  91646C97  E6635C01
   50  -  6B6B51F4  1C6C6162  856530D8  F262004E
   54  -  6C0695ED  1B01A57B  8208F4C1  F50FC457
   58  -  65B0D9C6  12B7E950  8BBEB8EA  FCB9887C
   5C  -  62DD1DDF  15DA2D49  8CD37CF3  FBD44C65
```

Listing 18-1. (cont.)

```
60  -   4DB26158   3AB551CE   A3BC0074   D4BB30E2
64  -   4ADFA541   3DD895D7   A4D1C46D   D3D6F4FB
68  -   4369E96A   346ED9FC   AD678846   DA60B8D0
6C  -   44042D73   33031DE5   AA0A4C5F   DD0D7CC9
70  -   5005713C   270241AA   BE0B1010   C90C2086
74  -   5768B525   206F85B3   B966D409   CE61E49F
78  -   5EDEF90E   29D9C998   B0D09822   C7D7A8B4
7C  -   59B33D17   2EB40D81   B7BD5C3B   C0BA6CAD
80  -   EDB88320   9ABFB3B6   03B6E20C   74B1D29A
84  -   EAD54739   9DD277AF   04DB2615   73DC1683
88  -   E3630B12   94643B84   0D6D6A3E   7A6A5AA8
8C  -   E40ECF0B   9309FF9D   0A00AE27   7D079EB1
90  -   F00F9344   8708A3D2   1E01F268   6906C2FE
94  -   F762575D   806567CB   196C3671   6E6B06E7
98  -   FED41B76   89D32BE0   10DA7A5A   67DD4ACC
9C  -   F9B9DF6F   8EBEEFF9   17B7BE43   60B08ED5
A0  -   D6D6A3E8   A1D1937E   38D8C2C4   4FDFF252
A4  -   D1BB67F1   A6BC5767   3FB506DD   48B2364B
A8  -   D80D2BDA   AF0A1B4C   36034AF6   41047A60
AC  -   DF60EFC3   A867DF55   316E8EEF   4669BE79
B0  -   CB61B38C   BC66831A   256FD2A0   5268E236
B4  -   CC0C7795   BB0B4703   220216B9   5505262F
B8  -   C5BA3BBE   B2BD0B28   2BB45A92   5CB36A04
BC  -   C2D7FFA7   B5D0CF31   2CD99E8B   5BDEAE1D
C0  -   9B64C2B0   EC63F226   756AA39C   026D930A
C4  -   9C0906A9   EB0E363F   72076785   05005713
C8  -   95BF4A82   E2B87A14   7BB12BAE   0CB61B38
CC  -   92D28E9B   E5D5BE0D   7CDCEFB7   0BDBDF21
D0  -   86D3D2D4   F1D4E242   68DDB3F8   1FDA836E
D4  -   81BE16CD   F6B9265B   6FB077E1   18B74777
D8  -   88085AE6   FF0F6A70   66063BCA   11010B5C
DC  -   8F659EFF   F862AE69   616BFFD3   166CCF45
E0  -   A00AE278   D70DD2EE   4E048354   3903B3C2
E4  -   A7672661   D06016F7   4969474D   3E6E77DB
E8  -   AED16A4A   D9D65ADC   40DF0B66   37D83BF0
EC  -   A9BCAE53   DEBB9EC5   47B2CF7F   30B5FFE9
F0  -   BDBDF21C   CABAC28A   53B39330   24B4A3A6
F4  -   BAD03605   CDD70693   54DE5729   23D967BF
F8  -   B3667A2E   C4614AB8   5D681B02   2A6F2B94
FC  -   B40BBE37   C30C8EA1   5A05DF1B   2D02EF8D
```

```
TestArray1 CRC == 0x784DD132
```

```
Reversed CRC32 of TestArray1+its CRC == 0xDEBB20E3
```

Listing 18-1. (cont.)

```
The CRC-32 Calculation is correct...

(TestArray1 + its CRC) Residual as Un-reversed Binary:
==> 1100.0111 0000.0100 1101.1101 0111.1011 <==


    *--------- Program Output End --------*
*/
```

Part IV

NetBIOS Technical Reference

Chapter 19

Network Control Block

As discussed in Chapters 3 and 4, applications access NetBIOS services using the Network Control Block (Ncb) which is identical to the IBM Token-Ring's Mcb. The following material assumes an IBM PC LAN Support Program implementation with one or more IBM LAN adapters present in a machine. In the case of more than one adapter, each adapter has its own NetBIOS interface and tables.

Ncb Fields

Table 19-1 outlines the Ncb format. USGC signifies unsigned char and USGI signifies unsigned int. Field names ending with "@" indicate an offset:segment address field. The Chain Send command uses the Ncb-CallName field to specify the length and location of a second data buffer.

NcbCommand

The NcbCommand field is a 1-byte field specifying the NetBIOS command. The high-order bit of the field specifies the command's wait/no-wait option.

The Wait/No-Wait Option
If the high-order bit of the value in the NcbCommand field is a binary zero, the wait option is specified (see Figure 19-1). Otherwise, the high-

---

The material in this chapter and Chapter 20 is excerpted and paraphrased from IBM's *Technical Reference PC Network Manual*, with the permission and courtesy of IBM.

Table 19-1. Ncb Format

Offset	Field Name	Len	MASM Type	C Type	Description
+00 +00h	NcbCommand	1	DB	USGC	Command
+01 +01h	NcbRetCode	1	DB	USGC	Return code
+02 +02h	NcbLsn	1	DB	USGC	Local Session Number
+03 +03h	NcbNum	1	DB	USGC	Name number
+04 +04h	NcbBuffer@	4	DD	char far *	Buffer pointer
+08 +08h	NcbLength	2	DW	USGI	Buffer length (in bytes)
+10 +0Ah	NcbCallName	16	DB	char[]	Local/Remote NetBIOS name
+26 +1Ah	NcbName	16	DB	char[]	Local NetBIOS name
+42 +2Ah	NcbRto	1	DB	USGC	Receive time-out value
+43 +2Bh	NcbSto	1	DB	USGC	Send time-out value
+44 +2Ch	NcbPost@	4	DD	void far *( )	Post routine pointer
+48 +30h	NcbLanaNum	1	DB	USGC	Adapter number
+49 +31h	NcbCmdCplt	1	DB	USGC	Command status
+50 +32h	NcbReserve	14	DB	char[]	Reserved area

USGC = unsigned char. USGI = unsigned int.

order bit is a binary one and the no-wait option is specified. The Cancel, Reset, and Unlink commands have only a wait option.

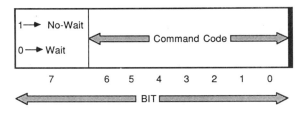

Fig. 19-1. Format of the NcbCommand field.

Selecting the wait option requests NetBIOS to return control when the adapter completes the command. In this sense, a no-wait NetBIOS option behaves like an ordinary application program subroutine call.

When the command completes, the AL register and the NcbRetCode field contain the completion code. Care must be taken to assure that the command completes within a satisfactory period of time because NetBIOS enters an enabled spin-loop and does not resume application processing until the command completes.

Selecting the no-wait option requests that NetBIOS return control to the application while the command is pending completion. The post routine, if specified, is given control when the adapter completes the command.

Selecting the no-wait option allows maximum throughput by permitting several simultaneous pending commands. However, while a command is pending, application programs must not change either the Ncb or any data field (e.g., the post routine address) associated with the command.

Immediate and Final Return Codes

When the no-wait option is selected, two return codes may be returned. The first return code, referred to as the *immediate return code*, returns after the command is initially scanned by NetBIOS. The other return code, referred to as the *final return code*, returns when the command is completed.

If the first return code is not 00h, NetBIOS has rejected the command and does not proceed with processing the command. In this instance, NetBIOS does not provide a second return code, nor does it invoke a post routine. In any case, all immediate return codes are also valid final return codes.

NcbRetCode

The NcbRetCode field is a 1-byte field containing a value of FFh while a no-wait option is pending. It also contains the command's final completion code when NetBIOS completes the command.

If the no-wait option is used without specifying a post routine, both the NcbCmdCplt field and the NcbRetCode field contain the final return code after command completion:

- A return code value of 00h indicates successful command completion.
- Return code values of 1 through 254 (FEh) indicate an unsuccessful command completion.

Applications should never loop on the NcbRetCode field looking for command completion; they should loop on the NcbCmdCplt field. This is because the NcbRetCode field is set before the NcbCmdCplt field is set.

After completing the NcbRetCode field, the Ncb may be placed on an internal NetBIOS POST processing queue. The NcbCmdCplt is not set until the Ncb is dequeued from the POST processing queue. This applies to all Ncbs that have a no-wait option, even if the post routine address is 0000:0000. In the case that the post routine address is 0000:0000, the Ncb is dequeued and the determination is made not to invoke a post routine.

NcbLsn

The NcbLsn field is a 1-byte field referring to an existing Local Session Number (LSN). The LSN value must be between 1 and 254 (FEh) inclusive. NetBIOS assigns the LSN value in an incremental, modulo 255, roundrobin manner. The values zero and 255 (FFh) are never assigned.

An LSN value is valid only after a Call or Listen command successfully completes and is a session number the local application has with another application. It is logically equivalent to an application's open file-handle. The applications may be local or remote, and the LSN value assigned to one side of a session is independent of the value assigned to the other side. Two adapters within the same machine may have sessions with the same LSN value, but they are differentiated by their adapter's NcbLanaNum values.

The NcbLsn field is required for Send, Chain Send, Receive, Receive-Any, and Hang Up commands but is not used for datagram commands. For Reset commands, the NcbLsn value can specify the maximum number of sessions NetBIOS allows for the adapter. (See the Reset command description in Chapter 20 for details.)

NcbNum

The NcbNum field is a 1-byte field that NetBIOS completes after an Add Name or Add Group Name command successfully completes. This number, and not its associated name, is used with all Receive-Any commands and all datagram commands. NetBIOS assigns the value of NcbNum in an incremental, modulo 255, roundrobin manner. The values zero and 255 (FFh) are never assigned and the value 01h is always used by the permanent node name.

For Reset commands, the NcbNum value can specify the maximum number of pending commands the NetBIOS allows for the adapter. (See the Reset command description in Chapter 20 for details.) Specifying an NcbNum value of FFh with Receive-Any and Receive Datagram commands indicates that data can be received for any existing session or registered name, respectively.

NcbBuffer@

The NcbBuffer@ is a 4-byte field containing the address of an application buffer. This field is in offset:segment format and must be a valid memory address.

For Adapter Status and Session Status commands, the NcbBuffer@ field contains the address where NetBIOS should place the information it returns. The NcbLength field specifies the length of the buffer.

For Cancel commands, the NcbBuffer@ field points to an Ncb that should be canceled.

For Chain Send, Send, Send Datagram, and Send Broadcast Datagram commands, the NcbBuffer@ field specifies the address where the data resides that should be transmitted. The NcbLength field specifies how much data should be sent.

For Receive, Receive-Any, Receive Datagram, and Receive Broadcast Datagram commands, the NcbBuffer@ field specifies the address where received data should be placed; the NcbLength field specifies how much data should be placed at that location.

NcbLength

The NcbLength field is a 2-byte field indicating the length, in bytes, of an application receive or transmission buffer.

For Chain Send, Send, Send Datagram, and Send Broadcast Datagram commands, an application uses the NcbLength field to indicate the number of bytes to send.

For Receive, Receive-Any, Receive Datagram, Receive Broadcast Datagram, Adapter Status, and Session Status commands, an application uses the NcbLength field to indicate the size of the data-receive buffer. For these commands, NetBIOS updates the NcbLength field with the number of bytes actually received when the commands complete.

NcbCallName

The NcbCallName field is a 16-byte field containing a network name or second application buffer specification.

For Call, Listen, and Send Datagram commands, an application places a name the application wants to communicate with in the Ncb-CallName field. Usually the name is a remote name, though the name can be a local name for local sessions.

In the case of a Listen command, placing an asterisk (*) in the first position of the NcbCallName (byte 0) indicates that the Listen can be satisfied by any Call to the name specified in the NcbName field.

In the case of an Adapter Status command, placing the asterisk in the first position of the NcbCallName (byte 0) indicates that the Adapter Status command is for a local adapter.

For a Chain Send command, an application uses the NcbCallName field to specify the size and location of a second application buffer. In this case, only the first six bytes of the NcbCallName field are used and the others ignored. The first two bytes (bytes 0 and 1) specify the second buffer's length and the remaining four bytes (bytes 2 and 5) are the offset: segment address of the second buffer.

NcbName

The NcbName field is a 16-byte field containing a local network name.

For Add Name and Add Group Name commands, the NcbName field contains a name for which the application is requesting network registration. For the Delete Name command, the field contains a name that the application is requesting to be deleted from the NetBIOS name table.

For Call or Listen commands, the field contains a local network name that the application wishes to use to conduct a session.

For Session Status commands, placing the asterisk in the first byte (byte 0) of the NcbName field indicates that NetBIOS should return data for all sessions that the adapter currently supports.

Applications may use permanent node names as names. NetBIOS constructs permanent node names by appending the 6 bytes of an adapter's permanent ID ROM value to 10 bytes of binary zeros. The maximum number of names that an adapter may be known by is determined by the config.sys DXMT0MOD.SYS NAMES parameter. This value does not include the permanent node name as one of its entries.

NcbRto

The NcbRto field is a 1-byte field used by Call and Listen commands to specify time-out periods for Receive-Any and Receive commands associated with a requested, but yet unestablished, session.

A nonzero value specifies a time-out period in increments of 1/2 seconds. For example, a value of 255 (FFh) indicates a time-out period of 127.5 seconds. A value of 00h indicates there is no time-out.

Time-out periods may vary for each session, but are fixed for a given session and are not changeable once the session is established. In addition, time-out periods for both sides of a session may be different.

Unlike Send and Chain Send time-out expirations, if a Receive-Any or Receive command's time-out period expires, the session does not terminate (see NcbSto).

NcbSto

The NcbSto field is a 1-byte field that Call and Listen commands use to specify a time-out period for all Send and Chain Send commands associated with a requested, but yet unestablished, session. It has no effect on Send No-Ack and Chain Send No-Ack commands.

A nonzero value specifies a time-out period in increments of 1/2 seconds. For example, a value of 255 (FFh) indicates a time-out period of 127.5 seconds. A value of 00h indicates there is no time-out.

Time-out periods may vary for each session, but are fixed for a given session and are not changeable once the session is established. In addition, the time-out periods for both sides of a session may be different.

Send and Chain Send time-outs should be used with caution because they terminate the session when they expire. Canceling Send and Chain Send commands with a Cancel command also terminates the session associated with the canceled commands.

NcbPost@

The NcbPost@ field is a 4-byte field pointing to a routine, referred to as the post routine, NetBIOS executes when it accepts and subsequently completes.

The NcbPost@ field only applies to no-wait option and is ignored when the wait option is specified. This field uses an offset:segment format. If the post address is all zeros, NetBIOS does not call a post routine. In this case, the application must check the NcbCmdCplt field for a change from a value of FFh.

Alternatively, the post address is not all zeros and NetBIOS calls the post routine as an interrupt. NetBIOS enters the routine with the AL register set to the return code, the CS:IP registers set to the post routine entry point, and the ES:BX registers pointing to the completed Ncb. Post routine entry is made in a disabled state and the post routine should return to NetBIOS with an IRET instruction.

The post routine does not have to save or restore registers and can issue NetBIOS requests. However, it should not issue PC-DOS requests because PC-DOS is not reentrant and such a request may have been interrupted to invoke the post routine.

NcbLanaNum

The NcbLanaNum field is a 1-byte field indicating which adapter card NetBIOS should use to process the command.

The NcbLanaNum must contain either 00h for the first (primary) adapter or 01h for the second (alternate) adapter. The adapter must be initialized for the appropriate primary/alternate setting. The NcbLanaNum values 02h and 03h are reserved for IBM PC LAN adapters.

NcbCmdCplt

The NcbCmdCplt field is a 1-byte field indicating the status of a pending no-wait option command. A value of FFh signifies the command is still pending. Any other value indicates that the command has completed; the value is the final return code.

If a no-wait option is specified and the NcbPost@ is all zeros, NetBIOS places the command return code in both the NcbRetCode and the NcbCmdCplt fields when Ncb processing is complete. Applications should loop on the NcbCmdCplt field looking for command completion; they should never loop on the NcbRetCode field.

NcbReserve

The NcbReserve field is a 14-byte reserved area. NetBIOS uses this field for Ncb processing and to return extended error information.

Command Completion

When an application presents an Ncb to NetBIOS, NetBIOS provides a return code to the requesting application. The particular way it does this depends on whether the command specifies a wait option or a no-wait option. If the NcbCommand high-order bit has a value of binary 1, the no-wait option is selected. Otherwise, the wait option is specified.

Wait Option

If a command specifies a wait option, control does not return to the application until the adapter completes the command. When the command completes, the final return code is in the AL register as well as the NcbRetCode and NcbCmdCplt fields. Control returns to the instruction immediately following the NetBIOS request interrupt.

No-Wait Option

If a command specifies a no-wait option, NetBIOS presents two return codes. After initially scanning the Ncb, control returns to the instruction immediately following the NetBIOS request interrupt with an immediate return code in the AL register. If the immediate return code is not 00h, the adapter cannot successfully execute the command.

If the Immediate return code is 00h, the adapter queues the request pending final completion and provides a final return code when the adapter completes the command. If the NcbPost@ field of the Ncb is zero, NetBIOS places the final return code in the NcbCmdCplt field, which must be checked for change by the application program.

If the application checks the NcbCmdCplt field, a value other than FFh indicates command completion and this value is the final return code. Applications should never loop on the NcbRetCode field looking for command completion, but rather on the NcbCmdCplt field because the NcbRetCode field is set first. After completing the NcbRetCode field, the Ncb may be placed on an internal NetBIOS POST processing queue. The NcbCmdCplt is not set until the Ncb is dequeued from the POST processing queue. This applies to all Ncbs that have a no-wait option, even if the post routine address is 0000:0000. In the case that the post routine address is 0000:0000, the Ncb is dequeued and the determination is made not to invoke a post routine.

No-Wait Option with a Post Routine
If the NcbPost@ field is not zero, NetBIOS sets the final return code in both the AL register and the NcbRetCode field. NetBIOS then saves its registers, points the ES:BX register pair at the completed Ncb, pushes the

flags, disables maskable interrupts, and executes a far call to the post routine.

In the application post routine, the final return code may be obtained from either the AL register or the NcbRetCode field. The post routine should return to NetBIOS with an IRET instruction. The post routine does not have to save or restore registers and can issue NetBIOS requests. However, it should not issue PC-DOS requests because PC-DOS is not reentrant and such a request may have been interrupted to invoke the post routine.

No-Wait Option with No Post Routine

If the NcbPost@ field is zero, no post routine is specified. The final return code is in both the NcbCmdCplt field and in the NcbRetCode field. Again, applications should never loop on the NcbRetCode field looking for command completion, but should monitor the NcbCmdCplt field to see when it changes from a value of 0FFh.

Chapter 20

NetBIOS Commands

The following information applies to NetBIOS requests for PC-DOS and
NetBIOS. Appendix F contains additional information for OS/2 NetBIOS
requests.

The Commands

Adapter Status

33h Wait; B3h No-Wait

	In	Out	
	In	*Out*	*Immediate Return Codes*
NcbCommand	X		00h 03h
NcbRetCode		X	21h 22h 23h
NcbLsn			4Xh
NcbNum			50h-FEh
NcbBuffer@	X		
NcbLength	X	X	
NcbCallName	X		*Final Return Codes*
NcbName			
NcbRto			00h 01h 03h 05h 06h 0Bh
NcbSto			19h
NcbPost@	?		21h 22h 23h
NcbLanaNum	X		4Xh
NcbCmdCplt		X	50h-FEh
NcbReserve		?	

The Adapter Status command requests the NetBIOS status of either a local or remote adapter.

The NcbCallName field specifies from which adapter to obtain the status. The field may contain a permanent node name, group name, or unique name. If the first byte of the NcbCallName field contains an asterisk (*), the local NetBIOS status of the adapter specified by the NcbLanaNum field returns. The status information returns in the buffer pointed to by the NcbBuffer@ field.

The minimum buffer size is 60 bytes. The maximum status information size is 60 plus 18 times the maximum number of names. The maximum number of names is determined by the adapter's IBM LAN Support Program NAMES parameter.

A message incomplete status (06h) returns for two reasons:

1. The buffer is not large enough to hold all the generated data.
2. The status information generated for a remote Adapter Status command exceeds the maximum datagram length.

In either case, the final amount of data returning in the buffer is the lesser of the buffer's size or the maximum datagram length.

Token-Ring Adapter Status Information Format

I-Frame is an IEEE 802.2 term for an information frame, which is used in session communication. LLC logic transmits I-Frames and signifies their receipt with an acknowledgment (ACK).

UI-Frame is an IEEE 802.2 term for an unnumbered information frame, used for datagrams and query frames. LLC logic transmits UI-Frames but does not acknowledge their receipt with an ACK.

An appendage is similar to a NetBIOS post routine. It is defined by the CCB adapter handler interface. (Ncb commands are broken into CCB commands and passed to the adapter handler logic for processing.) Appendages are executed as part of CCB command completion processing.

The CCB DIR.OPEN.ADAPTER command RING.STATUS.APPENDAGE field pointer identifies an appendage. NetBIOS issues a DIR.OPEN.ADAPTER specifying a RING.STATUS.APPENDAGE as part of the command and uses the appendage to update status counters. However, NetBIOS does not open the adapter if it is already open. In that case, NetBIOS does define a RING.STATUS.APPENDAGE and consequently has no way of updating the status counters. In any event, there can only be one RING.STATUS.APPENDAGE for an adapter and there is no way for any other application to determine who owns it.

The Frame Rejected Receive Count is the number of received and rejected I-Frames. The maximum-size I-Frame used in a session is the smallest DHB.SIZE of the two communicating adapters and is determined at session start-up. Received I-Frames larger than the maximum value are received and rejected by LLC logic. When NetBIOS is used, the Frame Rejected Receive Count should always have a value of zero.

The Frame Rejected Transmit Count is the number of I-Frames rejected before transmission. The maximum-size I-Frame used in a session is the smallest DHB.SIZE of the two communicating adapters and is determined at session start-up. Requests to transmit I-Frames larger than the maximum value are rejected by LLC logic. When NetBIOS is used, the Frame Rejected Transmit Count should always have a value of zero.

The I-Frame Receive Error Count normally indicates the number of I-Frames received out of sequence. In this event, LLC logic enters a checkpointing state to establish data integrity.

The Transmit Abort Count should always have a value of zero since there is no way to abort a transmission.

The Successful Frame Transmit/Receive Count value includes the number of successfully transmitted/received I-Frames and UI-Frames.

The I-Frame Transmit Error Count is similar to the I-Frame Receive Error Count except that it reflects the number of out-of-sequence frames that were sensed by other adapters. This value may be nonzero since I-Frames may disappear before arriving at their destination, subsequently causing the next successfully arriving frame to appear out of sequence. The checkpointing sequence informs the local adapter the condition has occurred.

The Remote Request Buffer Depletion Count indicates the number of times NetBIOS has run out of SAP buffers. Because this cannot happen, this value should always be zero. Otherwise, this is a NetBIOS error.

The Expired T1 Timer Count indicates the number of times the Response Timer has expired. The response timer expires when a local link station has transmitted DLC.MAXOUT frames without receiving an ACK. In this event, the LLC logic enters checkpointing and requests an ACK from the remote link station. An excessive Expired T1 Timer Count value indicates an adjustment is required.

The Expired Ti Timer Count indicates the number of times the inactivity timer has expired. The inactivity timer expires when there is no activity on the session. The count is informational only and is no cause for concern. The returned Token-Ring Adapter Status command information is summarized in Table 20-1. All counters, except for the remote request buffer depletion count counter, roll over from F...Fh to 0...0h.

Table 20-1. Token-Ring Adapter Status Information Format

Offset		Size	MASM	C	Field Contents
+00	+00h	6	DB	char	Permanent node name [6]
+06	+06h	1	DB	USGC	NetBIOS major version number (low-order nibble-only)
+07	+07h	1	DB	USGC	Always set to zero
+08	+08h	1	DB	USGC	Lan adapter type
+09	+09h	1	DB	USGC	Minor version number
+10	+0Ah	2	DW	USGI	Reporting period in minutes
+12	+0Ch	2	DW	USGI	Frame rejected receive count
+14	+0Eh	2	DW	USGI	Frame rejected transmit count
+16	+10h	2	DW	USGI	I-Frame receive error count
+18	+12h	2	DW	USGI	Transmit abort count
+20	+14h	4	DW	USGL	Successful frame xmit count
+24	+18h	4	DW	USGL	Successful frame receive count
+28	+1Ch	2	DW	USGI	I-Frame transmit error count
+30	+1Eh	2	DW	USGI	Remote request buffer depletion count
+32	+20h	2	DW	USGI	Expired T1 timer count
+34	+22h	2	DW	USGI	Expired Ti timer count
+36	+24h	4	DD	far *	Local extended status information pointer
+40	+28h	2	DW	USGI	Free command blocks
+42	+2Ah	2	DW	USGI	Current maximum pending Ncbs
+44	+2Ch	2	DW	USGI	Maximum commands
+46	+2Eh	2	DW	USGI	Transmit buffer depletion count
+48	+30h	2	DW	USGI	Maximum datagram packet size
+50	+32h	2	DW	USGI	Pending session count
+52	+34h	2	DW	USGI	Maximum pending session count
+54	+36h	2	DW	USGI	Maximum sessions
+56	+38h	2	DW	USGI	Maximum session packet size
+58	+3Ah	2	DW	USGI	Name Table entry count
+60	+3Ch	??			Name Table entry(ies)

The Token-Ring extended status information address field at offset 36 (24h) is valid only for local status commands; the field's value is undefined for remote status commands. The field points to the fixed memory location of adapter-specified status. An application program should not modify the data, though it can inspect and use it. The extended status information address field has the following format:

Bytes 00-01: DIR.INITIALIZE bring-up error code

Bytes 02-03: DIR.OPEN.ADAPTER error code

Bytes 04-05: Latest ring status

Bytes 06-07: Latest adapter check reason code

Bytes 08-09: Latest PC-detected error (from the AX register)

Byte 10: Latest operational error code (4X or 5X)

Byte 11: Return code of latest implicit CCB command

Bytes 12-13: Line errors

Bytes 14-15: Internal errors

Bytes 16-17: Burst errors

Bytes 18-19: A/C error

Bytes 20-21: Abort delimiter

Bytes 22-23: Reserved

Bytes 24-25: Lost frame

Bytes 26-27: Receive congestion

Bytes 28-29: Frame copied errors

Bytes 30-31: Frequency errors

Bytes 32-33: Token errors

Bytes 34-35: Reserved

Bytes 36-37: Reserved

Bytes 38-39: Reserved

When NetBIOS initializes, DIR.INITIALIZE and DIR.OPEN. ADAPTER commands are sometimes executed followed by a DLC.OPEN. SAP command. Byte 10 provides the last of the executed CCB command codes and byte 11 contains its CCB return code. Bytes 10 and 11 help determine conditions resulting in certain 4Xh return codes.

Adapter counters (bytes 12 through 39) are valid only if a ring status appendage is defined and wraps from FFFFh to 0000h. When no appendage is defined, these counters are updated when a ring status counter overflow is reported. These counters are the same as obtained with a DIR.READ.LOG command through any application program. Issuing a DIR.READ.LOG command resets these counters. If an appendage is defined, it is the application's responsibility to maintain the adapter counters. The number of pending sessions (offset 50) is computed using the following procedure:

Pending sessions are

- pending Call and Listen commands
- pending and completed Hang Up commands
- established and aborted sessions

Each NetBIOS local name table (offset 60) entry is 18 bytes long and has the following format:

- The first 16 bytes (bytes 0-15) contain a NetBIOS name that has been added with an Add Name or Add Group Name command. The permanent node name is not included in the NetBIOS name table entries, but is reported separately.
- The 17th byte (byte 16) is the name's NetBIOS name number (NcbNum).
- The 18th (byte 17) byte is ANDed with 87h to provide the name's status.

Possible status values are (x = reserved bit, $N = 0$ if the name is a unique name, and $N = 1$ if the name is a group name):

Nxxxx000: The name is in the registration process

Nxxxx100: The name is registered

Nxxxx101: The name is deregistered

Nxxxx110: The name is a detected duplicate name

Nxxxx111: The name is a detected duplicate name that is pending deregistration

Registered Name: If a name is a registered name, it has been added to the local NetBIOS name table.

Deregistered Name: If a name is a deregistered name, a Delete Name command was issued for it while it had active session(s). When a name is deregistered, NetBIOS does not permit subsequent Call or Listen commands to use the name. After the session(s) terminates, NetBIOS removes the name from the local NetBIOS name table and the name can be added again for use by Call and Listen commands.

Duplicate Name: If a name is a detected duplicate name, it is a unique name added to two different NetBIOS name tables as a result of a network error. Duplicate names should be deleted as soon as they are detected.

PC Network Adapter Status Information Format

The returned PC Network Adapter Status command information has the format outlined in Table 20-2. The PC Network LANA adapter's external jumper status is illustrated in Figure 20-1.

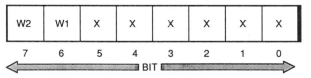

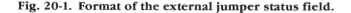

W2 = 1 → W2 Jumper on adapter (RPL-disabled)
W2 = 0 → W2 Jumper off adapter (RPL-enabled)

W1 = 1 → W1 Jumper on adapter (reserved)
W1 = 0 → W1 Jumper off adapter (reserved)

Fig. 20-1. Format of the external jumper status field.

The self test results values are

80h: Successful completion
81h: Processor test failed
82h: ROM checksum test failed
83h: Unit ID Prom test failed
84h: RAM test failed
85h: Host interface test failed
86h: +/− 12V test failed
87h: Digital loopback test failed
8Eh: Possible constant carrier
8Fh: Analog loopback test failed

When the reporting period, collision count, aborted transmission, successful transmission, successful receive, and retransmission counters reach FFFFh, they roll over to 0000h. When the CRC error, alignment error, and resource depletion counters reach FFFFh, they do not roll over to 0000h.

Table 20-2. PC Network LANA Adapter Status Information Format

Offset		Size	MASM	C	Field Contents
+00	+00h	6	DB	USGC	Permanent node name [6]
+06	+06h	1	DB	USGC	External jumper setting
+07	+07h	1	DB	USGC	Self test results
+08	+08h	1	DB	USGC	Adapter protocol layer major version number
+09	+09h	1	DB	USGC	Adapter protocol layer minor version number
+10	+0Ah	2	DW	USGI	Reporting period in minutes (rolls over)
+12	+0Ch	2	DW	USGI	CRC error count (does not roll over)
+14	+0Eh	2	DW	USGI	Alignment errors (does not roll over)
+16	+10h	2	DW	USGI	Collision count (rolls over)
+18	+12h	2	DW	USGI	Transmit abort count (rolls over)
+20	+14h	4	DD	USGL	Successful transmits (rolls over)
+24	+18h	4	DD	USGL	Successful receives (rolls over)
+28	+1Ch	2	DW	USGI	Retransmit count (does not roll over)
+30	+1Eh	2	DW	USGI	Resource depletion count
+32	+20h	1	DB	char	Reserved area1 [8]
+40	+28h	2	DW	USGI	Free command blocks
+42	+2Ah	2	DW	USGI	Current maximum Ncbs
+44	+2Ch	2	DW	USGI	Hardware maximum command blocks
+46	+2Eh	1	DB	char	Reserved area2 [4]
+50	+32h	2	DW	USGI	Pending session count
+52	+34h	2	DW	USGI	Current maximum pending sessions
+54	+36h	2	DW	USGI	Hardware maximum session count
+56	+38h	2	DW	USGI	Maximum packet size
+58	+3Ah	2	DW	USGI	NetBIOS name table entry count
+60	+3Ch	??			struct NetBIOS name table entry(ies) [16]

The local name table entries have the same format as discussed in the Token-Ring Adapter Status command.

Add Group Name   36h Wait; B6h No-Wait

	In	Out	Immediate Return Codes
NcbCommand	X		00h 03h
NcbRetCode		X	21h 22h 23h
NcbLsn			4Xh
NcbNum		X	50h-FEh
NcbBuffer@			
NcbLength			
NcbCallName			*Final Return Codes*
NcbName	X		
NcbRto			00h 03h 0Dh 0Eh
NcbSto			15h 16h 19h
NcbPost@	?		21h 22h 23h
NcbLanaNum	X		4Xh
NcbCmdCplt		X	50h-FEh
NcbReserve		?	

The Add Group Name command adds a nonunique 16-character name that the network adapter is known by to an adapter's NetBIOS name table. The name cannot be used as a unique name, but can be used as a group name, by any other network adapter.

NetBIOS processes this command by repeatedly broadcasting a network name query. The number of times it transmits the query is determined by the config.sys DXMT0MOD.SYS TRANSMIT.COUNT parameter.

If no reply to a name query request is received after a period determined by the config.sys DXMT0MOD.SYS TRANSMIT.TIMEOUT parameter, another name query is broadcast until TRANSMIT.COUNT queries have occurred. If still no reply has arrived, NetBIOS assumes the name is nonunique and adds it to the local NetBIOS name table as a group name.

The adapter returns the number of the name in the NcbNum field. This number is used in datagram support and for Receive-Any commands.

Add Name   30h Wait; B0h No-Wait

	In	Out	Immediate Return Codes
NcbCommand	X		00h 03h
NcbRetCode		X	21h 22h 23h
NcbLsn			4Xh
NcbNum		X	50h-FEh
NcbBuffer@			
NcbLength			
NcbCallName			*Final Return Codes*
NcbName	X		
NcbRto			00h 03h 0Dh 0Eh
NcbSto			15h 16h 19h
NcbPost@	?		21h 22h 23h
NcbLanaNum	X		4Xh
NcbCmdCplt		X	50h-FEh
NcbReserve		?	

The Add Name command adds a unique 16-character name to an adapter's NetBIOS name table. This is a name the adapter is known by and must be unique across the network.

NetBIOS processes this command by repeatedly broadcasting a network name query. The number of times it transmits the query is determined by the config.sys DXMT0MOD.SYS TRANSMIT.COUNT parameter.

If no reply to a name query request is received after a period determined by the config.sys DXMT0MOD.SYS TRANSMIT.TIMEOUT parameter, another name query is broadcast until TRANSMIT.COUNT queries have occurred. If still no reply has arrived, NetBIOS assumes the name is unique and adds it to the local NetBIOS name table as a unique name.

The adapter returns the number of the name in the NcbNum field. This number is used in datagram support and for Receive-Any commands.

Call

10h Wait; 90h No-Wait

	In	Out	*Immediate Return Codes*
NcbCommand	X		00h 03h
NcbRetCode		X	21h 22h 23h
NcbLsn		X	4Xh
NcbNum			50h-FEh
NcbBuffer@			
NcbLength			
NcbCallName	X		*Final Return Codes*
NcbName	X		
NcbRto	X		00h 03h 05h 09h 0Bh
NcbSto	X		11h 12h 14h 15h 18h 19h
NcbPost@	?		21h 22h 23h
NcbLanaNum	X		4Xh
NcbCmdCplt		X	50h-FEh
NcbReserve		?	

The Call command opens a session with a destination name specified by the NcbCallName field. The command uses a local name specified by the NcbName field. The destination name adapter must have a Listen command pending for successful session establishment.

Sessions may be established between any valid names whether they are local or remote names. Multiple sessions may be established with the same pair of names or even with the same name. All Send (and Chain Send) or Receive commands for sessions abort if they do not complete before their specified session time-out intervals expire (NcbSto and NcbRto, respectively). For session Send and Chain Send, this aborts the session. The session time-out intervals are specified in 1/2 second units. (A value of zero means that no time-out occurs.)

A Call fails if it is not successful before the system time-out expires. The system time-out is calculated by multiplying the system interval and system retry count. The values are NetBIOS constants that are determined by the config.sys DXMT0MOD.SYS TRANSMIT.TIMEOUT and TRANSMIT.COUNT parameters, respectively.

When a Call is completed, NetBIOS assigns a Local Session Number (LSN) to the established session. NetBIOS assigns the LSN value in an incremental, modulo 255, roundrobin manner. The values zero and 255 are never assigned. The LSN value must be between 1 and 254 (FEh) inclusive.

Cancel   35h Wait

	In	Out	*Final Return Codes*
NcbCommand	X		00h 03h
NcbRetCode		X	23h 24h 26h
NcbLsn			4Xh
NcbNum			50h-FEh
NcbBuffer@	X		
NcbLength			
NcbCallName			
NcbName			
NcbRto			
NcbSto			
NcbPost@			
NcbLanaNum	X		
NcbCmdCplt		X	
NcbReserve		?	

The Cancel command cancels the NetBIOS command, whose Ncb is at the address given by NcbBuffer@. Canceling pending Send or Chain Send commands always aborts their respective session, though you can cancel their No-Ack variants without aborting their respective sessions.

You cannot cancel the following NetBIOS commands:

- Add Group Name
- Add Name
- Cancel
- Delete Name
- Reset
- Send Datagram
- Send Broadcast Datagram
- Session Status
- Unlink

Chain Send
Chain Send No-Ack

17h Wait; 97h No-Wait
72h Wait; F2h No-Wait

	In	*Out*	*Immediate Return Codes*
NcbCommand	X		00h 03h
NcbRetCode		X	21h 22h 23h
NcbLsn	X		4Xh
NcbNum			50h-FEh
NcbBuffer@	X		
NcbLength	X		
NcbCallName*	X		*Final Return Codes*
NcbName			
NcbRto			00h 03h 05h 07h 08h 0Ah 0Bh
NcbSto			18h
NcbPost@	?		21h 22h 23h
NcbLanaNum	X		4Xh
NcbCmdCplt		X	50h-FEh
NcbReserve		?	

The Chain Send No-Ack command is a variant of the Chain Send command. Its differences are discussed in Appendix E.

The Chain Send command sends data on the session specified by the NcbLsn field value. The data is in two independent buffers pointed to by the NcbBuffer@ and the NcbCallName fields. NetBIOS concatenates the second buffer's data to the first buffer's data and sends the aggregate data as a single, seamless message. Each buffer can contain between zero and 64K-1 bytes inclusive.

The first 6 bytes of NcbCallName field specify the length (2 bytes) and address (4 bytes) of the second buffer in offset:segment format. When the remote side of the session closes a session with a Hang Up, all local Chain Send commands pending for the closed session return with a session-closed status.

If a local Hang Up command is issued with session-pending Chain Send commands, they complete before the Hang Up completes. If a session aborts, a session-ended-abnormally status is returned. If a Chain Send time-out expires, the session aborts and a command-timed-out sta-

---

*For NcbCallName: bytes 0-1 = NcbLength2, and bytes 2-5 =NcbBuffer2@ in offset: segment format.

tus is returned. The time-out value for a Chain Send command is determined when the session's Call or Listen completes and cannot be specified with this command.

The total message size must be between zero and 128K-2 bytes inclusive. If more than one Send or Chain Send is pending within a session, the data is transmitted in a first-in, first-out (FIFO) order. If the Chain Send cannot be completed for any reason, the session aborts to guarantee data integrity.

Chain Send commands without corresponding Receives at the session partner consume NetBIOS resources. It is not advisable to issue many Chain Sends without corresponding Receives.

Chain Sends canceled by a Cancel command terminate their session.

Delete Name   31h Wait; B1h No-Wait

	In	Out	Immediate Return Codes
NcbCommand	X		00h 03h
NcbRetCode		X	21h 22h 23h
NcbLsn			4Xh
NcbNum			50h-FEh
NcbBuffer@			
NcbLength			
NcbCallName			Final Return Codes
NcbName	X		
NcbRto			00h 03h 0Fh
NcbSto			15h
NcbPost@	?		21h 22h 23h
NcbLanaNum	X		4Xh
NcbCmdCplt		X	50h-FEh
NcbReserve		?	

The Delete Name command deletes a 16-character name from a NetBIOS name table.

If the Delete Name command is issued when the name has active sessions, the command completes after deregistering the name. (See the Adapter Status command.) The command's return code has a value of 0Fh, indicating the name has active sessions.

In this instance, the actual name deletion is delayed, with the name occupying an entry in the adapter's NetBIOS name table, until all sessions associated with the name are closed by a Hang Up command's abort. A deregistered name is not usable by subsequent NetBIOS Call and Listen commands. Send and Receive commands for existing sessions continue to work until the sessions end but datagram commands cannot use the name.

If the name has only pending nonactive session commands when the Delete Name command is issued, the name is removed and the command-completed status is returned to the user. The pending nonactive session commands terminate immediately with the-name-was-deleted (17h) status.

Nonactive session commands are:

- Listen
- Receive-Any
- Receive Datagram
- Receive Broadcast Datagram

Hang Up   12h Wait; 92h No-Wait

	In	Out	Immediate Return Codes
NcbCommand	X		00h 03h
NcbRetCode		X	21h 22h 23h
NcbLsn	X		4Xh
NcbNum			50h-FEh
NcbBuffer@			
NcbLength			
NcbCallName			*Final Return Codes*
NcbName			
NcbRto			00h 03h 05h 08h 0Ah 0Bh
NcbSto			18h
NcbPost@	?		21h 22h 23h
NcbLanaNum	X		4Xh
NcbCmdCplt		X	50h-FEh
NcbReserve		?	

The Hang Up command closes the session specified by the NcbLsn value.

When the session closes normally, a good-return status returns. A session-closed status or an illegal session number returns if the session does not exist (is already closed or never existed).

All local pending Receive commands for the session terminate and return with session-closed status in the NcbRetCode field when a Hang Up command is issued. They terminate whether they have received any data.

If local Send or Chain Send commands are pending for the session, the Hang Up command delays until the Send or Chain Send commands complete. This delay occurs whether the commands are transferring data or are waiting for the remote side to issue Receive or Receive-Any commands. The Hang Up completes when any of the following conditions occur:

1. The Send or Chain Send completes.
2. The Send or Chain Send aborts.
3. The Send or Chain Send fails because the session terminated in response to a Hang Up command issued by the other application.
4. The Send or Chain Send fails because the time-out specified at session creation expired.

If one of these conditions does not occur within the system time-out period after the Hang Up command is issued, the Hang Up command returns with a command-timed-out status and the session aborts. The system time-out is calculated by multiplying the system interval and system retry count. The values are NetBIOS constants that are determined by the config.sys DXMT0MOD.SYS TRANSMIT.TIMEOUT and TRANSMIT.COUNT parameters, respectively. When the session aborts, all pending commands on that session return to the issuer with session-ended-abnormally status.

When the session closes, all Send, Chain Send, and Receive commands pending on the terminated session return with a session-closed status. If a single Receive-Any command is pending on the local name used by the session, it returns with a session-closed status. However, if multiple Receive-Any commands are pending, only one returns with a session-closed status.

Note that just one (of possibly many) Receive-Any commands pending on the session returns, though all Send, Chain Send, and Receive commands pending on the session return.

When a session terminates, all remote pending commands on that session return to the issuer with a session-closed status.

Listen   **11h Wait; 91h No-Wait**

	In	Out	*Immediate Return Codes*
NcbCommand	X		00h 03h
NcbRetCode		X	21h 22h 23h
NcbLsn		X	4Xh
NcbNum			50h-FEh
NcbBuffer@			
NcbLength			
NcbCallName*	X	X	*Final Return Codes*
NcbName	X		
NcbRto	X		00h 03h 09h 0Bh
NcbSto	X		11h 15h 17h 18h 19h
NcbPost@	?		21h 22h 23h
NcbLanaNum	X		4Xh
NcbCmdCplt		X	50h-FEh
NcbReserve		?	

The Listen command opens a session with the name specified in the Ncb-CallName field, using the local name specified by the NcbName field.

If the first position of the NcbCallName field is an asterisk (*), a session is established with any network adapter that issues a Call to the local name. The name making the Call is returned in the NcbCallName field. A Listen command for a specific name has priority over a Listen for any name.

Sessions may be established with either a local or remote name. Multiple sessions may be established with the same pair of names. All Send and Chain Send commands, but not their No-Ack variants, for a session that are unsuccessful after the specified time-out interval specified by the Listen command's NcbSto field value abort the session. If a Send or Chain Send command is canceled by a subsequent Cancel command, the session aborts.

---

*NetBIOS returns the NcbCallName field if the application specifies an asterisk (*) as the first character of the NcbCallName field.

Time-out intervals are specified in 1/2 second intervals. A value of zero means that no time-out occurs. A Listen command does not time-out, but occupies a session entry and is reported as a pending session by Adapter Status commands. NetBIOS assigns the LSN value in an incremental, modulo 255, roundrobin manner. The values zero and 255 are never assigned. The LSN value must be between 1 and 254 (FEh) inclusive.

The name-conflict-detected error returns if, during the completion of a Listen command, a unique name exists in more than one table. All adapters with the name registered, except the one where the Call command returns successfully, report the name-conflict-detected error.

Receive   15h Wait; 95h No-Wait

	In	Out	Immediate Return Codes
NcbCommand	X		00h 03h
NcbRetCode		X	21h 22h 23h
NcbLsn	X		4Xh
NcbNum			50h-FEh
NcbBuffer@	X		
NcbLength	X	X	
NcbCallName			Final Return Codes
NcbName			
NcbRto			00h 03h 05h 06h 07h 08h 0Ah 0Bh
NcbSto			18h
NcbPost@	?		21h 22h 23h
NcbLanaNum	X		4Xh
NcbCmdCplt		X	50h-FEh
NcbReserve		?	

The Receive command receives data from a specified session partner that Sends or Chain Sends data on the session. A Receive command cannot detect that data may have been sent to it by a Send No-Ack or Chain Send No-Ack versus a Send or Chain Send command, respectively.

If more than one command that can receive data on a specific session is pending, they are processed in the following priority:

1. Receive

2. Receive-Any-for-a-Specified-Name

3. Receive-Any-for-Any-Name

Once the commands are sorted by priority, they are processed in a first-in, first-out order within a priority. The Receive time-out value is specified with the session Call or Listen command and cannot be specified with this command. Use the wait option with this command with care because all application processing stops until the command completes.

When a session closes, either by a local Hang Up command or by the remote Hang Up command, all Receives pending for the session return with a session closed status.

If the Receive buffer is not large enough for the message being received, a message-incomplete status (06h) is returned. To obtain the rest of the information before a Send time-out occurs at the other side of the session, the local application should issue another Receive or Receive-Any command. However, if the data was sent with a Send No-Ack or Chain Send No-Ack, the data is lost already, though the session continues.

Receive-Any   16h Wait; 96h No-Wait

	In	Out	*Immediate Return Codes*
NcbCommand	X		00h 03h
NcbRetCode		X	21h 22h 23h
NcbLsn		X	4Xh
NcbNum*	X	?	50h-FEh
NcbBuffer@	X		
NcbLength	X	X	
NcbCallName			*Final Return Codes*
NcbName			
NcbRto			00h 03h 06h 07h 0Ah 0Bh
NcbSto			13h 17h 18h 19h
NcbPost@	?		21h 22h 23h
NcbLanaNum	X		4Xh
NcbCmdCplt		X	50h-FEh
NcbReserve		?	

---

*NcbNum = FFh = Receive-Any-for-Any-Name.

The Receive-Any command receives data from any session partner that Sends or Chain Sends data on a session associated with a specified local name. A Receive-Any command cannot detect that data may have been sent to it by a Send No-Ack or Chain Send No-Ack command versus a Send or Chain Send command, respectively. The local application specifies the local name with the name's NcbNum when issuing this command. If the application program sets NcbNum field to FFh, the Receive is for any remote name the adapter has a session with, for any of its names. This is referred to as a Receive-Any-for-Any-Name command.

If more than one command that can receive data on a specific session is pending, they are processed in the following priority:

1. Receive

2. Receive-Any-for-a-Specified-Name

3. Receive-Any-for-Any-Name

Once the commands are sorted by priority, they are processed in a first-in, first-out order. When the return code is presented, NetBIOS sets the NcbNum field to the number of the name for which the data was received. The Receive time-out value is specified with the session's Call or Listen command and cannot be specified with this command.

When a session terminates by a Hang Up command (session-abort), one Receive-Any or Receive-Any-for-Any-Name returns with session-closed (aborted) status, regardless of the number that may be pending. The NcbLsn field of the returning command contains the terminating session number. A Receive-Any-for-Any-Name returns only if no Receive-Any is pending for the terminating session.

If the Receive buffer is not large enough for the message being received, a message-incomplete status (06h) is returned. To obtain the rest of the information before a Send time-out occurs at the other side of the session, the local application should issue another Receive or Receive-Any command. However, if the data was sent with a Send No-Ack or Chain Send No-Ack, the data is lost already, but the session continues.

Application programs should use the Receive-Any-for-Any-Name command with caution because it may receive messages for other programs running in the workstation. Use the wait option with this command with care because all application processing stops until the command completes.

Receive Broadcast Datagram   23h Wait; A3h No-Wait

	In	*Out*
NcbCommand	X	
NcbRetCode		X
NcbLsn		
NcbNum	X	
NcbBuffer@	X	
NcbLength	X	X
NcbCallName		X
NcbName		
NcbRto		
NcbSto		
NcbPost@	?	
NcbLanaNum	X	
NcbCmdCplt		X
NcbReserve		?

Immediate Return Codes

00h 03h
21h 22h 23h
4Xh
50h-FEh

Final Return Codes

00h 03h 06h 0Bh
13h 17h 19h
21h 22h 23h
4Xh
50h-FEh

The Receive Broadcast command receives a datagram message from any adapter issuing a Send Broadcast Datagram.

There is no time-out associated with this command. A message-incomplete status (06h) returns if the receive buffer is not large enough to receive all the data, and the remaining data is lost. Use the wait option with this command with care because all application processing stops until the datagram is received.

Receive Datagram   21h Wait; A1h No-Wait

	In	Out	Immediate Return Codes
NcbCommand	X		00h 03h
NcbRetCode		X	21h 22h 23h
NcbLsn			4Xh
NcbNum*	X		50h-FEh
NcbBuffer@	X		
NcbLength	X	X	
NcbCallName		X	*Final Return Codes*
NcbName			
NcbRto			00h 03h 06h 0Bh
NcbSto			13h 17h 19h
NcbPost@	?		21h 22h 23h
NcbLanaNum	X		4Xh
NcbCmdCplt		X	50h-FEh
NcbReserve		?	

The Receive Datagram command receives datagrams directed to the local name associated with the value in the NcbNum field. Any network name can transmit the datagram and the local name can be a unique (including the permanent node name) or group name.

Though this command does not receive broadcast datagrams, if the NcbNameNum field contains the value FFh, the command receives a datagram directed to any local network name. Receive Datagram commands for a specific name have priority over a Receive Datagram for any name.

If the local application does not have a Receive Datagram command pending when the datagram is transmitted, the message is not received. If the receive buffer is not large enough to receive all the data, a message incomplete status (06h) returns and the remaining data is discarded. If an adapter has several Receive Datagram commands pending for the same name, the next Send Datagram command satisfies only one of the Receive Datagram commands.

There is no time-out associated with this command. Use the wait op-

---

*NcbNum = FFh = Receive Datagram for any name.

tion with care because all application processing stops until a datagram is received.

Reset   ## 32h Wait

	In	Out	Final Return Codes
NcbCommand	X		00h 03h
NcbRetCode		X	23h
NcbLsn	X		4Xh
NcbNum	X		50h-FEh
NcbBuffer@			
NcbLength			
NcbCallName			
NcbName			
NcbRto			
NcbSto			
NcbPost@			
NcbLanaNum	X		
NcbCmdCplt		X	
NcbReserve		?	

The Reset command resets the specified adapter by clearing the NetBIOS name and session tables and aborting any existing sessions. This also sets the next available LSN value and NcbNum value to 01h and 02h, respectively. Whether the Reset command closes and reopens the adapter depends on the IBM LAN Support Program CLOSE.ON.RESET (CR) parameter. If it is specified as NO, then NetBIOS does not close the adapter, leaving all existing DLC communication facilities intact. If the CLOSE.ON.RESET parameter is specified as YES, then the adapter is closed and reopened, aborting existing DLC communication.

In either case, if the RESET.VALUES parameter is specified as YES:

- When the number of sessions specified in the NcbLsn is zero, the default maximum number of sessions is the IBM LAN Support Program SESSIONS parameter rather than the normal default value of 6.
- When the number of commands specified in the NcbNum field is

zero, the default maximum number of pending commands is the IBM LAN Support Program COMMANDS value rather than the normal default value of 12.

Otherwise, the RESET.VALUES parameter is specified as NO and the adapter is reset with the maximum number of sessions specified by the lesser of the NcbLsn field value and the SESSIONS parameter. This maximum is specified by the lesser of the NcbNum field value and the COMMANDS parameter. Note that the network traffic and statistics are reset for Token-Ring Adapters, but not for PC Network Adapters.

| **Send** | | | **14h Wait; 94h No-Wait** |
| **Send No-Ack** | | | **71h Wait; F1h No-Wait** |

	In	*Out*	*Immediate Return Codes*
NcbCommand	X		00h 03h
NcbRetCode		X	21h 22h 23h
NcbLsn	X		4Xh
NcbNum			50h-FEh
NcbBuffer@	X		
NcbLength	X		
NcbCallName			*Final Return Codes*
NcbName			
NcbRto			00h 03h 05h 07h 08h 0Ah 0Bh
NcbSto			18h
NcbPost@	?		21h 22h 23h
NcbLanaNum	X		4Xh
NcbCmdCplt		X	50h-FEh
NcbReserve		?	

The Send No-Ack command is a variant of the Send command. Its differences are explained in Appendix E.

The Send command sends a message to the session partner specified by the LSN value in the NcbLsn field. The NcbBuffer@ field points at the data to send.

When the remote side closes a session with a Hang Up command, all local Send commands pending for the closed session complete with a session-closed status. If a local Hang Up command is issued with any pending Send commands, the Send commands complete before the Hang Up command completes. If a session aborts, a session-ended-abnormally status returns.

If the Send time-out expires, the session aborts and a command-timed-out status returns. The time-out value for a Send command is determined when the session's Call or Listen completes and cannot be specified with this command. The message size must be between zero and 65,535 (64K-1) bytes inclusive.

If more than one Send or Chain Send is pending for a session, the data is transmitted in a first-in, first-out order within the session. If the Send does not complete for any reason, the session aborts to guarantee data integrity.

Send commands without corresponding Receives at the session partner consume NetBIOS resources. It is not advisable to issue many Sends without corresponding Receives.

Sends canceled by a Cancel command terminate their session.

Send Broadcast Datagram   22h Wait; A2h No-Wait

	In	Out	Immediate Return Codes
NcbCommand	X		00h 03h
NcbRetCode		X	21h 22h 23h
NcbLsn			4Xh
NcbNum	X		50h-FEh
NcbBuffer@	X		
NcbLength	X		
NcbCallName			*Final Return Codes*
NcbName			
NcbRto			00h 01h 03h
NcbSto			13h 19h
NcbPost@	?		21h 22h 23h
NcbLanaNum	X		4Xh
NcbCmdCplt		X	50h-FEh
NcbReserve		?	

The Send Broadcast Datagram command sends a datagram message to every network adapter.

Remote adapters not having a Receive Broadcast Datagram command pending do not receive the message. If an adapter issues a Send Broadcast Datagram and has a Receive Broadcast Datagram pending, the adapter receives its own message. If an adapter has several Receive Broadcast Datagram commands pending, the next Send Broadcast Datagram command satisfies all Receive Broadcast Datagram commands.

Send Datagram   20h Wait; A0h No-Wait

	In	*Out*	*Immediate Return Codes*
NcbCommand	X		00h 03h
NcbRetCode		X	21h 22h 23h
NcbLsn			4Xh
NcbNum	X		50h-FEh
NcbBuffer@	X		
NcbLength	X		
NcbCallName	X		*Final Return Codes*
NcbName			
NcbRto			00h 01h 03h
NcbSto			13h 19h
NcbPost@	?		21h 22h 23h
NcbLanaNum	X		4Xh
NcbCmdCplt		X	50h-FEh
NcbReserve		?	

The Send Datagram command sends datagrams to specified network names. The specified name may be a unique (including a permanent node name) or group name.

Adapters having the name but not having a pending Receive Datagram command for that name discard the datagram. If an adapter has a Receive Datagram pending for a name and issues a Send Datagram for that name, the adapter receives its own message. The Send Datagram command satisfies only one pending Receive Datagram command if an adapter has several Receive Datagram commands pending for the same name.

Session Status   34h Wait; B4h No-Wait

	In	Out	Immediate Return Codes
NcbCommand		X	00h 03h
NcbRetCode		X	21h 22h 23h
NcbLsn			4Xh
NcbNum		X	50h-FEh
NcbBuffer@	X		
NcbLength	X		
NcbCallName			*Final Return Codes*
NcbName	X		
NcbRto			00h 01h 03h 06h
NcbSto			15h 19h
NcbPost@	?		21h 22h 23h
NcbLanaNum	X		4Xh
NcbCmdCplt		X	50h-FEh
NcbReserve		?	

The Session Status command obtains the status of one or all sessions associated with a local name. If an asterisk (*) is specified as the first byte of the NcbName field, this command obtains the status for all of the names in the NetBIOS name table.

The minimum valid buffer length is 4 bytes. An illegal buffer length status (01h) is returned if the NcbLength field is less than 4. A message incomplete status (06h) is returned if the NcbLength field is less than the generated status data. To obtain all status data, the buffer length must be at least 4 plus 36 times the number of reported sessions.

A remote Adapter Status command fails if it is not successful before the system time-out expires. The system time-out is calculated by multiplying the system interval and system retry count. The values are Net-BIOS constants that are determined by the config.sys DXMT0MOD.SYS TRANSMIT.TIMEOUT and TRANSMIT.COUNT parameters, respectively. The returned data has the format outlined in Table 20-3.

If adequate buffer space is available, the contents of bytes 4-39 are repeated for every session associated with the specified name (36 bytes for each session). Otherwise, the excess data is lost.

The session state field has the following values:

01h: Listen pending

02h: Call pending

03h: Session established

04h: Hang Up pending

05h: Hang Up complete

06h: Session aborted

Table 20-3. Returned Data Format

Offset	Length	MASM	C	Field Contents
00 00h	1	DB	USGC	Name Number for reported sessions
01 01h	1	DB	USGC	Number of sessions associated with this name
02 02h	1	DB	USGC	Number of pending Receive Datagram and Receive Broadcast Datagram commands
03 03h	1	DB	USGC	Number of pending Receive-Any commands
04 04h	1	DB	USGC	Local Session Number
05 05h	1	DB	USGC	Session state
06 06h	16	DB	char[ ]	Local name
22 16h	16	DB	char[ ]	Remote name
38 26h	1	DB	USGC	Number of pending Receive commands
39 27h	1	DB	USGC	Number of pending Send and Chain Send commands

Unlink

70h Wait

	In	Out	Final Return Codes
NcbCommand	X		00h 03h
NcbRetCode		X	21h 22h 23h
NcbLsn			4Xh
NcbNum			50h-FEh
NcbBuffer@			
NcbLength			
NcbCallName			
NcbName			
NcbRto			
NcbSto			
NcbPost@			
NcbLanaNum	X		
NcbCmdCplt		X	
NcbReserve		?	

The Unlink command provides compatibility with the original PC Network LANA NetBIOS which uses the Unlink command to disconnect from an RPL server.

00h is the only valid NcbLanaNum value for an Unlink command. A value of 01h may appear to be accepted, but only because NetBIOS does not inadvertently reject the value during processing.

If the Unlink command is for an original PC Network LANA adapter and RPL is active, NetBIOS subsequently issues an internal Hang Up command with a wait option using an internal Ncb located in high memory. This Ncb contains a value of 00h in its NcbLanaNum field because NetBIOS RPL activities use the primary adapter exclusively.

Alternatively, the adapter may not be an original PC Network LANA adapter or an original PC Network LANA adapter with RPL active. In this case, NetBIOS does not execute a Hang Up command for an RPL session, but treats the command as a no-operation and simply returns a good-return code. In any instance, 00h virtually always returns as the return code for any Hang Up command that specifies a valid NcbLanaNum field value.

Special Value Summary

NetBIOS treats four values as special values. Their NetBIOS meaning varies by the context of their use.

Special Value 00h

00h is invalid as a first character of any name except a permanent node name.

00h is an invalid NcbLsn value.

00h is an invalid NcbNameNum value.

Using 00h in a Call or Listen command's NcbRto field indicates session Receive and Receive-Any commands should not time-out.

Using 00h in a Call or Listen command's NcbSto field indicates that session Send and Chain Send commands should not time-out.

Using 00h in the NcbLsn and NcbNum fields for a Reset Command indicates NetBIOS should determine the maximum number of allowable simultaneously existing sessions and pending control blocks, respectively.

00h is the only valid NcbLanaNum value for an Unlink command. A value of 01h may appear to be accepted, but only because NetBIOS does not inadvertently reject the value during processing.

Special Value 01h

NetBIOS reserves 01h for the permanent node name NetBIOS name number. The permanent node name is always used in NetBIOS communication even if the value is overridden for use as a LAN address.

For the original PC Network LANA adapter, the RPL session always has an LSN value of 01h because it is always the first NetBIOS session.

Special Value FFh

FFh is an invalid NcbLsn value.

FFh is an invalid NcbNameNum value.

Using FFh as the NcbNum value in a Receive-Any command specifies the command is a Receive-Any-for-Any-Name command.

Using FFh as the NcbNum value in a Receive Datagram command specifies the command can receive a datagram directed to any local name.

Special Value *

Using an asterisk (*) as the first character of a Listen command's Ncb-CallName field indicates that any adapter calling the name specified in the Listen's NcbName field is a valid session partner.

Using * as the first character of an Adapter Status command's Ncb-CallName field indicates the status request is for the local adapter specified by the NcbLanaNum field value.

Using * as the first character of a Session Status command's Ncb-CallName field indicates the status request is for all names in the local adapter specified by the NcbLanaNum field value.

Complex Hang Up Scenario

Assume two workstations are conducting a communication session. Assume further that each station has two Receive commands, two Receive-Any commands, a Chain Send command and a Send command pending on their respective side of the session. Finally, assume that one station, station XXX, issues a Hang Up command specifying the given session. The following discussion illustrates the various outcomes of this situation.

First, all Receive commands for the session at station XXX are immediately completed with a session-closed NcbRetCode, but only one of the Receive-Any commands is completed with a session-closed NcbRet-Code. The absence of these pending commands may cause pending Send and Chain Send commands to time-out on the other side of the session, immediately aborting the session.

Alternatively, the Hang Up command is delayed at station XXX until the local pending Send and Chain Send commands complete. In the event they do not complete before the system time-out period expires, the Hang Up command itself times-out and the session is aborted. The system time-out period is computed by multiplying the system interval and system retry count. The values are NetBIOS constants that are determined by the config.sys DXMT0MOD.SYS TRANSMIT.TIMEOUT and TRANSMIT.COUNT parameters, respectively.

Return Code Summary

For wait option commands, the *AL register* contains the final command return code. Alternatively, for no-wait option commands, the AL register contains the immediate return code. If the return code is not 00h, then no further processing is done on the command. Finally, the AL register provides the final return code to the post routine if the command is initially accepted and specifies a post routine.

The *NcbRetCode Field* contains the final return code for commands that specify the wait option or the no-wait option without a post routine.

The *NcbCmdCplt Field* contains the final return code if a no-wait command option is used with an accepted command that does not specify a post routine.

Appendixes

NetBIOS2.h Listing

```
#define TRUE   1
#define FALSE  0

#define SUCCESS 1
#define FAILURE 0

#ifndef USGC
#define USGC   unsigned char
#endif

#ifndef USGI
#define USGI   unsigned
#endif

#ifndef USGL
#define USGL   unsigned long
#endif

#define NetbiosInt21FunctionCode    ((USGC) 0x2A)
#define NetbiosInt5C                ((USGC) 0x5C)

#define COMMAND_PENDING             ((USGC) 0xFF)

#define Mcb Ncb

#define MAX_ADAPTER_NUMBER      1
#define MAX_SESSION_COUNT       254
#define MAX_NAMES               254
#define MAX_COMMAND_COUNT       255
```

```
#define NO_WAIT                      ((USGC) 0x80)

#define NETBIOS_RESET_WAIT_ONLY      ((USGC) 0x32)
#define NETBIOS_CANCEL_WAIT_ONLY     ((USGC) 0x35)
#define NETBIOS_ADAPTER_STATUS       ((USGC) 0x33)
#define NETBIOS_UNLINK_WAIT_ONLY     ((USGC) 0x70)
#define NETBIOS_TRACE                ((USGC) 0x79)

#define NETBIOS_ADD_NAME             ((USGC) 0x30)
#define NETBIOS_ADD_GROUP_NAME       ((USGC) 0x36)
#define NETBIOS_DELETE_NAME          ((USGC) 0x31)
#define NETBIOS_FIND_NAME            ((USGC) 0x78)

#define NETBIOS_CALL                 ((USGC) 0x10)
#define NETBIOS_LISTEN               ((USGC) 0x11)
#define NETBIOS_HANG_UP              ((USGC) 0x12)
#define NETBIOS_SEND                 ((USGC) 0x14)
#define NETBIOS_SEND_NO_ACK          ((USGC) 0x71)
#define NETBIOS_CHAIN_SEND           ((USGC) 0x17)
#define NETBIOS_CHAIN_SEND_NO_ACK    ((USGC) 0x72)
#define NETBIOS_RECEIVE              ((USGC) 0x15)
#define NETBIOS_RECEIVE_ANY          ((USGC) 0x16)
#define NETBIOS_SESSION_STATUS       ((USGC) 0x34)

#define NETBIOS_SEND_DATAGRAM        ((USGC) 0x20)
#define NETBIOS_RECEIVE_DATAGRAM     ((USGC) 0x21)
#define NETBIOS_SEND_BDATAGRAM       ((USGC) 0x22)
#define NETBIOS_RECEIVE_BDATAGRAM    ((USGC) 0x23)

#define NETBIOS_INVALID_COMMAND      ((USGC) 0x7F)

/* LAN Adapter Types */

#define TOKEN_RING_ADAPTER ((USGC) 0xFF)
#define PC_NETWORK_ADAPTER ((USGC) 0xFE)

/* NETBIOS Version Numbers */

#define VERSION_MASK ((USGC) 0x0F)

#define PARM_MASK ((USGC) 0xF0)
#define OLD_PARMS ((USGC) 0x10)
#define NEW_PARMS ((USGC) 0x20)
```

```
struct Ncb
   {
     USGC    NcbCommand;          /* command code                  */
     USGC    NcbRetCode;          /* return code                   */
     USGC    NcbLsn;              /* local session number          */
     USGC    NcbNum;              /* Datagram ADD NAME table entry  */

     char *  NcbBufferOffset;     /* I/O buffer offset             */
     USGI    NcbBufferSegment;    /* I/O buffer segment            */

     USGI    NcbLength;           /* length of data in I/O buffer   */

     char    NcbCallName[16];     /* remote system name for CALL    */
     char    NcbName[16];         /* local adapter network name     */

     USGC    NcbRto;              /* receive timeouts in 1/2 second units */
     USGC    NcbSto;              /* send    timeouts in 1/2 second units */

     char *  NcbPostRtnOffset;    /* offset  of post routine       */
     USGI    NcbPostRtnSegment;   /* segment of post routine       */

     USGC    NcbLanaNum;    /* network adapter number to execute cmd  */
     USGC    NcbCmdCplt;    /* 0xFF ==> command pending, else cmplted */

     char    NcbReservedArea[14]; /* work area for network card     */
   } ZeroNcb;                     /* prototype NCB for sizeof calcs */

#define MIN_NAME_NUM        2
#define MAX_NAME_NUM      254
#define ILLEGAL_NAME_NUM   0

#define MIN_LSN          1
#define MAX_LSN        254
#define ILLEGAL_LSN      0

struct NameTableEntry {
             char EntryName[16];      /* symbolic network name     */
             USGC EntryNameNum;       /* associated name number    */
             USGC EntryNameStatus;    /* & with 0x0087 for status   */
             };

struct DlcStatus {
   /* +00 */    USGC PermanentNodeName[6];
   /* +06 */    USGC MajorVersionNumber;  /* low-order nibble only */
   /* +07 */    USGC AlwaysZero;
```

```
        /* +08 */    USGC LanAdapterType;
        /* +09 */    USGC MinorVersionNumber;
        /* +10 */    USGI ReportingPeriodMinutes;
        /* +12 */    USGI FrameRejectedReceiveCount;
        /* +14 */    USGI FrameRejectedXmitCount;
        /* +16 */    USGI I_FrameReceiveErrorCount;
        /* +18 */    USGI XmitAbortCount;
        /* +20 */    USGL SuccessfulFrameXmitCount;
        /* +24 */    USGL SuccessfulFrameRcvCount;
        /* +28 */    USGI I_FrameXmitErrorCount;
        /* +30 */    USGI RmtRqstBufferDepletionCount;
        /* +32 */    USGI ExpiredT1TimerCount;
        /* +34 */    USGI ExpiredTiTimerCount;
        /* +36 */    struct LocalTrAdapterStatus far * LocalExtStatPtr;
        /* +40 */    USGI FreeCommandBlocks;
        /* +42 */    USGI CurrentMaxNcbs;
        /* +44 */    USGI MaximumCommands;
        /* +46 */    USGI TransmitBufferDepletionCount;
        /* +48 */    USGI MaximumDatagramPacketSize;
        /* +50 */    USGI PendingSessionCount;
        /* +52 */    USGI MaxPendingSessionCount;
        /* +54 */    USGI MaximumSessions;
        /* +56 */    USGI MaximumSessionPacketSize;
        /* +58 */    USGI NameTableEntryCount;
        /* +60 */    struct NameTableEntry TableEntry[MAX_NAMES];
                } ;


struct LocalTrAdapterStatus {
        /* +00 */    USGI DirInitBringUpErrorCode;
        /* +02 */    USGI DirOpenAdapterErrorCode;
        /* +04 */    USGI LatestRingStatus;
        /* +06 */    USGI LatestAdapterCheckReasonCode;
        /* +08 */    USGI LatestPcDetectedErrorCode;
        /* +10 */    USGC LatestOperationalErrorCode;
        /* +11 */    USGC LatestImplicitCcbReturnCode;
        /* +12 */    USGI AdapterLineErrors;
        /* +14 */    USGI AdapterInternalErrors;
        /* +16 */    USGI AdapterBurstErrors;
        /* +18 */    USGI AdapterAcError;
        /* +20 */    USGI AdapterAbortDelimiter;
        /* +22 */    USGI AdapterReserved1;
        /* +24 */    USGI AdapterLostFrame;
        /* +26 */    USGI AdapterReceiveCongestion;
        /* +28 */    USGI AdapterFrameCopiedErrors;
        /* +30 */    USGI AdapterFrequencyErrors;
```

```
/* +32 */    USGI AdapterTokenErrors;
/* +34 */    USGI AdapterReserved2;
/* +36 */    USGI AdapterReserved3;
/* +38 */    USGI AdapterReserved4;
             };

struct LanaStatus {
/* +00 */    USGC PermanentNodeName[6];
/* +06 */    USGC ExternalJumperSetting;
/* +07 */    USGC SelfTestResults;
/* +08 */    USGC SoftwareVersionMajor;
/* +09 */    USGC SoftwareVersionMinor;
/* +10 */    USGI ReportingPeriodMinutes;
/* +12 */    USGI CrcErrorCount;
/* +14 */    USGI AlignmentErrors;
/* +16 */    USGI CollisionCount;
/* +18 */    USGI XmitAbortCount;
/* +20 */    USGL SuccessfulXmits;
/* +24 */    USGL SuccessfulRcvs;
/* +28 */    USGI RetransmitCount;
/* +30 */    USGI ResourceDepletionCount;
/* +32 */    char ReservedArea1[8];
/* +40 */    USGI FreeCommandBlocks;
/* +42 */    USGI CurrentMaxNcbs;
/* +44 */    USGI HwMaxCommandBlocks;
/* +46 */    char ReservedArea2[4];
/* +50 */    USGI PendingSessionCount;
/* +52 */    USGI CurrentMaxPendingSessions;
/* +54 */    USGI HwMaxSessionCount;
/* +56 */    USGI MaximumPacketSize;
/* +58 */    USGI NameTableEntryCount;
/* +60 */    struct NameTableEntry TableEntry[16];
             } ;

struct DateTimeStruct { USGI DateCX;
                        USGI DateDX;
                        USGI TimeCX;
                        USGI TimeDX;
                      };

#define NB_ILLEGAL_BUFFER_LENGTH     0x01
#define NB_INVALID_COMMAND           0x03
#define NB_COMMAND_TIMED_OUT         0x05
#define NB_MESSAGE_INCOMPLETE        0x06
#define NB_NO_ACK_FAILURE            0x07
```

```
#define NB_ILLEGAL_LSN                0x08
#define NB_NO_RESOURCE_AVAILABLE      0x09
#define NB_SESSION_CLOSED             0x0A
#define NB_COMMAND_CANCELED           0x0B
#define NB_DUPLICATE_LOCAL_NAME       0x0D
#define NB_NAME_TABLE_FULL            0x0E
#define NB_NAME_HAS_ACTIVE_SESSIONS   0x0F


#define NB_LOCAL_SESSION_TABLE_FULL   0x11
#define NB_SESSION_OPEN_REJECTED      0x12
#define NB_ILLEGAL_NAME_NUMBER        0x13
#define NB_CANNOT_FIND_CALLED_NAME    0x14
#define NB_NAME_NOT_FOUND_OR_ILLEGAL  0x15
#define NB_NAME_USED_ON_RMT_ADAPTER   0x16
#define NB_NAME_DELETED               0x17
#define NB_SESSION_ENDED_ABNORMALLY   0x18
#define NB_NAME_CONFLICT_DETECTED     0x19
#define NB_INCOMPATIBLE_RMT_DEVICE    0x1A


#define NB_INTERFACE_BUSY             0x21
#define NB_TOO_MANY_COMMANDS_PENDING  0x22
#define NB_INVALID_ADAPTER_NUMBER     0x23
#define NB_CMD_COMPLETED_DURING_CANCEL 0x24
#define NB_RESERVED_NAME_SPECIFIED    0x25
#define NB_CMD_NOT_VALID_TO_CANCEL    0x26


#define NB_LANA_SYSTEM_ERROR          0x40
#define NB_LANA_REMOTE_HOT_CARRIER    0x41
#define NB_LANA_LOCAL_HOT_CARRIER     0x42
#define NB_LANA_NO_CARRIER_DETECTED   0x43
#define NB_UNUSUAL_NETWORK_CONDITION  0x44


#define NB_ADAPTER_MALFUNCTION        0x50


#define NB_COMMAND_PENDING            0xFF



#define MAX_SESSION_BUFFER_SIZE       8192
struct SessionMsg { USGL TextLength;
                char Text[MAX_SESSION_BUFFER_SIZE];
           };
```

C Post Routine Listing

```
#define LINT_ARGS

#include <dos.h>
#include <stdio.h>
#include "netbios2.h"

struct SREGS SegRegs;

struct Ncb  DatagramNcb;

char Buffer[1];

char ClientName[16] = "WDS-DG";

#if defined(LINT_ARGS)
extern  int main(int argc,char * *argv);
extern  void SendNoWaitDatagram(void);
extern  void cdecl interrupt far PostRoutine(
                        unsigned int es, unsigned int ds,
                        unsigned int di, unsigned int si,
                        unsigned int bp, unsigned int sp,
                        unsigned int bx, unsigned int dx,
                        unsigned int cx, unsigned int ax,
                        unsigned int ip, unsigned int cs,
                        unsigned int flags);
extern  void NetbiosRequest(struct Ncb *NcbPointer);
extern  void Logo(void);
#endif

USGC PostRoutineDriven = FALSE;
```

```
int main(argc, argv)
int   argc;
char *argv[];
{
   Logo();

   SendNoWaitDatagram();

   while(PostRoutineDriven == FALSE)
    ;   /* spins here until PostRoutineDriven == TRUE */

   printf("\n\nThe return code was %02Xh...",
                        DatagramNcb.NcbRetCode);

   printf("\n\nProgram ending.....\n");

   return 0;
}

void SendNoWaitDatagram()
{
  USGI temp;

  char far * BufferPtrFar      = (char far *) Buffer;
  void (far *PostRoutinePtr)() = (void (far *)()) PostRoutine;

  DatagramNcb.NcbCommand = NETBIOS_SEND_DATAGRAM + NO_WAIT;

  DatagramNcb.NcbLength  = 1;

  DatagramNcb.NcbBufferOffset  = (char *) FP_OFF(BufferPtrFar);
  DatagramNcb.NcbBufferSegment = (USGI)   FP_SEG(BufferPtrFar);

  DatagramNcb.NcbPostRtnOffset  = (char *) FP_OFF(PostRoutinePtr);
  DatagramNcb.NcbPostRtnSegment = (USGI)   FP_SEG(PostRoutinePtr);

  DatagramNcb.NcbNum     = 0x01;  /* use Permanent Node Name NameNum */

  for (temp = 0; temp < 16; temp++)
      DatagramNcb.NcbCallName[temp] =  ClientName[temp];

  NetbiosRequest(&DatagramNcb);
}
```

```
void cdecl interrupt far PostRoutine(es, ds, di, si,
                                     bp, sp, bx, dx,
                                     cx, ax, ip, cs,flags)
USGI es, ds, di, si, bp, sp, bx, dx, cx, ax, ip, cs, flags;
{
   PostRoutineDriven = TRUE;              /* no DOS calls allowed!!! */
   printf("\nNcb SEG:OFF == %04X:%04X", es, bx);      /* tsk tsk   */
}


void NetbiosRequest(NcbPointer)
struct Ncb *NcbPointer;
{
 union  REGS  InRegs, OutRegs;  /* defined in dos.h */
 struct Ncb far *NcbPtr = (struct Ncb far *) NcbPointer;

   segread(&SegRegs);

   SegRegs.es  = FP_SEG(NcbPtr);
   InRegs.x.bx = FP_OFF(NcbPtr);

   printf("\n\nNcb SEG:OFF == %04X:%04X", SegRegs.es,
                                          InRegs.x.bx);

   int86x(NetbiosInt5C, &InRegs, &OutRegs, &SegRegs);
}


void Logo()
{
   printf("\n  NetBIOS C Post Routine Sample Program");
   printf("\n © Copyright 1988 W. David Schwaderer");
}
```

Error Codes, Reasons, and Actions

Return Code	Meaning
00h	Successful completion, good return
01h	Invalid buffer length
03h	Invalid command
05h	Command timed-out
06h	Incomplete received message
07h	Local No-Ack command failed
08h	Invalid Local Session Number
09h	No resource available
0Ah	Session has been closed
0Bh	Command was canceled
0Dh	Duplicate name in local NetBIOS name table
0Eh	NetBIOS name table full
0Fh	Name has active sessions and is now deregistered
11h	NetBIOS local session table full
12h	Session open rejected because no Listen is outstanding
13h	Illegal name number
14h	Cannot find name called or no answer
15h	Name not found, or cannot specify asterisk (*) or 00h as first byte of NcbName, or the name is deregistered and cannot be used
16h	Name in use on remote adapter
17h	Name deleted
18h	Session ended abnormally
19h	Name conflict detected
1Ah	Incompatible remote device (PC Network)

Return Code	Meaning
21h	Interface busy
22h	Too many commands outstanding
23h	Invalid number in NcbLanaNum field
24h	Command completed while cancel occurring
25h	Reserved name specified for Add Group Name
26h	Command not valid to cancel
30h	Name defined by another process (OS/2 Extended Edition only)
34h	NetBIOS environment not defined (OS/2 Extended Edition only)
35h	Required operating system resources exhausted (OS/2 Extended Edition only)
36h	Maximum applications exceeded (OS/2 Extended Edition only)
37h	No SAPs available for NetBIOS (OS/2 Extended Edition only)
38h	Requested resources not available (OS/2 Extended Edition only)
40h	System error (PC Network)
41h	Hot carrier from a remote adapter detected (PC Network)
42h	Hot carrier from this adapter detected (PC Network)
43h	No carrier detected (PC Network)
4Eh	Status bit 12, 14, or 15 on longer than one minute (Token-Ring)
4Fh	One or more of status bits 8-11 on (Token-Ring)
50h-F6h	Adapter malfunction
F7h	Error on implicit DIR.INITIALIZE
F8h	Error on implicit DIR.OPEN.ADAPTER
F9h	IBM LAN Support Program internal error
FAh	Adapter check
FBh	NETBIOS program not loaded in PC
FCh	DIR.OPEN.ADAPTER or DLC.OPEN.SAP failed—check parameters
FDh	Unexpected adapter close
FFh	Command-pending status

00h, Successful Completion, Good Return

Meaning: The command completed without error.

Required Action: No action is required. This is normal after each successful command.

01h, Invalid Buffer Length

Meaning: A Send Datagram or Send Broadcast Datagram command cannot send more than 512 bytes. For Adapter Status and Session Status commands, the specified buffer length was less than the minimum required.

Required Action: Specify the correct size for the buffer and try the command again.

03h, Invalid Command

Meaning: The command code used is incorrect.

Required Action: Reissue the correct command code.

05h, Command Timed-Out

Meaning: For a Call or an Adapter Status command, the system time-out elapsed before the command completed. For Send, Chain Send, or Receive commands, the time-out period specified in the Call or Listen command establishing the session expired. For a Hang Up command, the time-out period expired for an outstanding Send or Chain Send to complete.

Required Action: For a Call, try again later. For an Adapter Status command, use a correct name. For a Send command, the session has been aborted. Establish another session, synchronize the session, and reissue the Send making sure a receive is outstanding on the other side of the session.

06h, Incomplete Received Message

Meaning: Part of a message was received because the specified buffer length is not big enough to receive the full message.

Required Action: For Receive and Receive-Any command: Issue another Receive to get the rest of the message before the remote side times-out, but not if the data was sent using a Send No-Ack or Chain Send No-Ack. (It is already discarded.) For Status, Session Status, Receive Datagram, and Receive Broadcast Datagram commands, the remaining data is lost.

If the command was a remote Status command, the error occurs when the remote side cannot transmit the entire status data because it is larger than the maximum-length transmittable UI-frame.

07h, Local No-Ack Command Failed

Meaning: One or more Send No-Ack and/or Chain Send No-Ack commands issued within this workstation for this LSN was unsuccessful.
   Required Action: The session is still active. Resynch the data flow however possible and continue.

08h, Invalid Local Session Number

Meaning: The specified session number is not for an active session.
   Required Action: Reissue the command specifying an active session number.

09h, No Resource Available

Meaning: A session cannot be established with a remote application program because there is no more room in its session table.
   Required Action: Reissue the command at a later time.

0Ah, Session Has Been Closed

Meaning: The session partner closed the session.
   Required Action: None.

0Bh, Command Was Canceled

Meaning: The command was canceled by a Cancel command.
   Required Action: None.

0Dh, Duplicate Name in Local NetBIOS Name Table

Meaning: An Add Name command specified a registered name that is currently in the local name table.
   Required Action: Reissue the command and specify another name or use the name without trying to add it.

0Eh, NetBIOS Name Table Full

Meaning: The number of names in the NetBIOS name table already equals the value previously specified in the DIR.OPEN.ADAPTER command.

Required Action: Wait until a name is deleted causing an available entry.

0Fh, Name Has Active Sessions and Is Now Deregistered

Meaning: The name specified in a Delete Name command is active in a session, but is now marked as deregistered. The name is unusable for any new sessions though it still active-sessions and occupies a slot in the table.

Required Action: Close all the sessions using this name so the name can be deleted and its name table slot can be freed.

11h, NetBIOS Local Session Table Full

Meaning: There are no available entries in the local session table. (The number of sessions is user-specified in Reset or DIR.OPEN.ADAPTER commands.)

Required Action: Wait until a session closes making an entry available.

12h, Session Open Rejected because No Listen Is Outstanding

Meaning: No Listen command is pending on the remote NetBIOS Interface.

Required Action: Wait until a Listen command is issued at the remote NetBIOS Interface.

13h, Illegal Name Number

Meaning: The specified name number no longer exists or was never specified.

Required Action: Use the most recent number that was assigned to the name.

14h, Cannot Find Name Called or No Answer

Meaning: No response to the Call command was received.
Required Action: Try the Call command later.

15h, Name Not Found

Meaning: The specified name is not in the NetBIOS name table, or the first character of the name is either an ASCII asterisk or 00, or the name is deregistered and cannot be used.
Required Action: Try a valid name.

16h, Name in Use on Remote Adapter

Meaning: The specified name is already registered as a unique name on another table.
Required Action: Specify another name or have the name deleted and changed at the other adapter.

17h, Name Deleted

Meaning: The name has been deleted and cannot be used.
Required Action: Add the name to the NetBIOS name table again and reissue the command.

18h, Session Ended Abnormally

Meaning: A Send command terminated because of a time-out or hardware problem.
Required Action: Issue a remote Adapter Status command for the other adapter and check your adapter's cable. Reestablish and synchronize the new session.

19h, Name Conflict Detected

Meaning: Network protocols have detected two or more identical unique names on the network.
Required Action: Remove the identical network names.

1Ah, Incompatible Remote Device

Meaning: An unexpected protocol packet has been received.
Required Action: Verify that all adapters on the network observe the network's protocols.

21h, Interface Busy

Meaning: The NetBIOS Interface is either busy or out of local resources. This condition can also be caused by having any of the ring status bits 12, 14, or 15 on.
Required Action: Try the command later.

22h, Too Many Commands Outstanding

Meaning: The number of commands currently pending equals the maximum number allowed.
Required Action: Try the command later.

23h, Invalid Number in NcbLanaNum Field

Meaning: The only valid values for the NcbLanaNum field are 0x00 and 0x01, or the specified adapter is not present.
Required Action: Verify that the adapter is present, or correct the value and retry the command using 00 for the primary adapter and 01 for the alternate adapter.

24h, Command Completed while Cancel Occurring

Meaning: A command completed that was in the process of being canceled by a Cancel command.
Required Action: None.

25h, Reserved Name Specified for Add Group Name

Meaning: An Add Name or Add Group Name command specified an IBM reserved name.
Required Action: Undocumented.

26h, Command Not Valid to Cancel

Meaning: The command specified in a Cancel command is not valid to cancel.

Required Action: Verify the correctness of the cancel command.

30h, Name Defined by Another Process (OS/2 Extended Edition only)

Meaning: The command refers to a locally defined NetBIOS name. Resources reserved for a given process within the workstation can only be used by that process and the specified local NetBIOS name is already reserved for another process.

Required action: Use another name or remove the process using the specified name.

34h, NetBIOS Environment Not Defined (OS/2 Extended Edition only)

Meaning: The Reset command must be the first command issued by a process. This return code value does not apply to the Reset command.

Required action: Issue the Reset command.

35h, Required Operating System Resources Exhausted (OS/2 Extended Edition only)

Meaning: NetBIOS cannot initiate the requested command because OS/2 Extended Edition resources are not available to support the command. This return code does not apply to the Reset command.

Required action: Retry later.

36h, Maximum Applications Exceeded (OS/2 Extended Edition only)

Meaning: NetBIOS services requested in the Reset command are not available to this process because the number of processes it is currently serving is the maximum allowed by the NetBIOS load time parameters. This return code value only applies to the Reset command.

Required action: Eliminate a process that is using NetBIOS services or increase the value of the NetBIOS Application (APP) load time parameter and reboot.

37h, No SAPs Available for NetBIOS (OS/2 Extended Edition only)

Meaning: Another process has allocated an insufficient number of SAPs in its DIR.OPEN adapter request. All allocated adapter SAPs are already in use and none are left for NetBIOS. Thus, NetBIOS services are not available to any process. Note that NetBIOS requires only one SAP to support all its processes. This return code value only applies to the Reset command.
Required action: Fix the first process.

38h, Requested Resources Not Available (OS/2 Extended Edition only)

Meaning: The requests for NetBIOS resources exceeds the number specified at NetBIOS load time. The resources are names, commands, sessions, and the use of name number 01h which can only be used by one process. NetBIOS is available for the application but with fewer resources. This return code value only applies to the Reset command.
Required action: Adjust the necessary load time parameter.

40h, System Error

Meaning: Undocumented.
Required Action: Undocumented.

41h, Hot Carrier from a Remote Adapter Detected

Meaning: A remote adapter has a hot carrier.
Required Action: Remove the offending adapter from the network and turn off your machine before trying to use the network again.

42h, Hot Carrier from This Adapter Detected

Meaning: A local adapter has a hot carrier.
   Required Action: Remove the offending adapter from the network and replace it.

43h, No Carrier Detected

Meaning: A local adapter cannot detect a carrier signal from the translator unit.
   Required Action: Determine why the adapter cannot detect a carrier signal and turn off your machine before trying to use the adapter again.

4Eh, Status Bit 12, 14, or 15 on Longer than One Minute (Token-Ring)

Meaning: One or more of the ring status bits (12, 14, or 15) have been on longer than 60 seconds. This return code is not reported at all if ring status bits 8 through 11 are also on.
   Required Action: Check the extended status last ring status code. The only NetBIOS Interface command that may be issued is Reset.

4Fh, One or More of Status Bits 8-11 On

Meaning: One or more of ring status bits 8 through 11 are on.
   Required Action: Check the extended status last ring status code. The only NetBIOS Interface command that may be issued is Reset.

50h-F6h, Adapter Malfunction

Meaning: A local adapter is producing an invalid error code.
   Required Action: Use another adapter.

F7h, Error on Implicit DIR.INITIALIZE

Meaning: NetBIOS experienced an error when it attempted to initialize the LAN adapter.

Required Action: Check the extended status bring-up error code. The only NetBIOS Interface command that may be issued until this is done is Reset.

F8h, Error on Implicit DIR.OPEN.ADAPTER

Meaning: NetBIOS experienced an error when it attempted to open the LAN adapter.

Required Action: Check the extended status bring-up error code. The only NetBIOS Interface command that may be issued until this is done is Reset.

There is a possibility that a DIR.OPEN.ADAPTER could fail because of a temporary timing condition. Because of this the DIR.OPEN. ADAPTER is retried twice at 30 second intervals before reporting this return code.

F9h, IBM LAN Support Program Internal Error

Meaning: The IBM Lan Support Program has experienced an internal error.

Required Action: Check the error code. The only NetBIOS Interface command that may be issued until this is done is Reset.

FAh, Adapter Check

Meaning: The adapter has experienced an internal error.

Required Action: Check the adapter check reason code. The only NetBIOS Interface command that may be issued is Reset.

FBh, NetBIOS Program Not Loaded in PC

Meaning: The IBM LAN Support Program is not loaded and available. However, it has received a control block with a value greater than X'03' in the first byte indicating a NetBIOS command has been issued.

Required Action: Load and start the IBM LAN Support Program and reissue the command or correct the control block.

FCh, DIR.OPEN.ADAPTER or DLC.OPEN.SAP Failed—Check Parameters

Meaning: As stated.

Required Action: Correct the parameters causing the error and execute the DIR.OPEN.ADAPTER command again. Note, the DLC.OPEN. SAP command is executed on initial start and restart of the NetBIOS Interface. The parameters used are obtained from the DIR.OPEN. ADAPTER command (executed either explicitly or implicitly).

There is a possibility that a DIR.OPEN.ADAPTER could fail because of a temporary timing condition, so before reporting this return code, the DIR.OPEN.ADAPTER is tried again twice at 30 second intervals.

FDh, Unexpected Adapter Close

Meaning: The adapter was closed while the NetBIOS interface was executing a command.

Required Action: Issue a Reset command.

F7h-FDh Error Notes

Required Action: The condition reported in the NcbRetCode is the last occurring error.

Extended status information, excluding adapter counters, is available in the NcbReserve field. For Reset commands, it is the status prior to the Reset.

Ring Status Information

If any of ring status bits 8-11 are on, they cause error code 0x4F.

If any of ring status bits 12, 14, or 15 are on for longer than 60 seconds, they cause error code 0x4E. 0x4F errors have priority over 0x4E errors.

Ring status bits 6 and 7 do not cause errors. If ring status bit 7 (counter overflow) is on, nothing is reported. Bit 6 (single station) is ignored.

If a ring status appendage is not defined, local NetBIOS Interface counters are updated via the DIR.READ.LOG command.

Ncb Command and Field Relationship

Commands Listed by Command Code

Command	Command Code	Retcode	LSN	Num	Buffer@	Length	Call Name	Name	Rto	Sto	Post@	Lana Num
Call	10h, 90h	O	O				I	I	D=O	D=O	C	I
Listen	11h, 91h	O	O				I/C (*)	I	D=O	D=O	C	I
Hang Up	12h, 92h	O	I								C	I
Send	14h, 94h	O	I		I	I					C	I
Receive	15h, 95h	O	I		I	I/O					C	I
Receive-Any	16h, 96h	O	O	I/C (FFH)	I	I/O					C	I
Chain Send	17h, 97h	O	I		I	I	I				C	I
Send Datagram	20h, A0h	O		I	I	I	I				C	I
Receive Datagram	21h, A1h	O		I (FFH)	I	I/O	O				C	I
Send Broadcast Datagram	22h, A2h	O		I	I	I					C	I
Receive Broadcast Datagram	23h, A3h	O		I	I	I/O	O				C	I
Add Name	30h, B0h	O		O				I			C	I
Delete Name	31h, B1h	O						I			C	I

Legend: I Input, O Output, C Conditional, (*) Asterick Accepted

Commands Listed by Command Code (cont.)

Command	Command Code	Retcode	LSN	Num	Buffer@	Length	Call Name	Name	Rto	Sto	Post@	Lana Num
Reset	32h	O	I	I								I
Adapter Status	33h, B3h	O			I	I	I (*)				C	I
Session Status	34h, B4h	O			I	I/O		I (*)			C	I
Cancel	35h	O			I							I
Add Group Name	36h, B6h	O		O				I			C	I
Unlink	70h	O										I
Send No-Ack	71h, F1h	O	I		I	I					C	I
Chain Send No-Ack	72h, F2h	O	I		I	I	I				C	I

Commands Listed by Categories

Command	Command Code	Retcode	LSN	Num	Buffer@	Length	Call Name	Name	Rto	Sto	Post@	Lana Num
					General							
Reset	32h	O	I	I								I
Adapter Status	33h, B3h	O			I	I	I (*)				C	I
Cancel	35h	O			I							I
Unlink	70h	O										I
					Name							
Add Name	30h, B0h	O		O				I			C	I
Delete Name	31h, B1h	O						I			C	I
Add Group Name	36h, B6h	O		O				I			C	I
					Session							
Call	10h, 90h	O	O					I	I	D=O	D=O	C	I

Commands Listed by Categories (cont.)

Command	Command Code	Retcode	LSN	Num	Buffer@	Length	Call Name	Name	Rto	Sto	Post@	Lana Num
Listen	11h, 91h	O	O				I/C (*)	I	D=O	D=O	C	I
Hang Up	12h, 92h	O	I								C	I
Send	14h, 94h	O	I		I	I					C	I
Receive	15h, 95h	O	I		I	I/O					C	I
Receive-Any	16h, 96h	O	O	I/C (FFH)	I	I/O					C	I
Chain Send	17h, 97h	O	I		I	I	I				C	I
Session Status	34h, B4h	O			I	I/O		I (*)			C	I
Send No-Ack	71h, F1h	O	I		I	I					C	I
Chain Send No-Ack	72h, F2h	O	I		I	I	I				C	I
Datagram												
Send Datagram	20h, A0h	O		I	I	I	I				C	I
Receive Datagram	21h, A1h	O		I (FFH)	I	I/O	O				C	I
Send Broadcast Datagram	22h, A2h	O		I	I	I					C	I
Receive Broadcast Datagram	23h, A3h	O		I	I	I/O	O				C	I

Send No-Ack and Chain Send No-Ack

When NetBIOS first appeared with the IBM PC Network LANA card, Net-BIOS insured data integrity for session traffic by sending an acknowledgment (ACK) for all messages successfully received with a Receive or Receive-Any command. When the IBM Token-Ring Network appeared, the IEEE 802.2 LLC layer also provided data receipt acknowledgments at a lower level in the communication layer hierarchy. However, the Token-Ring Network NetBIOS implementation continued to observe the practice of NetBIOS-to-NetBIOS ACKing as a legacy, though it was somewhat unnecessary in theory.

The Send No-Ack and Chain Send No-Ack commands, new with the IBM LAN Support Program version 1.02, are variants of the Send and Chain Send commands, respectively. Their purpose is to address the presence of redundant ACKing in IBM's NetBIOS implementations. Their use potentially provides modest performance improvements for session-oriented communication by eliminating both the theoretically unnecessary adapter NetBIOS session overhead and LAN traffic caused by IBM's NetBIOS-to-NetBIOS ACKing.

IBM recommends (but does not require) that these commands be used with the IBM PC LAN Program 1.3 and beyond. While the Send No-Ack and Chain Send No-Ack commands require the same input fields as the Send and Chain Send commands, their use has serious side effects that need to be completely understood by programmers.

Some NetBIOS implementations do not have these commands and the new 07h return code value they introduce. Use of these commands may produce nonportable results with side effects such as 03h (invalid command) return code values in NetBIOS implementations not recognizing their command codes.

A LAN may have different levels of NetBIOS in use. If a NetBIOS implementation is presented a local Send No-Ack or Chain Send No-Ack command and determines that the remote NetBIOS cannot respond to the request appropriately, the local NetBIOS treats the request as a Send or Chain Send command, respectively. In other words, there is no advantage in using the No-Acks in this scenario.

A No-Ack command is not guaranteed delivery of its data. When a No-Ack command fails, the session remains intact because the NcbSto parameter specified in the Call or Listen command that created the session has no effect on No-Ack commands. Moreover, a No-Ack command can be canceled without aborting the session.

In these senses, a No-Ack command is somewhat like a Send Datagram command. However, No-Ack commands differ from Send Datagram commands because the message size can be 64K-1 characters for a Send No-Ack command and 128K-2 characters for a Chain Send No-Ack command. In addition, No-Ack commands specify an NcbLsn value and Send Datagram commands specify an NcbNum value.

A No-Ack command may return with a final return code value of zero, but may have actually failed. The failure may be due to the target application's not having any Receive or Receive-Any command outstanding. Here, the command completely fails but may have already reported its "success." Or, if a Receive or Receive-Any command is outstanding, its buffer may not be large enough to hold all the arriving data. In this instance, the buffer is filled with data, and the remainder is discarded by NetBIOS.

No-Ack command failures are reflected in other session commands. No-Ack commands that failed but return a final return code with a zero value cause other local session commands associated with the same LSN value to fail with a 07h final return code value. These commands are the Send, Send No-Ack, Chain Send, Chain Send No-Ack, Receive, and Receive-Any commands.

Whichever command NetBIOS finds first gets the lucky number 07h as a final return code. Hence, failure determination logic is complicated by the fact that the failure detection point is generally not predictable. In this sense, NetBIOS's indiscrimination is most democratic.

A 07h return code value is ambiguous in many ways. The 07h return code value alerts an application that one or more No-Ack commands on the session have failed. No indication is given whether the command was one or more Send No-Ack command(s) and/or one or more Chain Send No-Ack command(s) or even how many No-Ack commands may have failed. One 07h return code represents all of them in unison. Finally, if only one failed, no indication is given regarding how much data was actually successfully received.

Receive or Receive-Any commands that receive data transmitted by a No-Ack command are given no indication that the data was transmitted by the No-Ack variant. If a Receive or Receive-Any command's buffer is not large enough, the command completes with a 06h (incomplete received message) return code value as it does if the data was sent by a Send or Chain Send command. However, the application cannot issue another Receive or Receive-Any to obtain the remainder of the data because it has already been discarded by the local NetBIOS. Yet the receiving application has no way of knowing this.

Applications such as the PC Network's RPL logic depend on the ability to issue a subsequent Receive to pending data. Here, as in many existing programs, the RPL logic issues a Receive to obtain a message header which indicates the remaining data size that should be received with a subsequent Receive command.

Conclusion

No-Ack commands generally have the curious characteristic of unpredictably reflecting their problems in other commands. Clearly, techniques that work with the Send and Chain Send commands cannot be used with their No-Ack counterparts. Oddly enough, when things go wrong while using No-Ack commands, the most straightforward approach is to use traditional Send and Chain Send commands to effect damage control. In any event, it is the application's responsibility to maintain data integrity in No-Ack error sessions.

It would seem that since traditional NetBIOS programming practices are generally inappropriate with the No-Ack commands, their use may be restricted to new applications. Otherwise, they may require significant restructuring of existing programs, exciting debugging opportunities, or both.

OS/2 Extended Edition
and LAN Manager

IBM's OS/2 Extended Edition and Microsoft Corporation's OS/2 Lan Manager contain extensions and changes to the PC-DOS NetBIOS Programming Interface. In both instances, NetBIOS functions are available via OS/2 dynamic linking. Processes present requests to NetBIOS using FAR CALL rather than PC-DOS INT 5Ch or 2Ah interrupts. Instead of pointing ES:BX to an Ncb and executing an INT 5Ch, OS/2 assembly language programs use the following sequence:

```
push NcbSelector    ; segment
push NcbOffset      ; offset
call NetBIOS        ; NetBIOS dynamic link
```

IBM OS/2 Extended Edition

Many PC-DOS NetBIOS device driver load time parameter keywords, including all "old parameters," are deleted and those that remain may have different defaults. Table F-1 lists the allowable parameters, their defaults, and their allowed values. The new APPLICATIONS parameter, specifies the number of processes that may simultaneously use the NetBIOS interface.

OS/2 Extended Edition Reset Command

In OS/2 Extended Edition, each process operates independently. A process obtains NetBIOS resources by a Reset command, which must be the first NetBIOS command a process issues. Processes cannot share names,

Table F-1. OS/2 Extended Edition Parameters

Keyword	Default	Valid Values
ADAP.ADDR.NOT.REVERSED (ANR)	NO	Y(es)/N(o)
APPLICATIONS (APP)	2	0 - 16
COMMANDS (C)	32	0 - 255
DATAGRAM.MAX (DG)	NO	Y(es)/N(o)
DLC.MAXIN* (MI)	-	0 - 9
DLC.MAXOUT* (MO)	-	0 - 9
DLC.RETRY.COUNT* (RC)	-	0 - 255
DLC.T1 (T1)	5	0 - 10
DLC.T2 (T2)	2	0 - 11
DLC.TI (TI)	3	0 - 10
NAMES (N)	17	2 - 254
RING.ACCESS (RA)	0	0 - 7
REMOTE.DATAGRAM.CONTROL (RDC)	NO	Y(es)/N(o)
REMOTE.NAME.DIRECTORY (RND)	0	0 - 255
SESSIONS (S)	32	0 - 254
STATIONS (ST)	32	0 - 254
TRANSMIT.COUNT (TC)	6	0 - 10
TRANSMIT.TIMEOUT (TT)	1	0 - 20

* The adapter and interface code determines the default values for these parameters

including the permanent name, and the right to use the permanent name is obtained using the Reset command. The OS/2 NetBIOS Reset command is significantly different from the PC-DOS Reset command and is the only command which has redefined command field meanings.

Storage Segment Seams

In OS/2 NetBIOS requests, storage segment adjustments cannot be made. If an offset plus the data length of a buffer exceeds 64K in a Receive, Receive-Any, Send, Send No-Ack, Chain Send, or Chain Send No-Ack command, the command completes with a return code value of 01h (invalid buffer length). Because OS/2 Extended Edition locks storage communication buffers, buffers should be maintained in as few data segments as possible.

Wait and No-Wait Options

Commands specifying the wait option are initiated and the requesting process threads are immediately blocked. When the command completes, execution returns to the requesting process's code. The effect is similar to PC-DOS NetBIOS commands that specify a wait option.

OS/2 Extended Edition processes no-wait commands by generating child threads that are immediately blocked. Execution then returns to the requesting process's thread. When the command completes, NetBIOS invokes a post routine if specified in the Ncb. Post routines return by executing a FAR RETURN instruction rather than an IRET instruction and do not have to save or restore registers.

Because commands specifying the no-wait option require more OS/2 Extended Edition resources than commands specifying the wait option, commands specifying the wait option may succeed when commands specifying no-wait fail with a 35h return code value (required operating system resources exhausted).

New Return Codes

OS/2 Extended Edition adds several NetBIOS return codes. These are fully explained in the return codes discussion in Appendix C.

30h: Name defined by another process

34h: NetBIOS environment not defined, Reset must be issued

35h: Required operating system resources exhausted

36h: Maximum applications exceeded

37h: No SAPs available for NetBIOS

38h: Requested resource(s) not available

Allocating and Deallocating NetBIOS Resources

Processes issue the Reset command to allocate (reserve) and use or to deallocate (relinquish) and terminate using NetBIOS resources.

Allocating Resources

A process must issue a Reset command as its first NetBIOS command. Processes use the Reset command to request NetBIOS to allocate resources for their exclusive use. These resources are taken from the Net-

BIOS resource pool created at NetBIOS load time from the load time parameter values. Allocated resources cannot be used by any other process until they are released by the owning process. The requested resources are collectively called an environment and include a quantity of sessions, commands, names, and the use of name-number one.

If the process subsequently issues a Reset command to redefine its environment, NetBIOS deallocates all resources currently reserved for the process and allocates the requested resources if they are available.

Resetting and Deallocating Resources

When a process issues a Reset command to deallocate its environment's resources, NetBIOS returns all the resources allocated to the process to the NetBIOS resource pool for subsequent use by other processes. For the requesting process, existing sessions are terminated and all added names are deleted from the NetBIOS name table(s). Because all processes operate independently, no other currently executing process is affected.

When an OS/2 Extended Edition process terminates, OS/2 EE implicitly issues a NetBIOS Reset to deallocate resources the process owns.

Microsoft Corporation's OS/2 LAN Manager

Microsoft Corporation's OS/2 LAN Manager contains new functions that allow processes to access more than one installed NetBIOS device driver. These drivers can support multiple LAN adapters of the same or different types and each type has its own load time parameters.

The new NetBIOS calls and their functions are

- NetBiosEnum( ): Determines the number of and names of all installed NetBIOS device drivers
- NetBiosGetInfo( ): Returns installed NetBIOS device driver information for the specified driver
- NetBiosOpen( ): Creates a device driver handle for sending Ncbs to a specified NetBIOS device driver. The process specifies one of three operating modes in the call:
    Regular mode is simultaneously usable by multiple processes. It does not allow use of the permanent name or Reset, Receive Any-to-Any, or Receive Broadcast Datagram commands.
    Privileged mode is only usable by one process (though other processes can use or open the adapter in Regular mode simul-

taneously). It does not allow use of Reset or Receive Any-to-Any commands.

Exclusive mode provides a process exclusive use of a NetBIOS device driver. This process can use any NetBIOS command.

- NetBiosClose( ): Cancels the device driver handle, cancels any outstanding Ncbs, and terminates access to a specified NetBIOS device driver,
- NetBiosSubmit( ): Passes one or multiple Ncbs to a specified Net-BIOS device driver. A chaining option specifies whether the request is for one or multiple chained Ncbs and is an efficient way to pass several requests to an individual NetBIOS device driver simultaneously.

For single Ncb requests, an error retry option specifies whether the LAN Manager should have the NetBIOS device driver retry a failing Ncb request a specified number of times. For chained operations, a 16-bit offset pointer precedes each Ncb that points to the next Ncb in the chain. All Ncbs must be in the same segment and a value of 0FFFFh specifies the end of the chain.

A chain can contain any Ncb sequence, but some are impractical. For example, a Send Datagram command may need an NcbNum value that is returned by an Add Name command positioned earlier in the chain. The Send Datagram command fails because the Lan Manager does not automatically place the NcbNum value in the Send Datagram Ncb.

For chained requests, an error retry option specifies whether the LAN Manager should have the NetBIOS device driver continue after an error (proceed-on-error) or terminate after an error (stop-on-error).

Whether an Ncb command specifying the no-wait option is an individual request or one within a chain, the LAN Manager implements no-wait requests with semaphore handles. Proceed-on-error chains typically are used for no-wait option Ncb commands. Stop-on-error chains are typically used with commands using the wait option. Ncbs not processed because of an earlier occurring error in the Ncb chain are posted with a return code value of 0Bh (command cancelled).

Bibliography

3Com Corporation. 1987. *NetBIOS Programmer's Reference (3260-00)*. Burlington, Massachusetts.

IBM Corporation. 1984. *IBM PC Network Technical Reference Manual (6322916)*. Armonk, New York.

—————. 1986. *Token-Ring Network PC Adapter Technical Reference (69X7862)*. Second edition. Armonk, New York.

—————. 1988. *Migration Considerations for NetBIOS*. IBM Washington Systems Center Internal Flash 8736.

—————. 1988. *New NetBIOS Commands in LAN Support Program V1.02*. IBM Washington Systems Center Internal Flash 8808.

Lai, Robert S. 1987. *Writing MS-DOS Device Drivers*. New York: The Addison-Wesley Publishing Company.

Microsoft Corporation. 1988. *Programming Interface for the OS/2 LAN Manager*. Microsoft Operating System/2 Software Development Kit Part Number 01396. Redmond, Washington.

Schwaderer, W. David. 1988. *IBM's Local Area Networks: Power Networking and Systems Connectivity*. New York: Van Nostrand Reinhold.

Index

C Programmer's Guide to Serial Communications

Joe Campbell

This book offers a comprehensive examination and unprecedented dissection of asynchronous serial communications. Written for C programmers and technically advanced users, it contains both a theoretical discussion of communications concepts and a practical approach to program design for the IBM® PC and Kaypro environments.

Topics covered include:

- The ASCII Character Set
- Fundamentals of Asynchronous Technology
- Errors and Error Detection
- Information Transfer
- Modems and Modem Control
- The UART—A Conceptual Model
- Real-World Hardware: Two UARTs
- The Hayes Smartmodem
- Designing a Basic Serial I/O Library
- Portability Considerations
- Timing Functions
- Functions for Baud Rate and Data Format
- RS-232 Control
- Formatted Input and Output
- Smartmodem Programming
- XMODEM File Transfers
- CRC Calculations
- Interrupts

672 Pages, 7½ x 9¾, Softbound
ISBN: 0-672-22584-0
No. 22584, $26.95

Portability and the C Language

Rex Jaeschke

Portability, the feature that distinguishes C from other programming languages, is thoroughly defined and explained in this definitive reference work. The book primarily addresses the technical issues of designing and writing C programs that are to be compiled across a diverse number of hardware and operating system environments.

Organized around the ANSI C Standard, it explains the C preprocessor and the run-time library and tackles portability from a C language perspective, discussing implementation-specific issues as they arise.

Topics covered include:

- Introduction and Overview
- The Environment
- Conversions, Expressions, Declarations, and Statements
- The Preprocessor
- Diagnostics, Character Handling, Errors
- Numerical Limits and Localization
- Mathematics, Non-Local Jumps, Signal Handling
- Variable Arguments and Common Definitions
- Input/Output, General Utilities, String Handling
- Date and Time
- Appendix: Keywords and Reserved Identifiers

400 Pages, 7½ x 9¾, Softbound
ISBN: 0-672-48428-5
No. 48428, $24.95

C Programmer's Guide to Microsoft® Windows 2.0

Carl Townsend

This intermediate-level programming guide shows the C programmer how to create applications under the Windows environment. Emphasizing the Microsoft C compiler, a sample application is presented along with the rationale behind its development.

Written as a tutorial, the book shows the experienced programmer how to exploit the extended features of Windows, providing an alphabetical list of functions and an easy-to-use guide to those extended features including printing, accelerators, and the GDI interface.

Topics covered include:

- Windows Overview
- The User Interface
- The Role of Messages
- The WinMain Program
- Managing Text with Windows
- Creating Menus and Using Dialog Boxes
- The Graphic Interface
- Windows, I/O, and Memory Management
- Creating and Managing Libraries
- Data Transfer
- Debugging Strategies
- Appendices: Installation, Message Boxes, Keyboard Interface, Function Summary, Using Windows with Pascal or Assembly Languages, Glossary

440 Pages, 7½ x 9¾, Softbound
ISBN: 0-672-22621-9
No. 22621, $24.95

QuickC™ Programming for the IBM®

Carl Townsend

This book is an entry-level tutorial for the beginning C programmer who desires to develop programs using the Microsoft® QuickC compiler. It will also acquaint the business professional or serious user with the basic aspects of programming in C.

The book includes hands-on interaction between the high-speed, low-cost compiler and the IBM® PC.

Topics covered include:

- Getting Started
- Representing Data
- Basic Input and Output
- Arithmetic Operations
- Program Control: IF, CASE, and Iteration Structures
- Using Functions and Macros
- Managing the Storage of Variables
- Arrays and Pointers
- Using Character Strings, Data Structures, Files and Other I/O, and Graphics
- Introduction to Structured Programming
- Developing Programs with QuickC
- Managing Databases with QuickC
- High-level Design: Menus
- Adding Database Records
- Editing and Deleting Records
- Reporting and Processing Programs

400 Pages, 7½ x 9¾, Softbound
ISBN: 0-672-22622-7
No. 22622, $22.95

**Visit your local book retailer or call
800-428-SAMS.**

To Order the Sample Programs Diskette

As a convenience and learning aid, you may order a diskette containing the current version of all C program source code and header files listed in this book, as well as errata and late-breaking NetBIOS news. The source code files are shipped on an unsupported, as-is basis. Neither Howard W. Sams & Company nor Sacramento Distribution Service assumes any liability with respect to the use, accuracy, or fitness of the information contained within the diskette.

Send this form with payment to:

Sacramento Distribution Service
P.O. Box 3014
Citrus Heights, California 95611-3014

- -

Diskette Order Form
Schwaderer, *C Programmer's Guide to NetBIOS*, #22638

Name _____ Company _____

Address _____ City _____ State _____

Country _____ Zip _____

Phone (for collect calls about order problems) (___) _____

Place of book   Type of computer
purchase _____   used _____

5 ¼″ Disks 360 KB (DOS 2.0 or higher)
Quantity:_____ @ $22.95 U.S.   Total: $_____

3 ½″ Disks 720 KB (DOS 3.2 or higher)
Quantity:_____ @ $24.95 U.S.   Total: $_____

California residents, add 6.5%
Santa Clara County, CA residents, add 7%   Tax: $_____

U.S. orders—$2.50   Shipping &
Foreign orders—$4.00   Handling: $_____

                                                 Total Order
_____ Check or money order enclosed.   Amount: $_____

Please allow six weeks for delivery within the U.S.

C
Programmer's Guide to
NetBIOS

REFERENCE CARD
©1988 by W. David Schwaderer

HOWARD W. SAMS & COMPANY
A Division of Macmillan, Inc.
11711 North College, Suite 141, Carmel, IN 46032 USA

Commands Listed by Categories

Command	Command Code	Retcode	LSN	Num	Buffer@	Length	Call Name	Name	Rto	Sto	Post@	Lana Num
General												
Reset	32h	O	I	I								I
Adapter Status	33h, B3h	O			I	I	I (*)				C	I
Cancel	35h	O			I							I
Unlink	70h	O										I
Name												
Add Name	30h, B0h	O		O				I			C	I
Delete Name	31h, B1h	O						I			C	I
Add Group Name	36h, B6h	O		O				I			C	I
Session												
Call	10h, 90h	O	O				I	I	D=O	D=O	C	I
Listen	11h, 91h	O	O				I/C (*)	I	D=O	D=O	C	I
Hang Up	12h, 92h	O	I								C	I
Send	14h, 94h	O	I		I	I					C	I
Receive	15h, 95h	O	I		I	I/O					C	I
Receive-Any	16h, 96h	O	O	I/C (FFH)	I	I/O					C	I
Chain Send	17h, 97h	O	I		I	I	I				C	I
Session Status	34h, B4h	O			I	I/O		I (*)			C	I
Send No-Ack	71h, F1h	O	I		I	I					C	I
Chain Send No-Ack	72h, F2h	O	I		I	I	I				C	I
Datagram												
Send Datagram	20h, A0h	O		I	I	I	I				C	I
Receive Datagram	21h, A1h	O		I (FFH)	I	I/O	O				C	I
Send Broadcast Datagram	22h, A2h	O		I	I	I					C	I
Receive Broadcast Datagram	23h, A3h	O		I	I	I/O	O				C	I

Commands Listed by Command Code

Command	Command Code	Retcode	LSN	Num	Buffer@	Length	Call Name	Name	Rto	Sto	Post@	Lana Num
Call	10h, 90h	O	O				I	I	D=O	D=O	C	I
Listen	11h, 91h	O	O				I/C (*)	I	D=O	D=O	C	I
Hang Up	12h, 92h	O	I								C	I
Send	14h, 94h	O	I		I	I					C	I
Receive	15h, 95h	O	I		I	I/O					C	I
Receive-Any	16h, 96h	O	O	I/C (FFH)	I	I/O					C	I
Chain Send	17h, 97h	O	I		I	I	I				C	I
Send Datagram	20h, A0h	O		I	I	I	I				C	I
Receive Datagram	21h, A1h	O		I (FFH)	I	I/O	O				C	I
Send Broadcast Datagram	22h, A2h	O		I	I	I					C	I
Receive Broadcast Datagram	23h, A3h	O		I	I	I/O	O				C	I
Add Name	30h, B0h	O		O				I			C	I
Delete Name	31h, B1h	O						I			C	I
Reset	32h	O	I	I								I
Adapter Status	33h, B3h	O			I	I	I (*)				C	I
Session Status	34h, B4h	O			I	I/O	I (*)				C	I
Cancel	35h	O			I							I
Add Group Name	36h, B6h	O		O				I			C	I
Unlink	70h	O										I
Send No-Ack	71h, F1h	O	I		I	I					C	I
Chain Send No-Ack	72h, F2h	O	I		I	I	I				C	I

Legend: I Input, O Output, C Conditional, (*) Asterick Accepted

The Ncb Fields

Offset	Field Name	Length in Bytes	Field Structure
+00	Command	1	☐
+01	Return Code	1	☐
+02	Local Session Number	1	☐
+03	Name Number	1	☐
+04	Buffer Address	4	☐☐☐☐
+08	Buffer Length	2	☐☐
+10	Call Name	16	☐☐☐☐☐☐☐☐☐☐☐☐☐☐☐☐
+26	Name (Local)	16	☐☐☐☐☐☐☐☐☐☐☐☐☐☐☐☐
+42	Receive Time Out	1	☐
+43	Send Time Out	1	☐
+44	Post Routine Address	4	☐☐☐☐
+48	LANA Number	1	☐
+49	Command Complete Flag	1	☐
+50	Reserved Field	14	☐☐☐☐☐☐☐☐☐☐☐☐☐☐

A C Ncb Structure

```c
#define USGC   unsigned char
#define USGI   unsigned
#define USGL   unsigned long


struct Ncb
   {
     USGC   NcbCommand;          /* command code                 */
     USGC   NcbRetCode;          /* return code                  */
     USGC   NcbLsn;              /* local session number         */
     USGC   NcbNum;              /* Datagram ADD NAME table entry */

     char * NcbBufferOffset;     /* I/O buffer offset            */
     USGI   NcbBufferSegment;    /* I/O buffer segment           */

     USGI   NcbLength;           /* length of data in I/O buffer  */

     char   NcbCallName[16];     /* remote system name for CALL  */
     char   NcbName[16];         /* local adapter network name   */

     USGC   NcbRto;              /* receive timeouts in 1/2 second units */
     USGC   NcbSto;              /* send    timeouts in 1/2 second units */

     char * NcbPostRtnOffset;    /* offset  of post routine      */
     USGI   NcbPostRtnSegment;   /* segment of post routine      */

     USGC   NcbLanaNum;     /* network adapter number to execute cmd  */
     USGC   NcbCmdCplt;     /* 0xFF ==> command pending, else cmplted */

     char   NcbReservedArea[14]; /* work area for network card    */
   } ZeroNcb;                    /* prototype NCB for sizeof calcs */
```

A MASM Ncb Structure

```
;               Ncb Structure

Ncb             struc
  Ncb_Command   db   00h          ;Ncb command field
  Ncb_RetCode   db   00h          ;Ncb return code
  Ncb_Lsn       db   00h          ;Ncb local session number
  Ncb_Num       db   00h          ;Ncb name number from AddName
  Ncb_BufferOff dw   0000h        ;Ncb message buffer offset
  Ncb_BufferSeg dw   0000h        ;Ncb message buffer segment
  Ncb_Length    dw   0000h        ;Ncb message buffer length (in bytes)
  Ncb_CallName  db   16 dup(0)    ;Ncb remote name
  Ncb_Name      db   16 dup(0)    ;Ncb AddName
  Ncb_Rto       db   00h          ;Ncb receive timeout
  Ncb_Sto       db   00h          ;Ncb send timeout
  Ncb_PostOff   dw   0000h        ;Ncb post routine offset
  Ncb_PostSeg   dw   0000h        ;Ncb post routine segment
  Ncb_Lana_Num  db   00h          ;Ncb adapter number
  Ncb_Cmd_Cplt  db   00h          ;Ncb OFFh ==> command pending indicator
  Ncb_Reserve   db   14 dup(0)    ;Ncb reserved area
Ncb             ends
```

NetBIOS Final Return Codes

00h	Successful completion, good return
01h	Invalid buffer length
03h	Invalid command
05h	Command timed-out
06h	Incomplete received message
07h	Local No-Ack command failed
08h	Invalid local session number
09h	No resource available
0Ah	Session has been closed
0Bh	Command was canceled
0Dh	Duplicate name in local NetBIOS name table
0Eh	NetBIOS name table full
0Fh	Name has active sessions and is now deregistered
11h	NetBIOS local session table full
12h	Session open rejected because no Listen is outstanding
13h	Illegal name number
14h	Cannot find name called or no answer
15h	Name not found, or cannot specify asterisk (*) or 00h as first byte of NcbName, or the name is deregistered and cannot be used
16h	Name in use on remote adapter
17h	Name deleted
18h	Session ended abnormally
19h	Name conflict detected
1Ah	Incompatible remote device (PC Network)
21h	Interface busy
22h	Too many commands outstanding
23h	Invalid number in NcbLanaNum field
24h	Command completed while cancel occurring
25h	Reserved name specified for Add Group Name
26h	Command not valid to cancel
30h	Name defined by another process (OS/2 Extended Edition only)
34h	NetBIOS environment not defined (OS/2 Extended Edition only)
35h	Required operating system resources (OS/2 Extended Edition only)
36h	Maximum applications exceeded (OS/2 Extended Edition only)
37h	No SAPs available for NetBIOS (OS/2 Extended Edition only)
38h	Requested resources not available (OS/2 Extended Edition only)
40h	System error (PC Network)
41h	Hot carrier from a remote adapter detected (PC Network)
42h	Hot carrier from this adapter detected (PC Network)
43h	No carrier detected (PC Network)
4Eh	Status bit 12, 14, or 15 on longer than one minute (Token-Ring)
4Fh	One or more of status bits 8-11 on (Token-Ring)
50h-F6h	Adapter malfunction
F7h	Error on implicit DIR.INITIALIZE
F8h	Error on implicit DIR.OPEN.ADAPTER
F9h	IBM LAN Support Program internal error
FAh	Adapter check
FBh	NetBIOS program not loaded in PC
FCh	DIR.OPEN.ADAPTER or DLC.OPEN.SAP failed—check parameters
FDh	Unexpected adapter close
FFh	Command-pending status